D1275689

A
Constant
Variable

New Perspectives
on the Community College

Arthur M. Cohen

with

Florence B. Brawer, John Lombardi

assisted by

John R. Boggs, Edgar A. Quimby, Young Park

A
CONSTANT
VARIABLE

Jossey-Bass Inc., Publishers
San Francisco · Washington · London · 1971

A CONSTANT VARIABLE
New Perspectives on the Community College
by Arthur M. Cohen and Associates

Published in Great Britain by
Jossey-Bass, Inc., Publishers
St. George's House
44 Hatton Garden, London E.C.1

Library of Congress Catalogue Card Number LC 76-168859

International Standard Book Number ISBN 0-87589-105-5

Manufactured in the United States of America

JACKET DESIGN BY WILLI BAUM, SAN FRANCISCO

FIRST EDITION

Code 7129

The Jossey-Bass
Series in Higher Education

A publication of the

EDUCATIONAL RESOURCES INFORMATION CENTER

ERIC **Clearinghouse For Junior Colleges**

UNIVERSITY OF CALIFORNIA, LOS ANGELES

The ERIC program is sponsored by the United States Department of Health, Education, and Welfare, Office of Education. The points of view expressed here do not necessarily represent official Office of Education position or policy.

Foreword

Educators are prone to make liberal use of the term *analysis* when discussing educational topics, although frequently their treatments are anything but analytical. In *A Constant Variable,* however, the authors have succeeded admirably in making a critical, analytical review of the community college.

The authors treat the history, ideology, and functions of the community junior college. They examine the institution itself, those who staff it, the students, and the educational processes employed. They thus provide those already working in the field with a basis for reassessing their roles and activities. Throughout, the authors identify conflicts in institutional values resulting from differences in perspective among those who support, staff, and attend these institutions.

A Constant Variable holds the reader's attention. The writing is alive and to the point. The review of the literature is thorough and its analysis incisive. The authors are not reluctant to attack sacred cows and to shatter shibboleths. But the book by no means lacks scholarship. The authors also refuse to be so irresponsible as to offer simple solutions to complex problems, although without doubt they intend to cause those associated with community colleges to reflect on their assumptions. As a consequence, some readers who are professionally involved with those institutions will experience discomfort, probably even taking objection to some of the conclusions.

For those planning to enter the community college as professionals, *A Constant Variable* will prove valuable both as a candid assessment of the institution and as a reference, giving direction and purpose to their activities. This is indeed recommended reading for graduate students and others engaged in research related to the community junior college; they will be well rewarded for their time.

Washington, D.C.   RAYMOND E. SCHULTZ
September 1971   Director, International Office
                    American Association of Junior Colleges

Preface

Our main purpose in *A Constant Variable* is to stimulate dialogue on current issues in community college education. By offering divergent perspectives, we hope to show the reader that it is possible to examine the community college as though it were something other than the social panacea the prevailing view holds it to be. If the book is widely heeded, people concerned with the community college will begin to examine the relationships between its premises and its operational procedures. Finding these to be frequently disparate, they will postulate alternative types of institutions. Thus, rather than being homogeneous, comprehensive colleges attempting to do everything, future institutions may have specific missions and operational procedures that work in concert.

A Constant Variable is directed toward all people interested in the community college. We hope that graduate students will find it indispensable; that their professors will find it a refreshing alternative to the bland promotional literature to which they are frequently subjected; and that community college leaders—directors of state systems, presidents, superintendents, state and national association directors—will find it challenges their views. Other administrators—deans, division chairmen—should find a new set of assumptions and may revise some of their favored practices accordingly or at least begin to examine them critically. We hope that faculty members will read it too and thereby show their ability to refute the perceptive critic who wrote: "They are prevented from reading the literature of higher education by a curious Catch-22 type of logic that says: education is an inferior discipline; therefore no real scholar will write an article on higher education, thus anyone who publishes an article on higher education is by definition not a true scholar and can safely be ignored" (Brann, 1970).

A note of caution: *A Constant Variable* is an analytical review and few professional educators are familiar with this form of critical writing. The sights and sounds of each era are normal to the people of the times. Acid rock is music to the contemporary young who can hear it, cacophony to their elders. The ear must be trained— and also the digestive system. An analytical review may be difficult fare for a generation of two-year college staff members who have been reared on a diet of promotional literature, platitudes, and tautology—an ahistorical hodgepodge that serves as the pap of the education world. Nevertheless, we prepared *A Constant Variable* because critical views of the community colleges are rarely seen. The prevailing position among community college leaders is that we need more of the same—more money, students, campuses. We see the institution through different eyes and believe that the colleges deserve no less than careful, independent analysis.

We do not purport to offer the definitive statement on the community college but a critical analysis based on the views of six people, all of whom have had experience with the community college in one or more capacities—as instructor, counselor, administrator, researcher, or consultant. At the time they worked on *A Constant Variable* all the contributors were affiliated with the ERIC Clearinghouse for Junior Colleges—sponsored by the United States Office of Education and described more fully in the Appendix. Florence B. Brawer, with the Clearinghouse since 1968, is a former junior college counselor who specializes in personality assessment and studies of people functioning in higher education contexts. She was responsible for the chapters on the students, and she co-authored the faculty chapters. John Lombardi joined the staff shortly after his retirement as assistant superintendent in charge of the College Division, Los Angeles City Junior College District, in 1969. His broad areas of interest include institutional management and special programs—hence his chapters on vocational education and black studies.

Other contributors to *A Constant Variable* are Young Park,

formerly assistant to the chancellor, North Orange Junior College District (California), who wrote a portion of Chapter One; Edgar A. Quimby, an instructor at Imperial Valley College (California) before he came to UCLA, who wrote another portion of Chapter One and co-authored the chapter on black studies; and John R. Boggs, formerly a junior college institutional research coordinator for the Regional Education Laboratory for the Carolinas and Virginia, who wrote Chapter Two. The bibliography was compiled by Jesse Overall, Aaron Zaidenberg, and Thomas Townsend, under the direction of Hazel Horn. Manuscript preparation was assigned to Katherine Gartin, Jane Epstein, and Kay Carfagna. Marcia Boyer assisted at several stages of the project.

A Constant Variable is, then, a Clearinghouse staff production, written by a select group of people who spend their time reading, thinking, writing, and worrying about the past, present, and future of the two-year college in America. Much imbalance and bias in selection and presentation of information naturally result from the fact that the staff does not represent an absolute cross-section of opinions. As if this imbalance alone were not sufficient to lend predilection to the work, Arthur M. Cohen conceived and edited the book, wrote portions of it, and had the last word on content.

Los Angeles   ERIC Clearinghouse for Junior Colleges
September 1971   ARTHUR M. COHEN, Director

Contents

Authors

JOHN R. BOGGS, who wrote the chapter on institutional research, is institutional research officer at Chaffey College (California). He was formerly at the National Laboratory for Higher Education, where he assisted in organizing the Educational Development Officer program.

FLORENCE B. BRAWER is a research psychologist in the ERIC Clearinghouse for Junior Colleges. A former community college psychometrist and counselor, her special interest in personality assessment of people in higher education led to her chapters on community college students. With Cohen, she also coauthored the chapters on the faculty and the book *Confronting Identity: The Community College Instructor.* She is coeditor of *Developments in the Rorschach Technique: Vol. III.*

ARTHUR M. COHEN is associate professor of higher education at the University of California, Los Angeles, and director of the ERIC Clearinghouse for Junior Colleges. He has written extensively on alternative patterns of curriculum and instruction in the community college.

His previously published works include *Dateline '79: Heretical Concepts for the Community College.*

JOHN LOMBARDI is a continuing consultant with the Clearinghouse and an examiner for the Commission on Institutions of Higher Education of the North Central Association of Colleges and Secondary Schools. He has served as president of Los Angeles City College and as assistant superintendent in charge of Los Angeles community colleges. His widespread interests are reflected in his chapters on black studies and vocational education.

YOUNG PARK was an instructor and an administrator with the Community College District, North Orange County (California), before coming to the Clearinghouse as an administrative analyst. He drafted the second portion of the chapter on the community college as an institution.

EDGAR A. QUIMBY is associate dean for curriculum and instruction at Genessee Community College (New York) and was formerly a research associate in the Institute for the Development of Educational Activities. He wrote the first portion of the chapter on the institution and assisted Lombardi with the chapter on black studies.

A
Constant
Variable

New Perspectives
on the Community College

A Constant Variable

Prologue

The fascination of a bonfire never ends. One flame, many flames. One can watch for hours seeing the whole fire and seeing each flicker. Always the same, always different. Like the ocean. Undulating waves. The water remains, the waves break. Never changing, always in motion. A constancy of action. A constant variable.

This book is about the community college, an institution that is always different yet always the same. How different? Each semester it revises its procedures, adopts new programs, reorganizes its operations. How the same? It always offers courses, credits, buildings, instructors.

How describe this constant variable, the two-year college? The college is many things. It is its history as reflected in the writings that have chronicled it. It is an institutional ethos that is the sum of the values, expectations, and aspirations of the people who comprise it. It is the potential of its students, the coherence of its programs, the images perceived by the people concerned with it. All this and more, it is a major social institution.

Even so, the moment its dimensions are described in answer to the question, "What is the college?", they become objects. They characterize the college but they are objects nonetheless, awaiting a perceiver to filter them through his own eyes and draw his own pictures. For no matter what is written about the institution, it must still be seen through a subject's eyes, and individual perceptions vary. To a single student, the college offers a way into the world—his own world. Two million students, two million private worlds. To an

1

instructor, the college is a job, a career, or merely a neutral housing that allows him to come into contact with young people. To an administrator, the college may be a mission; to a trustee, a status symbol that he wears to service club luncheons. To each individual it is any of these things or countless others that might be mentioned. It is thus impossible to characterize the college on an individual level; each person must do that for himself.

Nor is it any easier to speak of the institution as it appears to a class of individuals—students, staff members, or lay public. For which type of student can we speak? Full-time? Part-time? Occupational? Transfer? Upper-middle-class? Low socioeconomic status? High ability? Low previous achievement? The distinctions can be drawn in innumerable ways. The same is true for faculty members when taken in groups. Can one presume to speak for "the academic" or "the vocational" instructors? The short-termers or those who have been with the institution for decades? The instructors who perceive the college as a stopping-off place while they work on advanced degrees or those who have made it a long-term career? The militants? The boat-rockers? The apathetic time-servers? To presume to speak for "the faculty" is as audacious as to suppose that one can speak for "the students." Nor can one see the college through the eyes of "the administrators" or "the trustees." No vision of the institution serves adequately as a representation of the perception shared by a great many others. Like the blind men and the elephant, each person has his own truth. Each subcategory has its own reality.

This book is an analytical review—a review because it chronicles the apparent; an analysis because it goes behind the obvious to tease out a form of reality. From either standpoint, it is biased. A reviewer's biases are revealed in the topics he chooses and in his commentary—what he applauds or says we need more of. The analyst is biased because he begins with a vision of what could be and then assesses what is on the basis of how closely it approximates his model; viewing the apparent needs, the existing structures, and the people involved, he asks if they fit together, if they make sense. The reviewer gives his view of the news; the analyst asks what it means.

Because many biases have shaped this volume, it is fitting to state a few of them at the outset. First, an educational structure cannot perform optimally unless it has a large percentage of self-aware, well integrated staff members. No type of bureaucracy can of itself mandate top performance. Second, these staff members must think about each aspect of their operations on several levels. Each task must be assessed according to the way it serves the immediate situation, as it represents the tasks performed by the class of professional people that the individual represents, and as it fits the institution's ultimate purposes. Third, education is a field of thought; instruction is a discipline of knowledge. Both can be conceived apart from the context of what we call "school." Neither will advance without carefully structured inquiry. Fourth, no type of work or contact within the two-year college is unique or so remote from what has been studied in other contexts that its practitioners can justifiably ignore the literature of education. Fifth, adversary relationships do not befit an educational structure. Faculty versus administration, instructor versus student—any "us versus them" attitude runs counter to institutional purpose. Sixth, taken as a whole, the junior college in America lacks a coherent philosophy—but, for that matter, so do most other forms, types, and levels of educational structure. Several other biases and preconceptions are stated in the chapters themselves; others are left unstated, probably because they are unconsciously held. This is not an untoward effect, however, for the myth of value-free scholarly writing long has been debunked.

In examining the community college we find that, although it presents a remarkable success story, there are many tensions within the institution that bid fair to distort its purposes. Although the institution offers equality of opportunity, it does little to insure equality of educational effects. Herein lies one dilemma—of what enduring social value is an institution that provides opportunity without concomitantly accepting responsibility? We find also that the community college does much more than its leaders readily would admit in the way of sorting and certifying people, holding the young in custody, and indoctrinating them with the belief that some people are innately better than others. These disparate functions are in conflict with the institution's educational function and, in fact, may subvert ostensible institutional purpose. In short, the uncritical prevailing view that holds the institution to be a social panacea is shown to be unrealistic, shortsighted, and potentially debilitating.

The book includes sections on the institution, its people, and its processes. Selection of specific topics to cover was made on the basis of several criteria but primarily on the presumed amount of current interest in the subject, secondarily on the number of documents available for review. Some topics—for example, analysis of curricular effects and patterns of financial allocation—had to be omitted because, although many people are concerned with them, little information has been collected. Others were omitted because the book does not purport to be a fact book for the uninitiated. Hence, the tabulation of forms of governance and administrative structure or of the responsibilities assigned to staff members would have been inappropriate here.

The first section offers a view of the community college in other than functional terms. The institutional ideology is traced, and ways of personifying the college are postulated. The second chapter in the section examines institutional research for what it does and does not do. Institutional research is seen as an inchoate art, one which is often neglected completely, even by the individuals to whom it is nominally ascribed.

The second section describes some of the people within the community colleges. Faculty members are characterized in terms of who they are, what they do, and the way they approach their work. The rapidly growing literature on the students is examined in chapters Five and Six in order to provide bench marks regarding what is known now and to discuss trends for future studies.

Curriculum and instructional processes are reviewed in the third section. This is not a compendium of curricular functions and instructional techniques but an analysis of concepts in curriculum and an examination of instruction from the point of view of the disciplinarian in the field. Vocational education and black studies are treated in separate chapters—vocational education because many national leaders give it first priority for the community college, and black studies because it is a timely topic and because the introduction of black studies programs in the community college provides many insights into curriculum construction. The book concludes with an examination of some of the unstated social functions performed by the community colleges and a plea for new directions— points that will be elaborated in future volumes in this series.

Characterizing the College

After seven decades of phenomenal growth, community junior colleges are now commonplace institutions in the setting of American schooling and are fast becoming the mainstays of mass higher education in the United States. However, this growth has not clarified the role these colleges expect to play in the structure of American education. Witness the longstanding and much lamented identity crisis of the junior college. The issue of identity is not a peripheral concern for junior college professionals; many in the field regard it as a core topic deserving serious attention. Indeed, in Medsker's (1960) estimation, the necessity for delineating and establishing a distinct identity for the junior college has long been and is today the overriding problem of the field. Other writers also have called for comprehensive concepts of the instructional and educational functions of junior colleges.

The identity crisis of the two-year college is rooted in the enduring efforts of junior college leaders to fashion it into a unique educational institution. Note the widespread use of the term *unique* to describe virtually every facet and problem related to the institutional functioning of junior colleges—and note further the attempts by educational spokesmen to resolve the identity crisis of the junior college by promoting unique models or concepts that supposedly foreshadow future social reality. Foremost among these is Cohen's (1969) model of a learning institution built on a defined outcomes approach to instruction—a definitive statement on cognitive rationality in schooling.

All this concern for the identity and uniqueness of the junior college—the institutional personality, as it were—stems from two paradoxical assumptions. On one hand, at least some junior college spokesmen agree that the two-year college has not been a unique setting for education, notwithstanding the pervasive emphasis on uniqueness in the professional literature and in the institutional documents of junior colleges. On the other hand, many of the same spokesmen appear to assume that if the junior college is not unique, it has little or no claim to either the educational imagination or the financial support of the public. Given these assumptions, an enduring identity crisis in the junior college movement is not at all surprising.

The same assumptions point to an undercurrent of utopianism in the educational thinking of junior college leaders. The search for a distinct identity for the junior college is akin to other utopian quests—no less than a search for El Dorado. In fact, the sheer growth of junior colleges across the United States has undoubtedly been stimulated by visions of utopia. However, these visions running through much of the literature on the junior college obstruct efforts to explain its functioning and to reconstruct its past. It is arguable whether a reconstruction of the junior college past could explain much about the present functioning of junior colleges, but it is axiomatic that we will not understand the functioning of junior colleges until we can unravel their entanglement with educational utopias.

In the first part of this chapter, the image of the junior college is traced through the writings of those who have chronicled institutional development in an attempt to answer such questions as: From what doctrines did the idea of the college evolve? How has it, and the institutions it spawned, fit within its societal context? Next, the image is brought down to the level of a single institution; a useful way of characterizing each college is to personify it, to view it as an entity composed of the perceptions held by its staff members— that is, what they see becomes the institution. The first part of the chapter thus presents a sociohistorical interpretation of the junior college movement as a whole; the second part, a sociopsychological view of the colleges taken singly.

Historical Image

Since the 1920s several attempts have been made to pin down the functioning of junior colleges. By far the most important efforts have been book-length status reports on the emergence and development of these institutions. The first was Koos's *The Junior-College Movement,* published in 1925; one more recent is Reynolds' *The Comprehensive Junior College Curriculum,* published in 1969. Between those years, Eells, Seashore, Bogue, Hillway, Medsker, Fields, and others published similar status reports.

Although the status reports are not narrative histories, most of them are treated as such. With the possible exception of Medsker's book (1960)', they best serve as briefs in defense of junior colleges. All of them accept, if they do not always fully acknowledge, Lange's (1927)' programatic exposition of the tripartite functioning of junior colleges—transfer, terminal, and community service. Each status report is in reality an assessment of the junior college with respect to Lange's model. Reference group theory vis-à-vis both the four-year college and the high school forms much of the conceptual underpinning of this literature (though the use of this theory is explicit only in Medsker). From the vantage point of its author, the central issue in each report is the identity of junior colleges within the formal structure of American education. This viewpoint explains the use of reference group theory, besides highlighting an allegedly key issue about the identity and uniqueness of the junior college—is it part of secondary or higher education?

Koos, a long-time proponent of the 6-4-4 plan in mass education, viewed the junior college as the last stage of secondary schooling. He thought that junior college education should take place in the setting of secondary schools. Eells (1931), whose book was published only six years after Koos's, took the position that the junior college was properly a part of the higher learning and that it should not be viewed as a secondary school. In 1940 Seashore argued that the junior college was a transition institution between high school and college, thus giving the two-year college the unmistakable flavor of a European secondary school. The title of Bogue's book, *The Community College* (1950), published at mid-century, suggests that the junior college is a more-or-less autonomous institution in American education, capable of countervailing the conventionality of both high school and college curriculums. Eight years later, in 1958, Hillway pictured the junior college as a forcinghouse for equal educational opportunity. Fields' 1962 **report is** largely a sequel to the work of Bogue, while Reynolds' (1969) essay on the junior college curriculum recaptures Seashore's concept of the junior college as a transitional school.

Medsker's study is the only status report that attempts to formulate a genuinely empirical view of the junior college. He sets out to examine the functioning of junior colleges by assessing their utility against alternative schemes of schooling beyond the twelfth grade. In the end, Medsker defends the social utility of junior colleges as comprehensive institutions that project images of both high school and college. Significantly, his evidence regarding the educational functioning of the two-year college, together with Clark's (1960) investigations, led Jencks and Riesman (1968) to picture junior colleges in the disquieting image of antiuniversities.

Each of these status reports, even Medsker's, acknowledges the uniqueness of the idea of the junior college. And the emergence of the idea of the junior college has attracted an enormous amount of attention in other literature; in fact, it is at the heart of almost all writing on these colleges. University seminar papers, in particular, have so often recounted the ideas of the founding fathers of the junior college—Henry Tappan, William Folwell, William Rainey Harper, David Starr Jordan, and Alexis Lange—that an unfriendly observer might think that the same seminar paper keeps circulating throughout graduate programs in junior college education. Many doctoral dissertations similarly are worshipful essays celebrating the emergence of the idea of the junior college or chronicling the lives of the missionaries of the movement. If these papers are intended to be patristic exercises for neophyte junior college practitioners, they probably serve a good end; otherwise, they promote outmoded historiographical notions about the transformation of American education since the Civil War. At best, they recapitulate the perfectly serviceable summary of the founding fathers' ideas in Thornton's (1966) book.

One consistent theme on the beginnings of the junior college is that the idea originated from the efforts of two mid-nineteenth century university presidents—Tappan at Michigan and Folwell at Minnesota—to reform American education in the image of German schooling. A dissertation by Gallagher (1968) devotes considerable attention to this topic. The strategy of Tappan and Folwell was simple enough: they sought to create elite universities in the wilderness of pre-Civil War midwestern America by distinguishing between collegiate and university instruction. Both of them conceived college to be a preparatory institution not unlike the German *Gymnasium*; and both argued that the freshman and sophomore years of collegiate schooling were the capstones of secondary education. To free the university to perform its function properly, Tappan and Folwell urged secondary schools to assume the responsibility for providing freshman and sophomore course work—in other words, to emulate the *Gymnasium*. Their proposal on this point formed the backdrop for the turn-of-the-century debate over the same issue, in which Harper and Jordan argued in favor of the Tappan/Folwell position. The founding of Joliet College—the oldest continuously functioning public junior college in the country—under Harper's influence was not the beginning of the era of American junior college education as much as it was the last scene of Tappan and Folwell's dream of abolishing the four-year baccalaureate college. The junior colleges that were later founded in California and elsewhere were distinctly products of the twentieth century.

Treatments of the idea of the junior college are beginning to recognize that these colleges are an outcropping of the twentieth century and that they emerged from the search for order in American educational life during the Progressive Era. Gallagher emphasizes this point in his thesis; the introductory chapter is replete with fresh insights. Unfortunately, he apparently was not sufficiently interested in the historiography of the Progressive Era to flesh out his insights with appropriate evidence. Another recent dissertation, this one by Aldridge (1968), suggests the connection between the junior college movement and the Progressive Era by concentrating on the educational ideas of sixteen prominent spokesmen for the junior college since 1900. Aldridge compares the ideas of early junior college leaders (1900–1935) with those of later ones (1945–1960) and concludes that all the central notions about the functioning of junior colleges were outlined early in this century. He found only two main issues between the two generations of leaders: whether the junior college was part of secondary or higher education (the second generation held to the latter view) and whether the two-year college was best conceived as a transfer or a terminal institution (again, the second generation of leaders held to this second viewpoint). However, these differing points of view have generated much literature on the identity and uniqueness of the junior college—a point that Aldridge largely overlooks.

If neither Gallagher nor Aldridge fully understands the ideological impact that the idea of the junior college has had on either the study of the junior college or its functioning, it may be a consequence of dissertation research, which often yields a mass of trees but no concept of the forest in which they grow. However, in spite of their minimal explanatory power, these two studies are useful: they place the emergence of the junior college in its proper twentieth-century setting and concomitantly connect the development of the junior college with the Progressive Era.

One debilitating characteristic permeates the literature. Neither the authors of the status reports nor the historians of the idea of the junior college question the uniqueness of this institutional form; nor do members of either group clarify what is unique about the junior college. The changing perspectives of junior college educators and the changing emphases of junior college schooling are accepted as a linear evolution in ideology—a notion fully compatible with the utopian spirit in junior college thinking. But this barefaced historicism is sterile if not poverty-stricken since it contributes little to our understanding of the social and educational functioning of junior colleges either now or in the past.

The status reports are summative images of junior college schooling. And, ironically, although the authors of these reports were trying in most instances to avoid image-making, their work has hampered the efforts of others to ferret out reality from imagery in junior college education. The putative critics of utopian thinking in the junior college movement projected in turn their own utopianism. This unintentional entrapment, as McClellan (1968) argues, is the curse of most educational criticism. Thus, is it possible to understand the functioning of junior colleges and transcend both the idea that the junior college is unique and that it is destined for a distinct niche in the structure of American schooling? Is the junior college a part of secondary or higher education? Is it best conceived as a transfer or a terminal institution? Arguments over these questions have plagued much thinking and research on the junior college. Yet attempts to answer them have turned out to be points of departure, not points of reference, for discussing the distinctive functioning of junior colleges. The somewhat hazy concept of these institutions as community colleges since 1950 confirms this lack of consensus. Despite all the ink spilled on the questions, they are not very important; only the conventions of educational research, buttressed by the professional training of junior college leaders, have made them important.

The authors of the status reports and the idea-men in the junior colleges have tried to grapple with the social functioning of junior colleges in the face of those conventions—but a clearer picture of what the junior college is today and what it has been since 1900 will emerge only when we begin to look at it as a social institution. Besides, whether the junior college is a part of secondary or higher education is not important; the hazy concept of the community college tacitly recognizes its status. Undeniably, the legal status of public junior colleges has undergone a change from secondary schooling to higher education, but only as the result of an academic revolution in American society since 1945 in which junior colleges have been little more than passive participants. Sufficient evidence of diversity among American junior colleges suggests that some of them are, in most salient respects, secondary schools, while others are two-year versions of university colleges.

As a social institution, the two-year college syphons off people who are incapable of surviving the increasing rigors of undergraduate study in senior institutions, those who cannot secure remunerative and agreeable employment or who are seeking, as observed elsewhere in this book, a place to be. If the appellation *college* somewhat distorts the educational functioning of two-year institutions, it amply legitimatizes whatever reasons lead students to enroll. Going to college, after all, is a highly honored pursuit in American life. To be sure, some students purposely matriculate in junior colleges as an inexpensive way-station to the B.A., while others enroll to be trained in a skilled vocation. However, most junior college students with genuinely purposeful intentions (veterans, for example) are older than the college-age population—and they could be successfully schooled in almost any setting.

The junior college is the safety valve of the American educational scheme. It is the shock absorber for the jarring tensions generated by the victories of mass education and the academic revolution in American life. Its multipurpose comprehensiveness offers something for all who attend; it meets the needs of almost any student who can articulate them; and it fashions programs to meet the putative but unarticulated needs of its parent community. If the constant proliferation of courses, programs, and other offerings by the junior college is the despair of both its friends and critics, it is the touchstone of its success. For the junior college is the perfect expression of the theories of early twentieth-century social theorists —Arthur Bentley, John Dewey, and many others—who advocated permanent institutional settings that could deal with unending problems with an unending range of proximate solutions. It fulfills ideally the turn-of-the-century concept of how an industrial society should be organized. That it is today criticized for its universality only confirms its success.

Institutional Personality

The historical perspective and the societal context of the junior college offer certain ways of viewing this institution. There are others. Looking at it through a sociopsychological framework— as we do here—we can take the school out of its historical perspective and freeze it at one point in time. The college is thus removed from conventional imagery, and, instead, it is subjected to analyses stemming from different perceptions.

Our approach here is to personify the institution—to view it as having an ethos that is a composite of the perceptions of its various members. This *institutional personality* is based on the idea that the personality of the junior college is determined by the perceptions of the people who make up the institution and that the perceptions in turn are heavily influenced by the attitudes and values of the people concerned. A major contention here is that each institution is different from others because it is made up of unique student and faculty groups. Each is directly affected by individual (as well as social) values, perceptions, and needs. Each person is an input to the total institutional personality. The material presented here has four major purposes: (1) to establish the concept of institutional personality, (2) to identify the major inputs to institutional personality of junior colleges, (3) to examine literature and research projects conducted on these major inputs to institutional personality, and (4) to cite directions that should be taken in subsequent research on this concept.

Concept. The idea of an institution's having a personality is not original. The premise has seldom been explicitly stated but it has been discussed in various terms by writers in fields other than education—particularly by people concerned with the study of organizations in general. These writers suggest that the institutional personality is a composite of the perceptions of the important members of the institution. Parsons and Shils refer to this as a theory of action. They contend that the "frame of reference of the theory of action involves actors, a situation of actions, and the orientation of the actor to the situation" (1954, p. 56). By expanding this idea to educational systems, the analogy is here proposed that an institution is characterized by the way a teacher, student, or administrator regards his environment and his role in that environment. A person operates, or behaves, within a particular frame of reference that contains such different but important variables as values, perceptions, cognitive approaches, learning styles, and other dimensions determined both internally—intrapersonally—and externally. Such elements, part of the personality constellations of all people, influence their perceptions. Getzels supports this concept with his observation that each individual stamps the particular role he plays with the "unique style of his own characteristic pattern of expressive behavior" (1958, p. 154). Thus, the objects for study in institutional personality are largely the personality, perceptions, and values of the people who operate within the organizational structure—in the case of the community college, the students and staff.

What gives rise to the perceptions? Some writers feel that acquired habits and social presses determine perception of and responses to any given situation. In his study of college students, Newcomb concludes that people perceive situations "as they have learned to do." He states that this "learning process" or "habit of response" is a learned response to "right" and "wrong" ways of perceiving situations (1966, p. 3). Whatever the cause, the person has the power of selecting his perceptions—perceptions that are affected by motivation, prior experience, temporary external and internal

presses, and the like. As Hall and Lindzey state, "It is not objective
reality which serves as a determinant of behavior but rather objective reality as it is *perceived* or assigned meaning by the individual"
(1957, p. 25). As they apply to the members of a junior college,
perception and personality obviously involve much more than object stimulation. The personality interacts with the junior college
environment. These elements mingle, and each becomes a press that
both determines and is determined by the other.

One view of the junior college holds that its functions and
purposes are right and that those who learn and teach there are all
in agreement or are suited to roles predetermined by tradition.
Otherwise, why would they be there? Contrary to this line of thought
is the growing evidence of a serious lack of understanding among
members of the junior college community. If one were to concede
only that reality is what each individual perceives it to be, no two
individuals could reasonably see the junior college as the same thing.

Hard data verifying the uncommonality of perceptions were
produced in a study dealing with values held by students and faculty at three junior colleges (Brawer, 1971). It was revealed faculty
and students do not agree on many ways of dealing with educational problems and issues; further, faculty disagree among themselves on what is important in their roles as teachers. Thus, there
are great intra- and interinstitutional differences among the colleges and one way of determining these differences is to investigate
the perceptions and personalities that dominate any given institution. Each institution has its unique personality. The differences
stem from differences found in the perceptions and value orientations of the members of the institution. It is not enough to understand *the* junior college in general terms. The value of studying institutional personality is that an institution is shown to be what it
actually is, not what it is supposed to be (Park, 1970).

The study of institutional personality allows both researcher
and practitioner to understand their institution's educational functions. Moreover, it permits an exact evaluation of the institution's
achievement of objectives. The general and superficial goals of community service, transfer education, and vocational education are
but the functional goals of every institution. The perceived goals,
conditioned by value orientations, are the actual ones toward which

teachers and students strive—and they may or may not be in accord with catalog descriptions of institutional goals.

The identification and examination of all elements involved in an institution's personality would be a monumental task requiring the concerted efforts of a large research team. Since the number of inputs that can easily be studied obviously is limited, the problem of establishing a complete framework must await future effort. As a beginning, we approach the measurement of institutional personality by examining the individual value structures of the people constituting the institution, the composite of which is a major input to their perception of a particular institution.

Individual Values. Values are directly related to any selection process. Several people have attempted to explain this phenomenon. For example, Parsons and Shils (1954, p. 59) suggest: "Whenever an actor is forced to choose among various means objects, . . . among various goal objects, . . . whenever he is forced to make any choice whatever—his *value orientation* may commit him to certain norms that will guide him in his choices. The value orientations . . . are not random but tend to form a system of value orientations which commit the individual to some organized set of rules." In addition to individual value orientations, Kluckhohn feels that there are also social values. However, he asserts that each group value is inevitably given private interpretation by each person and becomes personally distinctive (1954, p. 395).

Jacob (1957) interprets the values held by college students as criteria of both personal and group conduct. The trend in student behavior indicates that change is taking place and values form a crucial part of that change. Spindler (1955) refers to emergent values that are replacing the traditional values associated with puritan virtue and individualism. These new values are supposed to represent a relativistic moral viewpoint and emphasize social contact.

The obvious question is whether the new values influence the behavior of the teachers, the administrators, and the establishment in general. This question must be answered, for values and attitudes constitute a predisposition to act in a particular manner when faced with certain situations. Thus, changes in values have important implications for changed behavior, or, as Carzo and Yanouzas point out, "values are the criteria or standards that guide individuals in their selection of the appropriate behavioral alternatives in a given situation" (1967, p. 147).

The assumption that values affect behavior is strongly supported by other experts in axiology. Kluckhohn states that values are "manifested in ideas, expressional symbols, and in the moral and aesthetic norms evident in behavioral regularities" (1954, p. 394). His view is further maintained by Rokeach, who feels that values tell us how to live, to justify our own actions, and to judge the actions of others. Moreover, according to Rokeach, if "you claim to have a 'value' and you do not want to influence anyone else under the sun to have it too, the chances are it is not a value. . . . Values . . . transcend specific objects and specific situations; values have to do with *modes of conduct* and *end-states of existence*. . . . To say that a person 'has a value' is to say that he has an enduring belief that a particular mode of conduct or that a particular end-state of existence is personally and socially preferable" (1968b, p. 550)'.

Rokeach concentrates on what he refers to as "preferable modes of conduct and preferable end-states of existence." The distinction between the two involves means and ends between instrumental and terminal values. The instrumental value is a personally desired mode of conduct, and the terminal value represents a personally desirable end-state of existence. Rokeach further proposes an organizational hierarchy of values for each individual that suggests a rank-ordering of values along a continuum of importance. He also suggests that institutions have value orientations, as do individuals; also that individuals have a priority of values, and, when they are faced with a decision, the value with the highest priority determines the choice to be made. Thus, institutions, which are made up of individuals, reflect the composite values held by the personalities within the institution.

Institutional Organization. In the educational environment, another approach to perceiving institutional personality is in terms of the institutional organization. Every teacher and administrator must make decisions—decisions involving not only teaching methods, tests, student abilities, and the objectives of a particular course but also the objectives of the institution itself. How these decisions are made determines the personality of the institution, to a large extent. Depending on what theory is favored, either the individual has the free will to make decisions or his behavior is predetermined by other factors.

Cohen concludes that this type of compulsion exists in the junior college: "Junior college teachers are told [that] they will be judged on the basis of their teaching. Coupled with the initial role-choice of the new teacher, the organizational climate exerts a force for 'teaching' too powerful, in most instances, for a single individual to overcome, no matter how much he wishes to be considered primarily as a member of an academic field" (1969, p. 97). Apparently the organization exerts a powerful influence over its members; yet what the organization is and where it obtains its power and values are undefinable.

In the Milo Study, Dalton (1961) found that the unofficial power struggle between members of the organization influences the personality of the institution. However, this inference still does not define the source of power and the rationale behind the desire for power. One may reason that an educational institution is, perforce, free of the power struggle and value differences found in industrial organizations. However, such is not the case. Martin writes on the fallacy of assuming that institutions are value free. Selection of subject matter, interpretations, application, and "a score of other academic decisions are shot through with value judgments. To fail to acknowledge them and face this situation openly is to fool the dull students and make the bright ones cynical" (1967, pp. 42–43).

Without doubt, the junior college is a very human institution, complete with manifestations of particular personal values and goals, as are all educational organizations. Personal perceptions of institutional goals and objectives create subcultures within educational institutions. They not only contribute to the total personality of the institution but also can be considered an idiosyncrasy of its personality.

Lines of Inquiry. Although elements contributing to the creation of an institution's personality are numerous and complex, several are more basic or have more research potential than others. These are the personalities and perceptions of teachers, administrators, governing boards, and students. Identifying these factors is an enormous task for any institution to assume, but it should not be an excessive chore when one considers the number of hours spent on other mundane counting projects. A series of studies coordinated by the Clearinghouse and reported in several publications (Park, 1971; Brawer, 1971b) indicates a trend toward consideration of personality and perception. This effort could serve as a research model for further study of institutional personality. Another model for studying junior college personnel is presented in the Clearinghouse Topical Paper *The Person: A Conceptual Synthesis* (Brawer, 1970). This work directs inquiry toward an understanding of the person in the institution. It presents a method of perceiving and appraising the individual and emphasizes that people must be viewed phenomenologically.

Among other approaches, a series of reports made to the Western Interstate Commission for Higher Education emphasizes certain dysfunctions in existing institutions and suggests guidelines for further study. One study reports that administrators have primarily an ethical-moralistic personal value orientation and secondarily a practical one (Martin, 1967). While the authors do not feel the instrument used in the study is refined enough for widespread use, their findings do support the image of the American system based on middle-class values. Another example of perception and organization can be found in Flizak (1968).

An extensive project was undertaken at the Center for the Advanced Study of Educational Administration at the University of Oregon. Ziller and his associates reported on several aspects of personality in *The Political Personality* (1969), *The Alienation Syndrome* (1969), *A Theory of Self-Other Orientation and Interpersonal Conflict* (1969), and *Complexity of the Self-Concept and Social Acceptance* (1969). These studies might serve as models for assessment of junior college staff members, much as Brawer's research model can be used for personality assessment.

Most general studies of perception and attitudes are reported in doctoral dissertations and seminar papers. While this work is valuable, the researchers usually seek large samples and, hence, do not relate the data to a particular institution. Some titles of recent work include: Wisgoski, *Attitudes of Community College Presidents, Chief Student Personnel Officers, and Faculty Toward the Student*

Personnel Point of View in Selected Illinois Community Colleges
(1968); Elsner, *The Presidential Prism: Four Views: A State Offi-
cer's View of the Community College President* (1969); and *The
Moraine Valley Resident: His Attitude Toward the Community
College and His Socio-Economic Characteristics,* a report by the
Moraine Valley Community College, Illinois (1969); Verbeke,
*The Junior College Academic Dean's Leadership Behavior as
Viewed by Superiors and Faculty* (1966); and Pratt, *Flexibility
of Personality as It Relates to the Hiring and Retention of Public
Community College Faculty, New York State University* (1966).

All these works relate to the existing junior college framework. Most suggest that further research is necessary, and many
recommend changes. However, what is lacking is a totality, or rationale, for a complete picture of what is to be investigated further
or what changes are to be made.

What an educational institution "is" is not always what it
"ought to be." Many members of the community, as well as professionals, pretend that the junior college is what it ought to be
without an examination of what it is. However, without study of
the institutional personality, alterations in the junior college will
continue to be superficial. There is no further need to cite the importance of these investigations, but there is a need to examine further the basis for the decision-making process and perceptions of
personalities in the junior college.

Missing in many reports of the attitudes of junior college
decision makers are the basic personality and perception factors that
underlie decisions. The Gilliland and Nunnery (1970) survey, for
example, indicates that school boards have both considerable freedom and knowledge of junior college affairs. Contrarily, studies reported in Rosenthal (1969) indicate that conformity and community pressures keep board members from learning about their
responsibilities. However, neither work is concerned with the factors
underlying the perceptions of the people studied.

The environment at a junior college reflects the values and
perceptions of the faculty, administration, students, and governing
board. If conflicts exist, they have a concurrent effect on the institutional personality. Several studies have been made of contrasting
attitudes: student versus faculty, faculty versus administration, and

administration versus students. An example is Milton's report on
faculty views of student participation in decision-making (1968).
The importance of values in decision-making and teaching and possible conflicts between teacher and student are dealt with by Barnes
(1968) and Oppelt (1967). Attitudes and opinions of faculty and
administration toward job descriptions of the junior college president are the topic of a doctoral dissertation by DeLoache (1966).
Such projects deal with perception but rarely reach the heart of the
institutional organism. They seem to concentrate on the accepted—
the ought-to-be institution—rather than on attempting to discover
what the institution is.

Those who are employed by junior colleges to work in offices of institutional research could help find ways and means of
determining what the institution is rather than merely gathering
statistical data on transfer students, for example. Personality assessment, schemes, and techniques to examine the organization could
provide guidelines for determining the personality of a particular
institution.

Of the many models and instruments available for introspective institutional research, Brawer's (1970) prototype for assessment
of personality, Pace's *College and University Environment Scales*
(1969), and Rokeach's *Values Scales* (1968b) are only a sampling.
The subjects for such introspective research are faculty, administrators, governing boards, and students. Since most junior college students remain at an institution for less than one year, they must be
considered less influential on the institutional personality than are
other subjects. The views, values, and personalities of the more-or-
less permanent members of an institution are the true indices of institutional personality.

Other forms of study are—or should be—influenced by the
study of institutional personality. It seems fruitless to conduct experiments on teaching methods, for example, when the people whose
judgments determine action in the classroom are unknown quanti-
ties. In this context, we suggest that the following areas be considered for further investigation by the university-based researcher and
by the junior college practitioner:

First, a study of values compared with Pace's CUES questionnaire. The *Values Scales* developed by Rokeach would be well suited

to this project. It could be compared with the junior college version of CUES (Hendrix, 1967), which contains items directly related to the junior college environment.

Second, a study of formal institutional goals and values as contrasted with informal institutional goals and values of the staff. Research could begin with the assumption that an informal organization exists, or an identification of the nature and characteristics of that informal organization might be made as part of the study.

Third, a study of individual personality classifications in the junior college, which would require some form of personality inventory or a device similar to the Rokeach *Values Scales*. Criteria must be established for the various personality groupings and specific questions devised to identify those within a particular group.

Fourth, a study of the junior college as an entity with personality traits that distinguish it from other institutions. Certain criteria must be established to identify the distinctive characteristics that place an institution in any of various classifications. The instrument would be similar to the *College and University Environment Scales,* but it would be directed toward identifying institutional personality traits instead of dealing with the college environment. This study not only would consider the personality of an institution but also would identify those who seem to contribute most to its creation.

This short list suggests only a small portion of research yet to be done in the identification of institutional personality. The purpose of this kind of research is to leave behind the commonly accepted ideas of what the junior college ought to be and to establish a framework for finding a more relevant perspective. Determination of institutional personality is important because perceptions derived from values are not stereotyped or superficial as are the commonly accepted goals of the junior college. Once institutional personality is identified, there can be a true assessment of objectives and the achievement of those objectives.

In sum, both types of study—sociohistorical examination and sociopsychological research—are needed. The sociohistorical investigator can place the junior college as a whole in the context of its society. The sociopsychological researcher can examine the single institution in order to determine its underlying value positions, the perceptions of its key people. Previous study of the junior college has all but neglected both modes of examination. Present research is almost invariably based on what the investigator feels the institution ought to be; the institutional rhetoric has attained its own form of reality. A new perspective demands new research bases.

Institutional Research

2

The dynamics involved in the advancement of knowledge result from the conflict between common sense and criticized knowledge. Common sense offers security and is composed of unquestioned cognitive "facts" we operate with from day to day. For example: students should be obedient; college students do better when they are required to pay for their education; competition is the best motivator; learning should not be easy; school administrators should have teaching experience; students do better if they like what they study; little boys do not do as well as little girls; everybody should not get A's; students who miss classes should lose grade points; there must be a time limit for dropping a course; certain courses must be required; courses in basic English and mathematics do not merit college credit; schools should run smoothly without incident; students must be tested before entering college; the degrees held by the staff are an index of the quality of the institution; the bigger the library (or anything else), the better.

As Pepper (1966) explains, conflict results when common sense "facts" are scrutinized and are frequently found to be unreliable. As a result, security is threatened, and the need for refined or criticized knowledge becomes apparent. This need is the important reason for promoting junior college studies and critiques of the problems, methods, and results of the studies. Without attempts to refine knowledge through studies to determine what knowledge and facts can be supported with adequate evidence, educational knowledge will remain primarily in the common sense realm—a secure haven, but one that is supported by such inadequate evidence as appeal to authority, self-evident principles, and dubious facts.

Refining knowledge is a fairly new and slowly expanding activity in the junior college. This activity, as in the whole field of education, rests on behavorial science research methodologies. There is no need for such restriction, but generally it exists. As behavorial science researchers, research personnel of junior colleges are sometimes in double trouble. They are frequently inexperienced in the use of standard research methodologies, and, while they are learning them, the methodologies themselves are being questioned.

This lag in expanding research activities, updating the methodologies, and providing direction for research activities is the general concern of an increasing number of junior college consortia, associations, and other groups. The Southern California Institutional Research Group, the ERIC Clearinghouse for Junior Colleges, the Florida Community Junior College Inter-institutional Research Council, the junior college special interest groups of the Association for Institutional Research and of the American Educational Research Association, and the Junior and Community College Consortium of the National Laboratory for Higher Education (North Carolina) are among groups that contribute to furthering practices in institutional research—here defined as applied study undertaken by or on behalf of a college to aid in understanding its own operations.

In this chapter we discuss institutional constraints that affect junior college studies; some of the studies themselves, including the topics, methodologies, and results; and general limitations in study design.

Institutional Constraints

Institutional constraints on intramural research are infrequently documented, if at all. They are revealed during discussions at conferences for junior college institutional research or for educational developmental officers, or in daily campus developments and staff interactions that affect the execution of a study. Frequently, these difficulties are reported only informally, and, unfortunately, their scope or prevalence is not easily discernible. However, from some examples of the problems, it is fair to assume that they contribute individually and collectively to the content and quality of junior college institutional studies and the reports about them. They should not be omitted or ignored when one is examining institutional studies and evaluating their quality or usefulness, for such omissions lead to premature conclusions for several reasons: institutional research studies lack sophistication on the part of those conducting them, research methods are not applicable to the institutional situation, and so on. These assumptions have some validity, but they are not sufficient for a complete evaluation. Extrinsic constraints must be considered.

The constraints are characterized by the following concerns of directors of institutional studies: (1) the only advantage to being a research officer on some campuses is to attend conferences and workshops; (2) the major function of some research officers is to write grant proposals, answer questionnaires, and reply to requests for data; (3) some administrators try to torpedo studies because they feel studies interfere with their authority; (4) sampling techniques can sometimes not be used because a higher authority does not trust samples and insists on using the total population; (5) some administrators grant permission for studies only if they are safe or will not have unpleasant repercussions; (6) members of accreditation teams sometimes feel changes are too liberal even if they are supported with data; (7) data are often either misinterpreted or not used; and (8) if reports of the studies are not reduced to two pages each, it is unlikely anyone will read them.

Despite the self-justification implicit in the above statements, the situations indicate a potential for affecting the character of junior college institutional studies. The statements are reducible to five problems that are not mutually exclusive: on some junior college campuses, the staff does not regard the director of institutional studies as having an important function; the director of institutional studies is frequently viewed as a convenience for handling routine chores rather than as a provider of information for changing routines; the design of and steps in conducting a study are strongly influenced by concerns irrelevant to the requirements of an objective study; common sense beliefs and conclusions preclude objective studies and the use of information obtained through them; and some decision-makers do not want to spend the effort or the time

necessary for adequate understanding and use of information that is or could be provided by institutional studies. Regardless of how such problems may be stated, they merit consideration for increasing the utility and returns of junior college studies. Many of them are unavoidable because of the politics and time pressures of institutions, but consideration of them, we hope, will not lead to attempts at an easy way out of objective institutional research.

Studies

The studies reviewed are, for the most part, 1970 additions to the ERIC collection. Approximately half these studies were conducted on the campuses of two-year colleges. The others came from graduate students training for the junior college, graduate faculty members coordinating junior college projects, federally funded organizations with a junior college focus, and district- and state-level junior college offices; a few came from private publishers of educational tests and materials.

The studies in the ERIC collection cover interests and problems that range in scope from topics affecting a single classroom to matters of general concern. The following examples of study objectives indicate the variety: to evaluate a new audio-tutorial class in general biology (Arnwine and Juby, 1969); to compare gain scores of students in large and small English classes (Silver, 1970); to obtain information on the use of field admissions representatives (Wesson, 1966); to develop an information storage and retrieval system (Orange Coast Junior College District, 1969); to investigate a reading-study skills program (Bossone, 1970); to investigate the work values of women to provide information for counseling (Blai, 1970); to describe a program for training junior college personnel (Zane, 1969); to examine problems in work-experience education (Hayes, 1969); to suggest practical approaches to augment public relations activities (Horvath, 1969); to determine the procedures for and present extent of admitting outstanding high school students to junior college courses for credit (Parker, 1970); to conduct a follow-up study to assess the success of the whole state system of junior colleges (Florida Community Junior College Inter-institutional Research Council, 1969); to establish guidelines for the preparation of industrial arts, vocational-industrial, and technical teachers (Feirer and Lindbeck, 1970); to get data on leaders in the junior college field and to determine what they feel the crucial issues will be in the next ten years (Ferrari, 1969); to provide an overview of state coordinating and control agencies for junior colleges (Wattenbarger and others, 1970).

Of the wide variety of problems and interests found in the ERIC documents, those that deal with the learning process and related student and instructor activities are infrequent. This infrequency is in contrast to numerous studies on student recruitment, student characteristics, student placement, student success, and similar topics. An increase in studies that deal with the learning process (or teaching effectiveness) on junior college campuses would fill an important gap in the concerns of many junior college administrators. In addition, the findings could avoid the type of situation revealed in Bossone's study from Hostos Community College (New York). In its foreword, Dispensieri states, "The desires of the social reformers have outdistanced the skills and techniques for teaching reading to a generation of educationally disadvantaged students who have been promised a higher education" (Bossone, 1970). That teaching skills and techniques need improvement is also shown by other studies reporting high failure rates (Arnwine and Juby, 1969; Roueche, 1968). Without studies of the learning process in the junior college setting, it is doubtful that there will be much refined information on which to base improvements.

Methodologies. While the problems and purposes of the studies are varied, the research methodologies used in them are few—a phenomenon noted by Thomson (1967). Some 20 to 25 per cent of the ERIC documents do not contain descriptions of research procedures. They are case histories of projects, reviews of documents, or first-hand descriptions of projects and practices. The other documents do contain some descriptions of procedures that represent identifiable research methodologies.

Three traditional methodologies from the social sciences are represented. First, and most common, are survey methods used for observational studies of populations. Survey techniques include sampling total populations, random and stratified random sampling, and selecting typical cases on the basis of expert opinion. Cluster and similar sampling techniques are not found. Two favorable trends are noted in studies using survey methods: researchers obtain higher response rates, and, more often, the important details of survey techniques are included in the studies. These details include pretesting the survey instrument, designating the sample size according to desired competence levels, providing methods for replacing missing units, and reporting the same error. (For examples, see Bossone, 1970; Florida Community Junior College Inter-institutional Research Council, 1969.) These merely indicate trends—many surveys lack sufficient rigor to determine the validity of the results.

The second methodological approach is that of group comparisons, that is, the comparison of groups that have received different treatments. Usually the comparison is done in a quasiexperimental fashion because naturally existing groups are most often used. Sometimes, matched groups and, less often, randomly assigned groups are compared. Another category of group comparisons introduces a treatment and compares the resultant values of the dependent variable with the predicted values or the values that would be expected in the absence of the treatment (Arnwine and Juby, 1969). Chi-squares and t-tests rank first as statistical techniques for the comparisons. Statistical models compatible with the manipulation of two or more independent or dependent variables are rarely used.

While the latter models are more complex, harder to implement, and harder to interpret than the previous ones, they have a potential advantage for the investigation of instructional effectiveness of alternative methods, especially in studies of larger institutions. The advantage is the inclusion of a large number of defined variables in the studies. As they stand, these studies tend to result in comparisons of total methods (for example, lecture, lecture-discussion, audio-tutorial, multimedia, team teaching), which are composites of many treatment variables left undefined in the global comparisons. When the many studies that make global comparisons are collected and analyzed, as they were by Dubin and Taveggia (1968), the results are confusing and indeterminate. One cannot decide which of two alternative teaching methods is most effective for which situation—not unsurprising if a given teaching method in one study can be an apple and in another can be a lemon.

Usually, student test scores and grades provide the criterion measures of comparison studies. Since statistical models for making comparisons often require variance or dispersion in the dependent or measured values, the application of the models (parametric, in particular) conflicts with the criterion-referenced approach, which strives to reduce the variance of achievement variables across students. One way to avoid conflict and still gain mileage from the models is to change the criterion measures used from test scores and grades to measures of efficiency, which remain varied or dispersed regardless of the approach used; for example, time required for students to meet the criteria.

The third methodology used in junior college studies is correlation, that is, the determination of relationship between variables. Its widespread use for predicting academic success from standardized tests is criticized by Sheldon (1970a). Sheldon points out that standardized tests add little or nothing to high school grade-point averages for the purpose of prediction, and he seriously questions the logic of their presence on the junior college campus. Among his criticisms he lists the following common faults in junior college research:

(1) The basic assumption that test items are nothing more or less than a sample of behavior (and test-taking behavior at that) seems to have been lost. (2) The concept of validity is frequently used with what appears to be no thought of what the test is valid for. Validity, it seems, is represented by the correlation coefficient between the test or subtest and grade-point average. The particular factors that influence the size of the validity coefficient, or any other correlation, appear to be ignored. (3) Descriptors of the sample used for correlations, such as range of talent or presence of extreme scores, are seldom reported in the studies, though they can frequently account for potentially spurious correlations. (4) The standard error of estimate, a much better concept of predictive validity, is seldom reported and, when it is, appears to be frequently misunderstood or misused. . . . (9) Few investigators seem to differentiate between the significance of a correlation and its meaning. Some colleges report hundreds of correlations and scores of t-tests with the same sample of less than a hundred students. They don't seem to know that the significance of a correlation depends almost entirely on the number

of cases used to compute it. (10) Though most junior college investi-
gators understand that coefficient of determination (r^2) represents
the proportion of the criterion variance accounted for by the predic-
tors, they lose sight of the fact that they have computed an r, *using a*
sample of students as opposed to a rho *of the true correlation for*
total population. As a consequence, with r = 0.31, *they assume they*
are accounting for 10 per cent of the criterion variance.

In general, the methodologies are composed of a restricted
number of research procedures, experimental designs, and statistical
models. Not included are many methodological approaches that
could sometimes apply to the purposes or situations of the studies,
for example: counterbalancing for experimental control, analysis of
covariance for statistical control, weighted subsamples for survey
studies, t-tests for groups with unequal variances, factorial designs
for multiple independent variables, multivariate designs for multiple
dependent variables. Also neglected are the nonparametric statistics
that would frequently serve as favorable alternatives to the Pearson
product-moment-correlation coefficient and the t-test.

Results.   Because of the popularity of the survey technique,
many studies result in descriptions of junior college students, staff, or
operational procedures. Some examples are the procedures used by
junior colleges to admit high school students, the programs for training junior college personnel, the concerns of junior college presidents,
and the demographic characteristics of students. In these cases, the
studies provide an information base for decisions.

Other studies offer suggestions or suggestive conclusions.
Some of these suggestions follow from the error of using the finding
of no difference as support. The following is a hypothetical example: Since there was no significant difference between the grades
obtained by students in large classes and those in small classes, the
data support the hypothesis that students do just as well in large
classes; therefore, it is suggested we should retain (or adopt) large
classes. This conclusion or suggestive conclusion is unproductive and
adds insult to injury: Restricted, unreliable measures, insensitive to
the independent variable, are used, and inferential statistical models
are misused. The logic of these models does not allow one to support

a hypothesis of no difference. Further, rejection of a null hypothesis is not tantamount to support for the reverse effect.

Fortunately, most conclusions found in junior college studies are pragmatic because they concern functional operations, frequently a specific operation of the total institution. Some examples of conclusions commonly found in junior college research studies are the use of self-appraisal for evaluating instructors, an emphasis on certain values when counseling women for employment, the addition of counseling and placement services for evening students, an augmentation of faculty orientation and development activities, and the development of new methods and materials for teaching reading to the disadvantaged. In addition, suggestions for further research on certain topics and for improvement in conducting the research are included in the studies. These conclusions stimulate interest in how something can or should be done; sometimes, however, because of the way the studies are initiated, they neglect to specify how to apply the suggestion. Frequently, each study stands alone. Only rarely do investigations stimulate systematic or integrative thought that allows one to generate new ideas and organize data across studies.

Designs. The major factor that prevents the derivation of new ideas or the integration of data from junior college studies is the absence of study designs initiated from a conceptual or theoretical base. Instead, most studies are casual inquiries that assume each topic to be independent: How successful are the transfer students? What is the drop-out rate? How do our local test norms compare with other norms? What are the characteristics, values, attitudes, and so on, of this particular group? What are the practices of other institutions? Answers to these questions are interesting, but the results of the studies do not mesh with each other; junior college topics remain isolated. In the studies, curriculum content remains isolated from the performance of transfer students. In another area, administration and counseling remain compartmentalized from instructional effectiveness, instructional effectiveness from teacher evaluation, teacher evaluation from drop-out rate, and so on.

In other words, logical ties between studies are infrequent, and arbitrary divisions for separating research topics are maintained. Without adequate conceptualization, each study of student characteristics or teacher effectiveness or attrition becomes a study for the sake of its own execution, following a mental set of how such a study should be done. While studies are grouped under the same topic, they do not allow for corroboration with one another or for new conceptual syntheses to redirect the mental set. Also, without broader conceptualization, it is difficult to distinguish the true divisions in the educational process from the divisions that serve mere linguistic or administrative convenience. As a result, the same research studies are done over and over again, adding little collectively to what refined knowledge there is in the junior college field.

The field of education is frequently criticized for its lack of theoretically or conceptually based research. As for psychological theory in educational settings, Cellura states, "There has been a notable tendency among educational researchers to avoid the use of theoretical systems in their research" (1969, p. 349). Furthermore, there is no explicit defense of an atheoretical approach. As examples applicable to educational research, Cellura suggests utility-expectancy theories that "tend to predict behavior as some function of the value or utility of a possible outcome and the expectancy that a desired outcome can be accomplished" (1969, p. 358). Frase (1970) labels the absence an affliction. He and Anderson (1970) suggest mathemagenic behavior (behavior that refers to activities relevant to the achievement of instructional objectives in specified situations) for the conceptual base.

Institutional research in the junior college has improved since Swanson (1965) made his national survey of the practice. Nevertheless, it has a long way to go before it attains a position of even minimal influence on college operations.

Characterizing the Faculty

3

College faculty members may be perceived in many ways. However, there is little research material available; most literature on the faculty includes only normative data such as academic backgrounds and previous work experiences. It is easy to see why. Colleges must collect information about their students—their funding sources demand it. And, along with routine data collection, it is easy to ask the students supplemental questions and thus build a bank of information. Furthermore, students are vulnerable targets for study—they have little choice in the matter—but instructors do not as readily lend themselves to investigation. Nevertheless, some attention has been paid to the special characteristics of two-year college instructors—and the literature is growing. Here, we deal with the junior college instructor, especially as viewed in the literature appearing between 1967 and 1970.

Studies in General

What do we know about junior college instructors? What do we need to know? May they be identified by special characteristics? How would such delineations relate to teaching effectiveness? Viewing the literature as a whole, one point is clear: there is not much from which to draw inferences about faculty functioning. We have certain gross data: In 1969–1970, for example, of the nearly 100,-000 two-year college instructors, fewer than 7 per cent had doctoral degrees while 69 per cent had earned the master's degree. Median annual pay scales for all ranks of instructors stood at just over

$8,000 in private colleges, nearly $11,000 in public two-year schools, ranging somewhat higher than public school pay and a bit lower than university rates. However, little more specific information pertaining to the entire group is available.

Called upon to teach courses often similar to those in the lower division of a university, the typical junior college instructor meets classes for twelve to fifteen hours weekly. He serves on college committees, selects materials, and engages in activities that fall within the commonly held definition of teaching. He is expected to be innovative—that is, to try various new media and approaches to instruction. He must teach students classified as remedial because junior colleges are enrolling ever-increasing numbers of untraditional students (a euphemism for "deprived" or "disadvantaged"). He must reconcile himself to a high percentage of drop-outs that either may have an impact on his morale or may lead him into questionable rationalizations. He must handle large numbers of students and may feel that he is being buried under a blizzard of paperwork. He must also realize that the community itself keeps a close eye on his manners and mores.

Although two-year college instructors prepare courses, meet classes, consult with students, assign marks, sit on committees—in short, do what instructors at all other levels of education do—we know little more about their professional activities. Further, the available information hardly distinguishes the individual from the mass; it allows us to sketch general descriptions but it does not enable us to portray a single entity.

Some systematic attempts have been made to assess the personal and professional situation of junior college instructors. Garrison's visits in twenty junior colleges throughout the country represented an ambitious initial effort to shed light on the lives of faculty members, their attitudes and perceptions. Although his report was generalized, it proved to be a landmark. Responses to several open-ended questions indicated that the institutions in which the instructors worked had such varied aims that the traditional criteria for college teachers seemed neither applicable nor accurate. Garrison determined that rapid expansion of post-secondary education made previous academic customs and attitudes wholly irrelevant to the the junior college. As he put it, "The junior college teacher is—or

may be becoming—a new breed of instructor in higher education"
(1967, p. 15)'.

Garrison implied that the use of categories such as student-
centered or subject-focused is thoroughly outdated. Indeed, many
frequent descriptors of the junior college as an institution that meets
the needs of the community through guidance services and transfer,
not-for-transfer, credit, or not-for-credit courses are as outdated as
the false dichotomy isolating academic and vocational-technical
offerings. Teachers cannot be understood in terms of these categories.

Since then, several other investigators have reviewed teachers
and teaching in the junior college. For example, the literature on
characteristics of college and university faculty members was sum-
marized by Brawer (1968) who discussed teacher typologies, images,
and personality dimensions. Updating an earlier study of junior
college faculty members, Medsker and Tillery collected data on
nearly 4,000 instructors in fifty-seven colleges (Cross, 1969). An
in-depth study of faculty members—as well as students and administrative staff—has been coordinated by the Clearinghouse (Cohen,
1970d; Brawer, 1970, 1971b; Park, 1971). Other studies focus on
issues related to the teacher's professional situation—for example,
patterns of faculty orientation (Kelly and Connolly, 1970) and the
evaluation of instructors (Cohen and Brawer, 1969).

Several studies attempt to draw comparisons of instructors
who may be differentiated by subject matter or who adopt various
groups as their point of reference. Hamill (1967)' found that certain
teachers who had greater academic preparation and had academic
assignments were dissatisfied with their institutions; they regard
four-year colleges and universities as their reference group. Conversely, teachers of applied subjects, women, and teachers with five
or more years of experience in their fields adopt the community college concept. Along a similar line, "high potential" instructors in
senior college transfer programs support senior college norms and
practices and favor reforms of junior colleges to the senior college
mode. On the other hand, "low potential" instructors in junior college vocational programs favor expansion of comprehensive roles
(Hunt, 1964)'. Rogers (1965)' compared junior college instructors
who were retired military personnel and who had attended service

academies with former military men who had not attended such
institutions, and he found that the latter group of instructors was
rated higher by administrators than was the former.

Comparison of the effective with the noneffective instructor
accounts for a plethora of material, some of which will be cited in
the chapter on teacher evaluation. The special characteristics on
which effectiveness may be assessed are also voluminous—but at
least one investigator (Pearce, 1966) suggests that the attributes
needed by effective teachers must point toward the tendency and
ability to help students develop and maintain their self-confidence.
Since it is unlikely that any given instructor could possess all necessary attributes to reach this goal—understanding, flexibility, patience,
practicality, sense of humor, creativity, and preparation—it is possible that if a balance among various faculty members could be
achieved, the staff as a whole could operate effectively.

Every era has special key words and concepts. These timely
issues invariably lead to special studies. Lately, no concept has
caught the fancy of educators as much as innovation. There have
been a few attempts to assess personal and institutional dimensions
related to innovation, for example: the role college administrators
take in establishing faculty attitudes toward instructional experimentation and innovation (Weber, 1966); a description of seminars
related to institutional readiness and faculty participation in developing instructional resources (Salatino, 1967); and the results of
questionnaires directed to perceptions about innovative procedures
(Campbell, 1968; Jensen, 1969; Wygal, 1966). However the question of which types of faculty member tend to accept change is
rarely asked. The finding that college instructors tend to shy away
from innovation has been noted by studies conducted in senior institutions (Evans and Leppman, 1967). Apparently the two-year college faculty is no exception.

The community colleges' concern with innovation brings up
many questions. With education's long heritage of rigidity, can
needed flexibility be injected into old systems? To discuss introducing innovation without consideration of such human dimensions as
flexibility, adaptability, and interactional effects is to deal with only
a small segment of the problem. Studies of faculty characteristics

are—or should be—basic to the innovation of changes within a college.

Activism also is a popular issue and has generated much concern in both the popular and professional presses. Little of a definitive nature, however, is known about the actual meaning of activism—student or faculty attitudes, what directions activism will take, how it might be used for good rather than to destroy. Some studies of student and faculty activism in the junior college have been undertaken. Discussing student activism from an administrator's point of view, Lombardi (1969) deals with issues such as activist groups, the definition of student rights, and the resultant reactions of students, faculty, and administrators. Gaddy (1970) surveyed the field and found 231 junior colleges reporting instances of overt student activism. Other writers have addressed themselves to activism by assessing the prevailing effect of the surrounding community and the faculty's recognition of the students' legitimate concern for curriculum reform (California Junior College Association, 1968). At least one report summarizes the responses of the staff to campus incidents during a student strike—Gold (1969) cites such offshoots of activist demonstration as the extent of class interruptions, verbal conflict, physical intimidation by those who interrupt classes, the degree of student support for and/or understanding of the strike, the faculty's understanding of the issues, and the administrator's role in handling the situation. Faculty militancy—clamorous demands for a greater voice in institutional governance—is less well chronicled. It is unclear whether such conflicts are interpreted as the result of desires to participate in institutional policy decisions rather than economic considerations (Wright, 1967) or whether faculty organizations themselves add to the militancy of the teachers and to the general unrest by the very way they compete for members (Riess, 1967).

The teacher of untraditional students is the subject of much conference rhetoric but little deliberate investigation. Exhortations directed toward him are easy to find. One example: "Teachers of remedial students must be both sensitive and subjective. They must be aware of many of the needs, appetites, problems, life and learning styles, and other dimensions of the students. In short, they must have the ability to empathize" (Moore, 1970, p. 71). Unfortunately, there is validity in the statements issued by Moore and others who also might be cited here, but we know practically nothing about who can best teach the untraditional student. Probably special training is desirable because, as Gleazer (1967) points out, instructors of remedial courses usually are inadequately prepared to deal with the problems they face. But for many reasons—not the least of which is that instruction is still viewed as an arcane art—no one quite knows how to arrange the special training sequences needed.

Typologies

A typological scheme groups people according to certain characteristics they have in common. Such schemes may be found in the literature of sociology and psychology, beginning with the earliest writings in these disciplines. Although typologies collapse many data into arbitrary categories, they can aid in understanding how roles, characteristics, and orientations merge.

Some attempts have been made to classify college instructors. Gusfield and Riesman's (1968) typology was formulated on the basis of the career orientations of instructors at two proximate colleges. Each school was affiliated with and developed under the auspices of a university in a large midwestern state, but each overtly attempted to depart from the mode of higher education posed by its parent institution. Explicitly dedicated to "average" state university students who were typically the first members of their families to go to college and who would normally pursue rigidly narrow vocational aims, the two colleges had much in common with the open-door community college.

Faculty members were categorized into three groups: *pioneer settlers, pioneer adventurers,* and *job holders.* The *pioneer settlers*— career-oriented planners in the image of Caplow and McGee's (1958) models—held firm professional orientations. Viewing the college as either a potentially permanent abode or as a way station toward a more settled career, they were considered to be conservative, career-oriented "young fogies" even though they had elected to teach in an experimental college. As a group, these instructors emphasized efficiency and insisted on teaching materials closely related to research and writing.

The *pioneer adventurers* expressed a dissident attitude toward the *settlers*. Focusing either on what they were getting away from in their former academic positions or on what they were moving toward in the future, they were attracted to their new positions by the college's innovative posture rather than by general career advantages accruing from the move. However, they appeared less committed than the *settlers* to values and standards of professional disciplines and while they might be—and indeed many were—competent scholars in their own special subject matter, they did not visualize their academic lives in a manner similar to the *settlers*. Instead, their roles appeared to be less a measure of dedicated attitude toward their subject fields than an orientation toward an interdisciplinary, more broadly defined, occupational interest.

The *job holder* differed from both the *settler* and the *adventurer* in that his academic position did not represent the central dimension of his life but was perceived rather as a means to other ends. He was motivated by neither the "academic marketplace nor the ideologies of missionary commitment to the experiment. . . . [This instructor] stands outside the diversities represented in the orientations of *settlers* and *adventurers*, getting his 'kicks' perhaps in the enjoyment of family, in the context of leisure time or in some other occupation" (Gusfield and Riesman, 1968, p. 278).

Dealing specifically with community college instructors, Friedman (1965, 1967) classified them in terms that suggest their prior institutional affiliation: *high schoolers, graduate students,* and *professors.* Most of the people in Friedman's sample had formerly taught in a secondary school, had earned the master's degree in a given academic field of specialization and were over thirty-five years old when they assumed their new careers as junior college instructors. Classified as *high schoolers,* they emphasized subject matter, prided themselves on their lack of identification with teaching methods, and frequently deprecated both methods courses in education and professors of education (although their own academic preparation had included approximately twenty hours in education courses and much of their conversation contained such "educationese" terms as "motivation," "units," and "supervised study").

Coming to junior college teaching directly from graduate degree programs and generally with no prior teaching experience, *graduate students* are usually in a state of transition. They spend much time in scaling down their expectations of acceptable student performance and filling in gaps in their own knowledge—particularly the difference between their academic specialties and the content necessary to build and teach freshman, sophomore, and remedial courses. On the whole, they are less committed to teaching as an occupation than either the *high schoolers* or the *professors:* they regard the junior college as an interim position until other jobs are attained or further studies are explored.

Friedman's third category is *professors*. Since they previously have taught large numbers of freshmen and sophomores, former four-year college professors continue to deal with similar course content at the junior college setting and adjust readily to teaching lower-division courses. They consider the switch to the junior college as permanent but a step downward—a failure or demotion. On the other hand, *high schoolers* view their move from secondary to higher education as a definite step upward in organizational mobility. Their attitudes are pinpointed by one individual in this group who suggests that his main reason for preferring the junior college to the high school is that the emphasis is on teaching rather than on maintaining classroom order. Classroom interaction is the chief source of work gratification for these instructors.

Friedman further differentiated instructors by placing them in *subject matterist* and *disciplinarian* categories. For the *subject matterist,* the sense of colleagueship is local and centered in the employing organization; for the *disciplinarian,* it is a cosmopolitan or nationwide association. Regardless of their former organizational affiliation, however, most instructors in Friedman's population are *subject matterists;* they see their professional purpose to be the transmission of information about their subject fields.

Systematic approaches to understanding teachers need not be contemporary to be relevant. A typology developed by Jung in the early 1900s is pertinent: all people are seen as possessing the attitudes of introversion and extraversion as well as the four functions of thinking, feeling, sensation, and intuition. The dominance of one function over the others gives a special character to an individual's basic orientation and thus leads to the specification of type.

The fact that Jungian typology depends on underlying processes as well as conscious posture suggests its applicability to dimensions of teaching. Just as one's attitudes and functions may shift with age and situational press, so portions of the teacher's role—counselor, classroom manager, test-maker—bring many aspects of his personality to the fore. If the various functions a teacher must assume do have a consistent underlying feature, it is conceivable that teaching may be handled best by special types of people. But what types?

In a study based on the conceptual scheme developed by Jung and using the Myers-Briggs Type Indicator (1962)—an objective technique developed from Jung's typology—certain personality dimensions of beginning junior college teachers were examined by Cohen and Brawer (1968). Subjects indicating preferences high in the "feeling" dimension were more likely to be employed as first-time teachers than were candidates with a different orientation. And, after several months as junior college instructors, "feeling" types were rated higher by supervisors than candidates demonstrating a preference for the "thinking" dimensions. These results corroborated the statement that "intuitive-feeling people . . . may excel in teaching (particularly college and high school) [and] . . . their best chance of success and satisfaction lies in work which involves the unfolding of possibilities . . . for people" (Myers and Briggs, 1962, p. 55). Although the "feeling" type predominated in the teachers studied, no one type was employed as a first-time junior college instructor to the exclusion of others. No evidence of clustering around a single type suggests that a heterogeneous junior college student population is matched by the heterogeneity of first-time teachers and teaching applicants, at least for the small group examined in this study.

Junior college teachers also may be classified according to their own behavior as disciplinarians within whatever field they represent—for example, biology, anthropology, and history—and within the field of instruction itself. According to a typology developed by Cohen (1970a), a person may work in an academic discipline on various levels of involvement, such as *discoverer, synthesizer, translator, practitioner,* or *commuter.*

The *discoverer* (or *researcher*) stands at the peak of the discipline. He develops theory, designs and conducts original studies, and frequently, invents tools or techniques of investigation in his field. The *synthesizer* draws on the findings of the *discoverer,* combining them into new knowledge suitable for use by others in the discipline. He is the writer of original textbooks, the one who repackages information and concepts, and frequently he injects a few of his own ideas. Both the *synthesizer* and the *discoverer* contribute to first-line journals, merging and reforming knowledge within their field. The *translator* defines areas of work by reviewing the publications and ideas transmitted by the *synthesizer* and transforming them into modes of practice by selecting relevant portions from the synthesized knowledge. Although he may occasionally read the leading journals in his field, he contributes to second-line journals only. The *practitioner* uses the tools of the discipline as his own. He accepts ideas from others at more involved levels but rarely, if ever, contributes his own ideas to the field. He stands as the mediator between his area and the layman and, accordingly, has considerable contact with students and other clientele. The *commuter* is affiliated with the discipline only by ascription. He reads popularized information readily understandable to any layman and operates within the boundaries of his discipline as it was taught to him.

By the nature of his position, the junior college instructor holds a dual disciplinary membership; he is affiliated with both his subject field and with the discipline of instruction. However, his levels of involvement vary. The biology instructor, for example, may be only a *commuter* in biology whereas he is a *translator* in instruction. If he is involved with his discipline at a level higher than that of *translator,* it is unlikely that he will find much support in the junior college and, therefore, must go to the university. Conversely, the university professor who works at a level below *translator* is not likely to be supported at his institution; if he does not act as a *discoverer* or *synthesizer* at least part of the time, he may well find it difficult to obtain advancement in rank and concomitant reward.

A typology developed especially for the junior college has been outlined on the basis of the roles typically assumed by faculty members: the *end-of-the-roaders,* the *ladder-climbers,* the *clock-punchers,* and the *defined-purpose routers* (Brawer, 1968). The *end-of-the-roaders* group is an amalgamation of Gusfield and Reisman's *settlers* and Friedman's *high schoolers* and *professors,* but here the designation is based on the teachers' actual behaviors rather than on their backgrounds. Whether they come to the junior college from high school or university teaching positions, directly from graduate schools, or from nonacademic positions, they perceive junior college teaching as both a means and end and as their permanent station. This does not always imply an elective choice, however. Although many *end-of-the-roaders* see the junior college as the epitome of success, for others it represents a last resort—because they were unable to hold former positions or because they want to teach in a university but did not complete the doctorate, or because the community college pays more than the liberal arts college where they would prefer to work.This is consistent with Medsker's (1960) conclusion that 44 per cent of junior college faculty members would rather be in a four-year college or university.

Closest to Gusfield and Riesman's *pioneer adventurers,* the *ladder-climbers* see the junior college as a stepping-off place to be occupied for a limited period of time. They still may be enrolled as university students working toward advanced degrees or may be planning to spend only a few years at the college until they obtain a better job. Consequently, they hold themselves aloof from instructors who view the junior college as a terminal point. Since transitory steps sometimes have a way of becoming permanent, however, "temporary" positions may last for years.

Reasons for the *clock-punchers'* interest in education vary but, whatever they may be, they choose to work in an educational institution, and the junior college presents them with as good an occupational opportunity as any. However, their true devotions are to other fields or avocations—for example, the artist who teaches in the junior college for bread and butter is primarily interested in furthering his own professional image outside the school. The essential difference between these and other instructors is that they view their jobs only in terms of earning wages, not as opportunities to further themselves or their disciplines.

The *defined-purpose routers* are the closest to what one would hope most teachers might become—at all levels of education. They are like Heath's (1964) "reasonable adventurers"—people who have found a reason for being, and who have dedicated themselves to the integration of self and to the attainment of their goals. They see the junior college as a teaching institution, a place where diverse types of students come to seek satisfaction for different needs. They are able to define their subject matter in terms of specific learning objectives, and they help move their students toward a combination of goal-oriented, specified behavior and personality integration. Indeed, because they have found their own sense of identity, they are able to project their identity into a professional image.

Grouping people into various categories on the basis of typologies such as these is one way of viewing the teaching profession. Further typological studies should be conducted because they can be helpful in facilitating better understanding of both the people and the profession. In addition, they can aid the individual instructor to realize that he frequently holds orientations in common with both high school and college instructors. And eventually merging the teaching orientation of the ideal high school teacher with the professional orientation of the protoype university professor, an integrated junior college instructor may evolve.

Attitudes and Values

Although schools have always been engaged in the transmission of cultural values, few attempts were made to measure the values of academic populations—students, faculties, or administrators—until the mid-1950s. Lagging behind as it does in the systematic assessment of its personnel, the study of values among junior college personnel thus is limited, and only a few investigations have been reported.

Studies concerned with instructors' attitudes toward social and political issues, toward their profession, and toward their students contribute information about attitudes in general. Although most of these investigations are concerned with teachers in areas other than higher education, a report by Medsker (1960) points to existing differences between teachers who adapted and those who did not adapt to the goals of the junior colleges. Training experiences were hypothesized to be significant in the development of role orientations and to be related to teacher effectiveness—a position that continues to be tested.

Using a semantic differential, Oppelt (1967) evaluated differences in the degree of favorableness expressed by instructors toward occupational and academic students. Questions were posed to assess attitudes toward students in academic and vocational programs; to describe instructors possessing the most favorable attitudes; to make inter- and intrainstitutional comparisons of attitudes; to determine "attitudinal conditioning," which is dependent upon institutional settings; and to examine values as predictors of certain teacher attitudes. Favorable attitude was not found to be a function of sex, total teaching experience, or home origin. However, vocational instructors viewed all concepts more favorably than did academic instructors: a direct relationship was found to age, blue-collar experience, and multipurpose teaching experience; and an inverse relationship was found to college degrees held by instructors. Vocational concepts were favorably perceived by academic instructors in institutions having a high proportion of vocational programs. Similarly, the self-perception of vocational instructors was better in institutions where their academic colleagues regarded them favorably.

Certainly the attitudes of colleagues and college administrators influence the attitudes held by individual faculty members and their own feelings about the community college—but how one develops attitudes and values has not been definitely established. Morrison (1969) found that both graduate and in-service training "cultivates" attitudes toward student needs; that collective faculty attitudes influence the individual to accept the college concept and its concern for students; and that the individual accepts these views if they are consistent with his own mode of procedure. The conclusion seems to be, the greater the faculty member's belief in the role of the college, the greater his concern for his students.

A major part of a project coordinated by the Clearinghouse focuses on the value systems of students, faculties, and administrators in three diverse California community colleges. In his report on values and institutional perceptions, Park (1970, 1971) identified the value priorities of the faculties, determined their perceptions of the junior college environment, and rated their particular institutional roles. He also pointed out institutional differences in value rankings and the relationships that exist between staff values and their interpretations of the functions and purposes of the community college. Responding to Rokeach's Values Scales (1968b), which consists of separate scales for ranking instrumental and terminal values, 238 junior college staff members arranged the several values according to their own hierarchies of importance (Park, 1970, pp. 16, 17) :

According to the data collected, the subjects appeared to be "self-centered" in their value orientations and seemed to view the institution as an "obstacle" to the achievement of their desired "ends." . . . There was a discernible difference in the value ranking patterns of individual colleges. [The value lists and these] patterns may indicate a "transition" is taking place in value priorities. . . . The subjects separate themselves, as individuals, from their work and the institution. . . . They do not seem to feel "secure" in their understanding of the institution and many admit to not fully accepting the "junior college philosophy."

In a different investigation that utilizes the same data as well as student responses to a similar survey, Brawer (1971b) compared the 238 instructors with 1,877 students in the same three colleges. She found that role orientation discriminated between the student/ staff populations better than age, sex, teaching field, or designated major did.

The study of values and attitudes is interesting, but just how they lead to specified behaviors is unknown. Despite these initial attempts, we have much to learn both about the belief systems of faculties and students and about the belief systems of people generally. We also need to know just how values and attitudes relate to human functioning, how (or if) they can be changed, and where and when change appears necessary.

If schools do not as a rule gather systematic data about their faculty members, they do recognize certain traits and characteristics that are typically demographic in nature. For example, many schools pride themselves on the number of doctorates held by their staff members, while others recognize former schools attended or the number of failing marks the instructors dole out. Other sources stress the way the teaching game is played, duties of faculty members (Kelley and Wilbur, 1970), and the problems they confront (Garrison, 1967). Only a few reports deal with related issues: personality characteristics of junior college faculty (Brawer, 1968); procedures by which they can design their courses according to specified learning objectives (Cohen, 1970c) and instructors' attitudes toward the use of objectives (Cohen, 1970d); or their attitudes toward high-risk, disadvantaged youngsters (Moore, 1970). Yet questions of personality, attitudes, and goals are all intrinsically intertwined with the faculty member as a person. They relate to the student with whom he interacts and to the school as a whole.

Flexibility is one of the dimensions important enough for investigation because it relates to many facets of teacher behavior and satisfaction. Using authoritarianism as a dimension of flexibility, Pratt (1966) attempted to correlate characteristics of the junior college president with the degree of flexibility of his faculty. Although no significant relationship was found between the president's authoritarianism and the overall authoritarianism of the faculty, an inverse relationship was established between the personalities of the presidents and the range of authoritarianism represented by the faculty. Presidents initially tended to hire people who, as a group, were like themselves in authoritative personality; however, they retained those who, as a group, differed from the president in their manifest degrees of authoritarianism and flexibility.

If flexibility is a necessary quality of the beginning instructor, it could be hypothesized that the degree of flexibility among new instructors relates to supervisors' ratings; and, further, that the more flexible person is judged the better teacher. Based on these contentions, attempts were made to determine first, whether there were, indeed, particular types of individuals who would be considered "good" and "poor" teachers; second, the general adjustability of these individuals and their abilities to endure the transition from one situation to another; and, third, the degree of adaptive flexibility required by good instructors, as compared with that shown by instructors judged less effective as teachers (Cohen and Brawer, 1967; Brawer and Cohen, 1966). Two groups of junior college teaching interns were assessed at the beginning of their first year of teaching. Flexibility was definitely related to ratings by their deans at the end of the term. Although whether instructors exhibit variety in their teaching was not investigated as part of this study, such flexibility might be inferred if we assume that the measured characteristics are basic and reliable indices of underlying traits.

In at least one sense, dimensions of flexibility are also related to other attitudes and personality dimensions. However, investigations of characteristics consistent with the change-minded person are limited. One report identified junior college teachers as either "innovators" or "traditionalists" (Wygal, 1966), with innovators seeing themselves as deviating from the norms of their schools and traditionalists as those who do not so perceive themselves. Indeed, it may be that teaching as a profession attracts and holds people with authoritarian tendencies. Who, in his own career as a student, cannot recall a number of rigid, dogmatic instructors? Is it a function of age alone or of the perceived role? Authoritarianism may well be a general trait among instructors. "Scratch the surface of the collective faculty," writes Axen, and "it would appear you reach a substratum of authoritarianism only slightly disguised in moments of noncrisis by a thin patina of liberalism and intellectualism" (1968, p. 111). All people need a certain amount of authority and structure; the junior college instructor is no exception. He must be able to distinguish, however, between authority and authoritarianism.

Some of the issues discussed in this chapter can never be reconciled. They give rise to the same questions that were asked a generation ago—and doubtless it will take several more generations to formulate appropriate answers. Indeed, many of the questions raised here may not be amenable to empirical investigation. And the questions that are rarely asked are perhaps more important in any review of students, faculties, or administrators: What constitutes an effective faculty member? Should we look at instructors according to the procedures they adopt or the products they help develop? How can better understanding of junior college instructors be translated into better education for junior college students? And, finally, how can we help instructors to become mature individuals who are certain of their identities and aware of the depth of their professional roles?

Faculty Preparation and Evaluation

4

If one accurately can judge interest by the number of reports about a subject, faculty preparation and evaluation are of primary concern. Guidelines for special programs to prepare and procedures to evaluate junior college teachers are being drawn on local, state, and national levels. Some detail special degrees or preparation sequences; others propose elaborate mechanisms for gathering evidence on which to award tenure or dismiss instructors. Too often, however, such proposals are so general and so equivocal ("There's a need for. . . . It has been suggested. . . .") that their purpose becomes obscured. Still, they reveal conventional wisdom. Patterns of teacher preparation, including certification and in-service training, and issues in faculty evaluation are reviewed here.

Preparation Patterns

Although teacher training has been attacked as adding nothing of value to a teacher's art, it is still with us. The programs have much potential value for the individuals who complete them because, as Lidz states, "in the process of learning a trade or a profession, . . . [one] learns a way of life along with the knowledge and skills of the occupation. It will shape or help shape many facets of his personality" (1968, p. 380). And appropriate training puts the person in a position to focus on tasks rather than on self; it reduces

49

self-conscious wondering about adopting particular skills and attitudes; and it facilitates his transition from student to professional. Accordingly, teacher preparation sequences are deliberate influences on the people engaged in them. Such programs are also extensions of the process whereby one selects himself into a teaching role, serving this process in several ways. Although entry into a preparation program suggests that the individual has already made a commitment to a field, the program itself allows him to solidify his choice or to reject it. It gives him a chance to practice his trade before assuming a contractual obligation and to narrow down details of the profession. Whereas he may have made his initial choice on fairly vague notions, the degree and/or credential program makes him confront the specifics of his work—but, most important, it allows him to test his own resources and weigh his liabilities, to amplify his talents and question his directions.

The academic preparation of incoming junior college teachers varies slightly. Most instructors have master's degrees; only a few are prepared in special junior college programs. In fact, formerly such programs were rare. In 1954, only twenty-three universities and four-year colleges offered as much as one course in the junior college (Colvert and Baker, 1955). In 1968, approximately seventy-five institutions had not only one course but also whole sequences or programs for junior college staff preparation. By 1970, over 200 colleges and universities were interested in establishing preparation programs for junior college instructors; and it appears that the special sequence to prepare people for junior college instruction is to endure.

Many of these programs result from plans formulated by state agencies or by college consortia working in association with universities to serve particular geographical areas. Among these are the Ford Foundation-funded Midwest Technical Education Program (MTEC, 1967), which includes intern teaching, observation of master teaching methods, orientation to student personnel services, field experience, course work, case studies, and seminars. Eastern Washington State College has developed a method of inter-institutional exchange with on-campus internships and summer workshops that provide training and guidelines for participants, emphasizing development of "competence in the use of varied instructional techniques and media . . . dealing with diverse student abilities and for effective communication" (Gordon and Whitfield, 1967).

Other programs have different emphases; for example, the UCLA program is built on the specification of objectives and the teaching/learning paradigm emphasized by Cohen (1967). In this training sequence, students are expected to develop courses that fit into the total curricular pattern of the junior college, courses to translate to their students in a way to effect maximum learning. The program has a distinct rationale: first, teaching is the prime function of the junior college; second, teaching is the process of influencing learning; third, learning is the changed ability or tendency to act in particular ways; fourth, neither teaching nor learning may be assumed to occur unless observable changes are demonstrated by the learner; fifth, change may be observed only if there has been previous determination of the students' ability; sixth, specific measurable objectives must be set so that learning may be appropriately guided. In the monograph *Focus on Learning* (1968), Cohen and Brawer describe the program in detail.

All these programs have similar course and practice components. Some include work in programmed instruction, the use of other reproducible media, the specification of instructional goals and objectives, the sociological characteristics of junior college communities, and/or interdisciplinary curriculum construction. In all cases, there is a remarkable unanimity of format. The frequent calls for special preparation sequences have been answered by only superficial changes.

Certification and Selection. Teaching is a licensed activity. All publicly supported educational systems—and some colleges and universities—require various forms of instructor certification. These requirements range from elaborate state-mandated preparation sequences for elementary and secondary school teachers to simpler, locally developed rules for community college instructors. And, although the details vary from state to state, there is much consistency in junior college certification patterns: the norm requires a master's degree to teach academic subjects and equivalent trade experience to teach in vocational programs.

For the profession at large, certification is a passport to respectability. However, it has arguments both pro and con. Proponents of junior college teacher certification claim that state and local agencies must exercise control over practices in tax-supported institutions. Others insist that teacher certification guarantees nothing of value in an instructor's preparation; that it only perpetuates identification of the junior colleges with the local school districts from which, in most states, they arose; and that it detracts from the junior college as part of higher education. Gleazer (1967) expresses his own skepticism regarding the tendency of graduate degree-granting institutions to build satisfactory junior college teacher preparation sequences. Other educators want the schools themselves (together with their professional associations) to control selection and preparation directly, so that novitiates are properly imbued with a "junior college point of view." However, most arguments about teacher certification skirt issues of relevancy and junior college uniqueness by dealing with questions of authority and responsibility as well as with purpose.

There are less comprehensive issues in certification. Do requirements point the way toward effective instruction? A single certificate does not necessarily guarantee that an instructor can perform all required duties. Perhaps the junior college teacher needs to be so specialized that his tasks cannot be subsumed under a single requirement, and particular certificates may better indicate individual talents rather than generalized implications of superficial ability.

Certification, however, is a minor issue compared with patterns of teacher selection. The conventional judgment still mandates prior experience gained at college or high school levels. The tendency for employing administrators to prefer the experienced teachers rather than those trained in programs particularly addressed to junior college teaching also is reflected in institutional staffing patterns. Nationwide, more than sixty-four per cent of 3,283 junior college teachers surveyed in 1960 recorded previous secondary or elementary school experience (Medsker, 1960, p. 172). In California—with the nation's largest and most comprehensive system of higher education—300 of the 681 new teachers of academic subjects who entered junior colleges in 1963 had moved in from high school positions; only ninety-eight had come directly from graduate schools (California State Department of Education, 1963–1964). In 1968, a similar study reported that the pattern had not changed toward more specialized junior college teacher training. On the contrary, as the teacher shortage was alleviated during the 1960s, junior college administrators were even more likely to employ instructors with previous experience, if not at a community college, then at another educational institution (Phair, 1969).

New Degrees. The move toward a Doctor of Arts degree has many proponents. In 1970, more than seventy-five graduate institutions were either offering, developing, or considering programs leading to this degree. Support for this degree stems from a variety of reasons. The *Carnegie Quarterly* (Winter/Spring, 1970) foresees "an oversupply of Ph.D's" in the 1970s, but it points out that if large numbers of potential Ph.D. candidates could be redirected into [Doctor of Arts] programs, a new market would open up in the community colleges." Hechinger (1970) also feels that "an unprecedented number of Ph.D.'s will be available to teach in community colleges but that the traditional preparation of Ph.D's, with its stress on research makes them questionable assets." He fears "a massive infusion of the wrong kind of teaching staff." Dunham (1969) insists the state colleges should move quickly to establish Doctor of Arts programs to prepare people for service at all levels of higher education except graduate divisions of universities. Thus, any specialized training leading to research is played down, and the Doctor of Arts degree emphasizing interdisciplinary courses is regarded as a worthy solution to questions of teacher preparation.

Other alternatives have been proposed. For example, Singer (1968) has suggested a separate institute organized and staffed by junior college personnel. Conceived as the "West Point" of the community college movement, this institute would prepare instructors to understand "the unique role of the junior college" and would "provide a spiritual home for career junior college teachers." In addition to the Doctor of Arts, the degrees offered might include the Candidate or Master in Philosophy, Master of Arts in Teaching, and a variety of titles that suggest preparation sequences other than those found in the usual master's degree program.

Reporting the results of a nationwide study of junior college teacher preparation, E. Cohen (1970) has suggested a related pattern—the establishment of semi-autonomous "Master's College

units" within existing institutions staffed by and operated under the
direction of personnel experienced in junior college instruction.
Graduates of this college would be prepared to teach general studies,
academic disciplines, or occupational subjects singly or in combination. And Cohen and Brawer (1972) have proposed a combination
of institutions involved in preparing teachers, with certain tasks
allocated to each. However, the trend is toward new degrees to be
awarded at the end of course sequences and practice-teaching situations that differ little from present patterns.

   In-Service Training and Orientation.   Preservice sequences
are not the only concerns in faculty preparation. Many junior college groups realize that the colleges must forge ahead alone if appropriate specialized training is to be accomplished. Accordingly,
plans for in-service training have been developed in several states;
for example, Wyoming (Christopher, 1966); Arizona (University
of Arizona, 1969); Hawaii (Zane, 1969); Kansas (Good and
others, 1968); Illinois (Birkholz, 1969); Oregon (Loomis, 1964);
and Washington (Gordon and Whitfield, 1967).

   In-service training is seen as the answer to several problems.
Kilpatrick (1967), for example, perceives such programs as present-
ing new ideas and teaching methods to the faculty, keeping the instructors current on subject matter, and orienting them to new
philosophies. These goals can be met in many ways: institutes, conferences, conventions, workshops, faculty and departmental meetings,
consultant services, university courses, classroom visits, and professional on-campus libraries. According to one report (Ellerbrook,
1968), twenty-one of thirty-nine public junior college presidents
who were surveyed reported formal in-service programs at their institutions. Knowledge of one's own college was considered more important than knowledge of the junior college in general—a suggestion that implies the need for in-college preparation, regardless of
where or to what extent faculty members were previously prepared.
And, in a survey conducted by the Faculty Development Project of
the American Association of Junior Colleges (AAJC, 1969), junior
college presidents stressed the general deficiencies of in-service training, which they felt must be alleviated by both two- and four-year
institutions.

   Much in-service work continues—formally organized or not.

Compiled by the Faculty Development Project, a directory of such programs cites a variety of training workshops and short courses especially designed for the instructor's professional improvement (Gladstone, 1969). In responses to a questionnaire on such programs, Eaton (1964) found that new faculty acquired knowledge of their duties from many sources both official and otherwise. He also found that fellow faculty members were helpful, that adequate faculty handbooks were needed, and that more information should be given on college objectives. In-service orientation programs were considered important for several reasons—understanding the junior college philosophy, describing student personnel services, helping new faculty learn more about their students, informing the faculty of legal obligations and their own legal rights, and, finally, easing communication in classrooms and among fellow teachers.

Orientation programs, a form of in-service training, have been described separately. Kelly and Connolly (1970) assessed faculty orientation in several states and offered a useful rationale for program development. Apuzzo (1968) also offered a program model, and the three-week presession orientation sequence at William Rainey Harper College (Illinois) has been described in detail (WRHC, 1967).

Some formal orientation is warranted because of many unique problems faced by new junior college instructors. One of the largest studies of junior college personnel, conducted by Siehr (1963), surveyed 5,000 faculty members in 429 institutions. And although this study was done in 1963, later findings do not contradict its results. Among the problems identified by nearly 3,000 usable returns were: lack of time for scholarly study, adaptation of instruction to individual differences, dealing with students who require special attention to overcome deficiencies, obtaining adequate secretarial help, understanding institutional teacher load and curriculum development, obtaining needed instructional materials, and grading. Siehr suggests that orientation programs be related to problems identified in a specific institution. They should include both formal and informal processes and should be directed to helping the new faculty member toward a complete understanding of his role in the college.

Whether the development of professional maturity can be

facilitated by special degree programs, in-service training, and/or orientation sessions remains to be seen. However, these programs do provide what college administrators feel is lacking in the usual university and college preparation sequences. They also provide an incomparable way of learning about an individual institution. One thing is certain—as the community college matures, it is taking on a greater role in training its own people. In-service training in some form or other seems destined to increase.

Evaluating Instructors

Faculty evaluation is a ubiquitous practice that is rarely examined in terms of what it means to the individual instructor. The systematic study of teachers and teaching for purposes of evaluation may indeed be viewed by the instructor as an intrusion and about the last thing he is interested in. Nevertheless, although staff members often question and protest the techniques employed, the use of findings, and even the entire process, the practice continues. Every educational institution has some type of formal or informal instructor evaluation scheme, and every faculty member eventually must be involved in the process.

Reviewing the status of research on teaching and characteristics of teachers in the two-year colleges, Cohen and Brawer (1969) related these efforts to faculty evaluation and concluded that the two practices apparently were unrelated—research on instructors and instruction have little if any effect on the way teachers are evaluated. A merger of the two streams of study is needed, with the assessment of student learning as the channel that could bring them together. Unfortunately, such mergers are difficult to manage. The tendency to examine student learning as the criterion of teacher effectiveness is growing, but considerable credence is still given to assessment on other criteria.

Here, we deal with practices of faculty evaluation. Teacher evaluation forms and teacher evaluation on the basis of ratings by supervisors and colleagues, grants and degrees, students, and teachers themselves are discussed and student gain as the ultimate criterion for evaluation is postulated.

Forms and Procedures. No matter who the rater—administrator, division chairman, or student—teacher evaluation schemes employ nebulous criteria. No matter how solid or reliable the rating form, it cannot be considered appropriate if it does not relate to definitive criteria; yet evaluation studies based on vague assumptions continue to be reported. Indeed, some student groups and some university-oriented faculty organizations applaud rating schemes that the educational research community discarded as unworthy a generation ago.

Different variables and alternate approaches to evaluation have been postulated, but whether these have anything to say about specific problems of the junior college is dubious. Some guidelines for teacher evaluation and assessment procedures were proposed by Morin (1968): ostensibly to provide faculty acceptance, to improve instruction for the whole college, to establish objectivity in retention or dismissal of probationers, and to increase teacher job satisfaction. Hendrix (1964) examined junior college faculty members according to certain specified criteria, but he concluded that the presence or absence of tenure—one of his major criteria—gave no indication of the best evaluation policies to pursue. Four approaches to measurement—introspection, classroom observation, product examination, and student evaluation—were suggested by Bannister (1961), who noted that forms of evaluation should be distributed, monitored, and collected by students and not be read by teachers until final course marks were submitted. Other evaluation schemes are concerned with instructors' degrees and the size and kind of their degree-granting institutions—as if these actually indicate teaching effectiveness.

The list could go on, but merely tallying procedures and recommendations seems to be a wasted exercise. The process must be viewed in terms of purpose, practice, and potential outcome. Do different groups consistently see instructors in different ways? Is one evaluation scheme or one rater more reliable than another? Does evaluation facilitate—or even encourage—more effective instruction?

Rating by Supervisors and Colleagues. The methods employed to rate teachers are instructive in themselves. Perhaps the oldest and most popular way is through supervisor ratings, and it continues to be the best approach for some purposes. It does seem reliable. In a series of investigations conducted by Cohen and Brawer in 1966 and 1967, several groups of junior college teaching candi-

dates were assessed in depth. Using the Rorschach Technique, the
Adaptive-Flexibility Inventory (Brawer, 1967), and the Myers-
Briggs Type Indicator, each subject was assessed during the summer
preceding his entry into teaching. At the end of his first year of
teaching, he was given independent ratings by his administrator
(president or dean of instruction). Responses to the three instruments were assessed for the purpose of understanding the personality characteristics of the new teachers and correlating the independent criteria (judgments of the program director and the college
supervisors) with the test material. Correlations were highest between the program director and the college supervisors, substantiat-
ing Ort's (1964) contention that evaluations by campus supervisors
consistently prove to be the best yardsticks available for predicting
success of neophyte instructors.

    Another method of rating instructors is based on faculty
members' appraisals of their associates. On the surface, this procedure seems to contain much merit. However, where the process is informal, its value is undocumented, and even when peer evaluation
procedures are highly systematized, as detailed in faculty association
recommendations (NFA, 1968), their value is open to question. It
has one advantage, however; "it is the scheme least likely to meet
with resistance" (Cohen and Brawer, 1969, p. 10).

    Student Evaluations. Students know when they have been
well taught, and teacher evaluation by students has long been popular. Indeed, in spite of the somewhat cynical opinion of some teachers that very little value can be placed on student judgments, increasing attention is given to student ratings. Questionnaires, checklists, and rating forms are used extensively at different levels of education and in hundreds of school settings. However, ratings by
students are subject to many of the same criticisms that relate to
other measures of judgment based on nebulous criteria.

    In practice, the dimensions on which students rate instruc-
tors vary widely. Students at St. John's River Junior College
(Florida) evaluated their instructors in 500 class sections on the
basis of four measures: positive personal traits, scholarship, skill of
presentation, and accuracy in evaluating students (Overturf and
Price, 1966). Responses to a student questionnaire suggested that
instructors who awarded higher grades did not rate higher than in-

structors awarding lower grades; honor students responded more strongly (favorably or unfavorably) to teacher performance; and students did not rate instructors who taught at "perferred" hours more highly than other instructors. Furthermore, instructors who were rated most highly were those who taught toward clearly defined and communicated objectives; they used only relevant materials and were always in charge of their classes.

Other studies of students' reactions to their instructors have been used for other purposes. Coming out of a student opinion survey administered to Grossmont College (California) students, a fourteen-point statement was issued regarding improvement of faculty/student relations (Heinz, 1967). Schmidt (1968) used a five-point student rating scale for the specific purpose of improving instruction, not for criticizing the instructor.

Criteria for rating also include the relevancy of the textbook, the extent to which it fulfills its objectives, and the currentness of the subject matter. The instructor may be judged on his presentation of material, tolerance of students' appearance, the kind and purpose of the assignments he gives, and the difficulty and frequency of the tests he administers. All such schemes open themselves to certain questions, perhaps the most important being how competent is any person—administrator, colleague, or student—to evaluate another? If rating ability is a skill that requires some degree of training, it is unfortunate that so much attention is given to ratings by untrained people. Raters or not, people are people, and thus students and supervisors alike allow irrelevancies or personal prejudice to influence their assessments of good teaching. The instructor's mannerisms are invariably given undue emphasis to the detriment of more pertinent dimensions. Rater training—one way around the problem—at least leads to reliable measurement, but it is a rare dean or department chairman who bothers to concern himself with such an issue.

Self-Evaluations. Ultimately, the most rewarding evaluation —although, perhaps the most difficult—is evaluation of self. This assumes a degree of maturity and a concomitant need for objectivity that are difficult for all, and for some impossible, to attain.

The American Association of Colleges for Teacher Education (Simpson and Seidman, 1962) attempted to further efforts at devising self-evaluation tools by publishing sample rating items, plus suggestions for their use. Where ratings were to be made by colleagues, students, administrators, or self, the instructor alone determined what he would do with the findings. Unfortunately, no attempt was made to follow up the effect of this list by determining whether anyone changed his teaching practices as a result of what he learned about himself.

At Columbus College (Georgia), twenty-six full-time faculty members voluntarily participated in a study of self-evaluation (Anderson, 1964). Teachers rated themselves on seven points and recorded two class sessions during a two-week period. This effort was followed by a review of tapes and other self-rating devices. According to the researcher, after listening to tapes of their classes, over half of the participants were sensitive to the information obtained from the tapes.

Considering the emphasis on both evaluation and good teaching, little attention has been paid to self-evaluation by junior college people. Brown and Thornton (1963a) take the position that college teachers can evaluate themselves through introspection, product assessment, class recordings, appraisal of student participation in class, and attending to ratings by students. Still, since these exercises are employed privately, we know little about the effects of such examinations. If changes—either positive or negative—take place, how can we measure them?

Student Gain. In evaluation practice, there is a growing tendency to look at the product, the dependent variable, the extrinsic result. Much of this work uses student gain as the criterion of teacher effectiveness. Justiz (1968) developed a scheme for measuring teacher evaluation, and a subsequent report by O'Connor and Justiz (1970) presents a reliable measure to evaluate junior college instructors. When the teacher's subject knowledge and a student's ability levels are held constant, teaching ability may be measured by testing students with a scale specified by the instructor's educational objectives. Thus, evaluation is based on student learning.

If evaluation proposes to recognize superior teachers rather than to search for fault, it probably will meet with minimal resistance from faculty. Accordingly, Kilpatrick (1967) suggests that initial evaluations become a part of the hiring process and that they be made on the basis of transcripts, recommendation, placement by application forms, and interviews. Subsequent evaluation of teaching effectiveness is also proposed to discover new ideas or techniques to be shared with others, as well as weaknesses to be corrected.

A supervisory scheme that promises both enhancement of communication and assessment of instructional effects was introduced in 1967 at Golden West College (California) (Cohen and Shawl, 1970). Designed particularly to gain information for properly allocating resources and assessing institutional effects, it was also intended as a curriculum-planning aid and as a way of leading instructors to specify their objectives—a worthy enterprise in its own right. The Golden West College scheme of instructional supervision begins at the initial employment interview. At that time, instructors are informed about the college's move toward the definition of specific objectives in all courses and curriculums, and they are encouraged to specify objectives in their own work. A twice-yearly series of scheduled interviews is arranged for both new and experienced instructors. At these meetings, the division chairman and the dean of instruction review the instructor's objectives and the student learning he has effected. Tests are examined and criticized; test scores are analyzed; objectives and media are reviewed. Suggestions for alternative strategies are made, and help in the form of paraprofessional aides, test-scoring services, and so on is offered. The entire operation takes place in a supportive context; that is, no one is being judged, no one is being threatened. The plan began on an experimental basis with volunteers from the faculty invited to participate. It since has been adopted by the district as an acceptable alternative to class visits for teacher evaluation. Junior college instruction will probably be enhanced as other districts abandon evaluation in favor of this type of mutually rewarding activity.

The entire matter of supervision, evaluation, examination, or conversation about instructors boils down to a simple point. What is to be done with the information collected? That is, for what purposes are the data about the instructor or the nature of his instruction being gathered? That question must be answered before an instructor evaluation scheme is organized. The common practice of using data compilation methods built on vague definitions to serve multiple purposes (award tenure, threaten instructors, satisfy administrators, enhance public relations) dooms any procedure before it is begun.

The gap between informal and formal evaluation of instructors is narrow. The evidence afforded by a scheduled "class visitation" differs little from the results of an administrator's conversation with a few of the instructor's students. Both are strongly biased by the perceptions of the observers. The perusal of grade marks earned by students who transfer to a university provides no more information on the quality of the instructors than does a conversation with a university professor. After viewing present evaluation practices, Cohen and Brawer conclude, "In its current form, the reasons for faculty evaluation are invalid, and the criteria upon which it is based are nebulous. It fails to differentiate between the teacher as a social being and the effects of his teaching. It serves no useful purpose. It is time to abandon it and replace it with something of value" (1969, p. 56). That "something of value" should be the assessment of instructional effects.

The Students in Review

5

How can we characterize 2,000,000 people? By height, weight, prior academic achievement, personality characteristics, or parents' income and country of national origin? Possible categories are unlimited. But why would we want to characterize 2,000,00 people? That is, what would we do with the information? Would we change our educational programs, bar the doors to certain types, or file it away to have on hand in case someone asks? Ways and reasons, means and ends. The how and the why of assessing students is in flux. Yet we measure them and produce an unwieldy number of reports that draw pictures of the "typical" junior college student, pictures that often are vague and confusing—particularly in regard to their usefulness. The ambiguity, however, may lie not in the pictures themselves but in the suggestion that one can attribute a quality of "typicalness" to the great number of individuals who make up junior college student populations.

Students, the constant variable. Each one differs from the others; all are the same. What are some of the differences? Some of the similarities? Can we accurately appraise the students? How can we understand them? For years, student assessment practices have attempted to answer these questions. Students are examined in order to tabulate data regarding their previous achievements, predict their academic potential, select into and select out of particular programs, determine individual characteristics, evaluate their perceptions of the college environment, counsel into special occupational programs, and assess institutional effect. At any college, any or all of these aims may be pursued simultaneously. Probably every school in existence gathers information about its students—the ERIC collection, for example, includes far more documents describing students than it does any other category. The problem is how to sort out these data to yield usable information.

Despite some obvious—and some subtle—drawbacks to certain studies, many investigations are useful. Several are cited here to represent the kinds of research reported, not as examples of either good or inadequate investigations. Documents were selected on two criteria—the date the material appeared and its representativeness. After determination of the material to be included, the literature from 1968 to 1970 was searched—particularly the ERIC documents unlikely to be widely disseminated in books or journal articles.

This three-year period was chosen for two reasons: first, research on the junior college student before 1968 was generally indigenous to a single institution or was included with material primarily on the four-year college and university student. This is still true, to some extent; however, the trend is to more specific examinations of those enrolled in community colleges. Second, before the middle 1960s, reports about students in general were quite different from subsequent reports—whether of national or regional scope, whether or not they were well executed, whether or not they employed precise methodology and definite criteria. Since 1964, the date of the Free Speech Movement at Berkeley, a new breed of college student has appeared. And, since there is an apparent three- or four-year lag between major events in a university and their impact on other schools, information obtained about junior college students before 1968 may not accurately describe those who have since entered college.

Drop Out or Persist?

Whether the phenomenon is called drop out, withdrawal, student mortality, attrition, or academic failure, dropping out of college has widespread ramifications, both educational and social. It has generated much concern on the part of educators, psychologists, sociologists, economists, the students themselves, their parents, and the general public.

However, the question of dropping out of school cannot be

examined in isolation. It is related to our entire social structure and is tied to the broader topic of goals and objectives for both the institutions and the people who attend them. Whether studies of drop out deal with single schools and thus are considered parochial in nature, or whether they are of nationwide scope and concern many institutions, what we know today differs little from what we knew in the past. In fact, Summerskill's 1962 statement that the percentage of drop out remained the same over forty years is still applicable. Yet, oddly, despite the consistency of these attrition figures, we continue to spend time and effort in reemphasizing them.

Disregarding merely numerical accounts, perhaps we can better understand both persistence and withdrawal from college if we look at other aspects of the problem. Thus, even so-called parochial or regional studies may have interesting and broader implications. Orange Coast (California) Junior College District's (1969b, 1970) series of follow-up studies comparing the nonreturning students of two quite different schools in a single district offers a case in point. Of special interest is the finding that students who left junior college at the end of the spring semester were more likely to matriculate in a four-year college than those who left after the fall semester. Perhaps students who leave after completing the spring semester lay their transfer plans more carefully than those who withdraw after the fall term and, in this sense, are more "traditional."

Other studies stress economic reasons for student withdrawal from school. Whether one accepts this view as truly representative of the situation or whether he chooses to look for deeper reasons, many reports substantiate either position. Of the numerous studies that discuss the financial concomitants of attrition, we cite a few that couple economics with other variables.

In some cases, inadequate counseling and lack of stimulating learning experiences, along with financial difficulties, seem to cause student withdrawal (Dave, 1968). In others, dismissal or academic suspension, lack of funds or goals, and influence of parents or friends are given as reasons for leaving four-year colleges and entering junior colleges (Lamke, 1951). Bossen and Burnett (1970) reported that if a student is single and his father has a high socioeconomic status, he is more likely to return to school after withdrawing. Almost half of Foothill College's (California) drop outs eventually

returned to school. Whatever the reasons, there are multiple influences: sometimes job conflict (Thompson, 1969); sometimes
the interplay of actual and perceived ability on the part of the students with poor family and social backgrounds (Turner, 1970);
sometimes activities external to the school coupled with financial
pressures (MacMillan, 1970).

Still considering the economic factor but taking a different
slant, Cerritos College (California) examined attrition in terms of
ethnic differences (Robinson, 1968). Fifty-three Mexican-American
students were surveyed to shed light on their attitudes toward school
and to detect reasons underlying lack of interest in attending or
tendencies to drop out. Although 90 per cent of this small group
reported that they had not experienced any student/staff discrimination, 50 per cent said the staff did not understand their problems.
They also pointed to economic difficulties, problems with teachers,
and academic and language handicaps as basic causes of nonatten-
dance and/or attrition. Perhaps part-time employment and loans for
needy students as well as greater sensitivity to people from different
ethnic groups would alleviate some of the disparity between community composition and college attendance/persistence.

Other investigators point to different reasons for drop out,
either ignoring or minimizing the financial ones. At San Jose City
College (California), for example, only forty of 514 students listed
financial reasons for withdrawal from school; other reports find no
specific demographic differences predicting drop out (Aiken, 1968).
A predisposition for withdrawal has been postulated by Trent and
Medsker (1968) in terms of personality dimensions.

Whether the reasons are socioeconomic, academic, or multi-
dimensional, definite feelings about school are frequent concomitants
of drop out (Snyder and Blocker, 1969a)—and these feelings are
either positive or negative. If drop out does engender strong
emotions, different ways of looking at student attrition are warranted.
Grade-point averages, measures of academic ability, and other variables may be important, but they certainly do not tell the whole
story of either the withdrawing or the persisting student. Perhaps
school administrators, counselors, and faculty might view this problem in a different light, change their approaches and attitudes when
necessary and/or feasible, and consciously attempt to provide suc-

cessful experiences for their students—not experiences that defeat them. One study suggests that the counseling process itself might be a threat that tends to stimulate drop out (Kunhart and Roleder, 1964)'. This phenomenon deserves more attention.

Student attrition may have much less to do with the school per se than with other factors influencing the student. One such concern is the question of whether drop out is a permanent or a temporary condition (Hughes and others, n.d.)'. Certainly it is true that many dropouts eventually find their way back to the colleges they once left, and it is a fact that demands consideration (Mitchell and Moorehead, 1968)' before we assess numbers, attribute causes, and assign solutions.

Whatever the individual situation, certain dimensions within both the school environment and the person must be observed in any concern with attrition. Personality factors, dynamic interactions, and external demands must all be understood—although many of them have been ignored for too long. Attempting to look at qualities different from those usually examined, Cohen and Brawer (1970)' administered the Omnibus Personality Inventory (OPI) (Heist, 1968)', the Adaptive-Flexibility Inventory (Brawer, 1967)', and a questionnaire to entering freshmen at Los Angeles Pierce College. On the OPI scales, these students appeared more homogeneous than those who comprised both the normative sample and comparative groups of college freshmen. Yet no major differences were noted between persisters and dropouts on selected OPI scales. Responses to the questionnaire by students who later failed to return to school showed that most tended to be enrolled for fewer than twelve units and to be employed more time outside school than persisting students. Perhaps more fruitful for further study were the findings that these dropouts have mothers with less education and had lower mean scores on the A-F Inventory than did persisters. Further, they had attended more schools before the tenth grade than had non-dropouts. Whether the greater number of schools suggests an individual propensity for incompletion or whether it reflects a different type of instability is a subject for further investigation.

To what extent should we be concerned with students who drop out of school before completing their programs? The record-keeping alone is of dubious veracity. If a person returns to school two, three, or ten years after withdrawal, is his drop-out status re-classified? Is the person who attends only every second semester a repetitive dropout? Does the school depend on a certain ebb and flow, input and output? The whole issue of the dropout problem eventually must call into question not only inconsistent record-keeping but the total educational enterprise. How long can schools continue to operate as they do and have the same effects on their student populations?

Transfer Students

If all studies of junior college populations were laid end to end, those concerning the so-called transfer student would reach far beyond midpoint. Transfer programs are assessed to secure financial aid, to excuse certain types of curriculum offerings, and to edify the college image. While many studies of transfers from junior colleges to four-year colleges and universities are parochial, some are very valuable for people concerned with the impact of college on its student populations.

Knoell and Medsker's study (1965) of transfer students, cited as the "most significant analysis of [this type] in recent years" (Willingham and Findikyan, 1969), emphasized the articulation problems of junior college students who subsequently transferred to a group of forty-three senior institutions. A natural outgrowth of this work was the 1966 publication, *Guidelines for Improving Articulation Between Junior and Senior Colleges* (NFA, 1968).

Most studies of articulation are statewide (Kintzer, 1970), although some look at student transfers in a single institution or are a composite of studies. In this light, reviewing studies of articulation conducted from 1928 through 1964, Hills (1965) suggests that transfer students should expect to suffer an appreciable grade drop in the first semester after transfer, that their grades tend to improve in direct relation to their length of schooling, and that, as a group, native students perform better than transfers. When comparisons were made between students at Appalachian State University (North Carolina), the grades of native students were generally found to be higher than those of transfers (Appalachian State University, 1968). Although this finding is not unusual, other factors influence and affect transfer students.

Despite the probability of such transfer trauma, however, the articulation picture is not all bad—in fact, transfers from the junior colleges frequently become university honor students. Gold (1967b) describes such a situation in his follow-up of Los Angeles City College transfers who later earned academic honors. Considerable variety was apparent in terms of designated majors and certain personal measures. Perhaps most interesting was the finding that, of the two students who fell below a C average at UCLA after transferring from a junior college, the one who had been dismissed and subsequently was reinstated made the dean's honor list two years later.

Schultz and Garrett (1967) identify many junior college students who became university honor students. A provocative assumption is that many students earning honors in both junior and senior colleges might not go beyond high school if it were not for the existence of two-year schools in their communities. Many of these honor students come from large families and from homes with limited financial and educational background. Other reports also suggest that undergraduate students transferring from junior colleges perform as well as groups who are indigenous to the university (Phay and McCary, 1967). For example, the grade-point average of junior college transfers to the University of Missouri equalled those of native students and students who transferred from other states (C. E. Johnson, 1965).

Studies of junior-senior college articulation do not pertain to the United States exclusively. In the course of a three-year study of students transferring from Vancouver City College to the University of British Columbia, attrition and graduation rates of the students were found to vary with the particular university program in which they enrolled (Dennison and Jones, 1968). In general, students, especially those twenty-five years old and older, who had completed two years at the community college were more likely to graduate as scheduled than were students completing only one year before transferring. However, one-year transfers showed better academic performances than did two-year transfer students.

The inadequacy of controls over criteria and the inconsistencies in assessing student performance in senior institutions make it impossible to reach an unequivocal conclusion about transfer stu-

dents and their experiences in both junior colleges and four-year
institutions. Nevertheless, transfer students seem to be in an increasingly favorable position in the university and, insofar as transfer
admissions are concerned, the junior college model is working well.
Willingham and Findikyan reported data indicating:

*that students transferring from two-year institutions have almost the
same average college grades as students coming from four-year institutions. Despite this equality [there is] . . . the interesting fact that
the junior college transfer students were less likely to be rejected
than the four-year students (24 per cent versus 35 per cent). This is
heartening insofar as it may indicate that senior institutions, as a
group, have not thrown up barriers to junior college students. As a
further check we examined all transcripts of students with C-or-
better averages who were transferring from public junior colleges to
public four-year institutions in the same state. Less than 10 per cent
of these students were rejected.*

*It is evident, . . . however, that very few junior college stu-
dents who have followed an occupational program attempt to transfer
to a four-year institution. Of those who do, few succeed. Obviously
the purpose of occupational programs is not to produce transfers
[1969, p. 7].*

The evidence on transfer students seems to favor junior colleges—not because students are taught particularly well or poorly
but because, in the absence of a two-year college at which they can
enroll, many would never get to college initially. In this respect the
junior colleges well serve their constituencies.

Activists

Another group of students—student activists—has aroused
considerable interest. The concern about campus unrest and about
those who instigate school disruption increases with the number of
espoused causes of such upheaval. The causes for activism usually
include the war in Indochina, racial discrimination, a breakdown
of family structure, political corruption, capitalistic exploitation of
the consumer, the weakening position of organized religion, and a
shift in the values of society. To this list Blocker (1969) adds the
development of an economy and a society based on the exploitation

of scientific knowledge, with virtually no comparable progress in the application of the social sciences to political institutions and processes. As appropriate responses to student unrest, he suggests that institutions engage in a thorough and critical examination of the philosophy and missions of the college and the extent to which all involved understand these concepts. They may also reconsider the organization and application of guidance services as well as the involvement of students, faculty, administration, and boards of trustees in institutional procedures and policy development.

Notwithstanding the fact that student uprisings are as old as the recorded history of education, Lombardi (1969, 1970, 1971) assumes a different view of student activism, tracing its developments from the Berkeley Free Speech Movement through to the 1970s. While junior college activists are decidedly influenced by their counterparts in senior institutions, he notes that their activities are usually more moderate. And, although activism is usually associated with the "far left," activist groups may be defined better according to their special interests. Thus, one might regard the New Left, the Rightists, and members of minority groups as potential or actual activists.

Zander (1969) proposes that administrators of college student affairs should be concerned with several variables: opening new channels for student participation to shape their educational experiences, recognizing relevant issues and reasonable dissent, insuring fairness and justice as well as order, understanding issues from students' viewpoints, using college resources to prevent disruption through promoting constructive alternatives, and making student attitudes known to the public. His approach varies from that of many other investigators concerned with student unrest. In fact, if administrators continue to stress practices that train students in the schools' philosophies and continue to emphasize their own powers of veto, disruption is far from being resolved.

Associated with any discussion of student activism are the reports of discipline and judicial decisions that occasionally—and increasingly—crop up in junior college literature. Several court decisions about student rights and privileges are considered in papers by Andes (1970) and Gaddy (1968), and, in view of student unrest, these appear pertinent. Because individual rights are guaranteed by the federal Constitution, when acting on disciplinary matters, the courts often have been called on to decide whether or not the student has been deprived of his rights under the due process clause. Andes's review presents brief examples from court cases concerning student discipline. Other reports point out certain student-rights clauses established by individual schools—for example, Monterey Peninsula (California) College (Bessire, 1969).

Despite these attempts, systematic studies of activism in the junior college await further study—perhaps such study as the investigation conducted in high schools throughout the country by Bailey (1971) and his associates from Syracuse University. And perhaps studies of activism should focus on steps that may be taken to alleviate tensions, not so much on figures and causes. Some of this study might follow the lines of comparison drawn by studies of other student groups.

Comparative Studies

In education, as elsewhere, we enjoy making comparisons. Students in different types of schools, professing different majors, transfer and terminal, representing different cultural and ethnic groups—all have been examined in an attempt to understand the varied dimensions inherent in the college experience. While in any comparative study there is inevitably some overlap between designated groups and specified dimensions, some investigations add potentially worthwhile inputs to our broader understanding of student populations.

Studies comparing transfer and terminal students are especially popular, although none of the findings are earthshaking. A case in point is Anthony's (1964). He found that transfer students generally come from higher socioeconomic levels and from academic high school backgrounds, score higher on college tests, are upwardly mobile, and place greater emphasis on prestige in selecting a career. Although the occupational choices of both transfer and terminal students are influenced by their parents, more higher ranking students go directly to four-year institutions than to junior colleges. And since the junior college's emphasis on guidance affects most students—albeit to varying degrees—we should examine in detail such related issues as the relative degree of influence of high school and college counselors on program choices for transfer and terminal students, ways to deal with students who hold unrealistic college goals, and comparisons of junior college students in both private and public institutions with their counterparts in four-year colleges and universities.

According to ACT composite scores (American College Testing Program, 1966), transfer students make higher scores than terminal students, for an obvious reason—in many colleges a student is not allowed to enter a transfer program if his test scores fall below a certain cutoff point. For some junior college groups, there are also differences between transfer and terminal students on high school and college grades—again, for the same reason. However, there are exceptions. Munday (1969) found it unusual for transfer students in the college group to achieve both higher test scores and higher high school grades than do terminal students. Although there were differences between test scores and grades, they were small; in fact, transfer and terminal students appear to be far more alike than different.

Also using ACT data, Fenske (1969) reported that although significantly more seniors falling in the lowest 30 per cent in scholastic ability indicated vocational/technical plans, the presence of a local vocational/technical institution had a greater influence on their plans than did lack of such an institution. The people graduating from high schools with a high propensity for vocational/technical plans were divided into two groups; one cluster consisted of seniors who ranked in the highest 30 per cent of their graduating class but whose parents had low occupational and educational status; the other group showed a converse pattern—seniors in the lowest 30 per cent of the graduating class had parents with both high educational and occupational status. Students in the latter group had a much stronger tendency toward vocational/technical plans than did seniors demonstrating higher scholastic ability. In general, vocational/technical students are likely to be "underachievers" with higher aptitude than achievement in high school. Their continuance in school is stimulated by the presence of a community vocational/technical institution.

To identify influences on the selection and completion of vocational/technical programs, McCallum (1968) studied male junior college students who made initial or deferred decisions about their school majors. Comparisons were already known of 327 students from six San Francisco area junior colleges—those who started in a vocational/technical program (initial group) and those who began in a transfer group and later changed their majors (deferred group). From school records and questionnaire responses, the groups were compared in terms of academic ability, educational achievement, and social and economic background. The initial and deferred groups differed in academic ability and educational achievement but not in socioeconomic factors. Initial students more often declared majors that had been initiated in high school; deferred students were less influenced by secondary school teachers or counselors and did not indicate their major in high school. Both groups were equally influenced by parents and college teachers, with 10 per cent expressing dissatisfaction with their majors. In terms of other attitudes and interests, the two groups generally agreed on occupations that were held in high or low esteem. Despite their vocational/technical orientation, more than 70 per cent of the students in both groups planned to transfer to four-year institutions.

Comparative studies of students are often indigenous to their own schools, remaining within institutional boundaries. Exceptions do occasionally crop up, however—as in Gold's (1967a) investigation of students' religious attitudes at three extremely different schools. Selected results, analyzed from previous studies conducted at Harvard, Radcliffe, and Los Angeles City College, 1946 to 1948, and again 1966 to 1967, indicated that all three institutions became more liberal after 1946, with both religious commitment and traditional religious behavior becoming less common (students professed less need for religious orientations and beliefs and fewer expressed belief in a personal God). Of the three institutions, students at Los Angeles City College indicated the most conservative attitudes toward religion, although changes in their attitudes were the same as at Harvard and Radcliffe, albeit less pronounced.

Looking at different characteristics among a broader sampling of institutions, Tillery (1964) examined University of California freshmen and their peers at California junior colleges by means of a questionnaire, the Omnibus Personality Inventory, aptitude scores, and their high school and first-semester college transcripts.

Although academic ability was definitely related to a choice of college or university, much diversity was found within each institution—a finding corroborated in many studies. The university student was usually better prepared academically, eligible to enter college at the end of seven rather than eight high school semesters and, providing his campus offered a self-challenging, liberal-cultural atmosphere, he was significantly higher in intellectual motivation. The junior college student, on the other hand, indicated greater interest in applied learning as demonstrated by his higher scores on the OPI's Practicality Scale. Further comparisons suggested that the greater social maturity of university students was matched by greater flexibility in ideas and values, while junior college students were less responsive to new experiences. The university student was more likely to come from a family in the higher education and income brackets, he gave greater weight to his academic standing and had higher aspirations for both degree and career than did his two-year counterpart.

Corroborating some of these findings, Hoyt and Munday found that junior college students representing eighty-five schools were less academically able than their peers at 205 four-year colleges. However, differences among junior colleges in academic potential were so great that the least able students in one college could be well above average in another. "Similarly, the average academic potential at several junior colleges was well above the average in typical four-year institutions" (Hoyt and Munday, 1969, p. 108). Students within individual junior colleges had more diverse academic talents than did those in four-year institutions, and college grades for the junior college students also were more varied.

Comparison of institutional and student traits is among the continuing attempts to predict academic success. An ACT report (Betz, 1969), documented by several studies, includes measures of thirty-six college characteristics intercorrelated for 581 junior colleges, findings about precise geographical areas, and the experiences and achievements of junior college graduates from twenty-nine specific colleges. In this study, the majority of students planned to transfer to a four-year college, worked for part of their two years of college, commuted to the campus, and were generally satisfied with their school. High school seniors choosing vocational education were also compared with those planning to go to college and with those having no educational plans.

Such studies are assumed to be worthwhile—else why continue doing them? But are they really? Would it not be better to establish common data and compare effects over a period of time? Merely viewing past and present status may really have nothing to do with the future—and how different people may react to and be influenced by different situations. We do need comparative information—but comparisons that point out new directions and are not primarily bound to the past, mirroring our early inadequacies and pointing to failures that painfully reflect our weaknesses.

Counseling and Personnel Services

As at other educational levels, the importance of counseling at the junior college is so often stressed that redundancy seems to outweigh value. Indeed, a plethora of material deals with counseling procedures, compares data about students who are or are not exposed to counseling, and describes alternative approaches to academic respectability and heightened awareness of self. Much of this information is parochial in nature; it is often indirect and unrelated to the students themselves, and, indeed, seems valuable only to the individuals generating the studies. However, other information is pertinent to the junior college as an institution of higher education and to the people with whom the school interacts—faculty, students, staff, community. Thus, implications drawn from some studies may be interesting to broader populations. For the many reports appearing in the literature before 1968, academic journals in addition to *Research in Education* may be searched. A few studies since 1968 will be cited here as examples of the approaches taken and the issues of concern in school guidance functions.

A group guidance program designed to provide a chance for self-assessment of personal strengths and weaknesses, improvement of attitudes in human relations, improvement of study habits and techniques, and the realistic assessment of vocational abilities is described by Witherspoon (1967). Conducted at Forest Park Community College (Missouri), this program is intended to supplement—not supplant—individual counseling procedures with both under- and nonachievers. It is built on the rationale that to be effective a counselor must understand the dynamics of group behavior; he must be a successful discussion leader and be alert to both individual and group reactions. He may choose to be directive or nondirective and may use any of several approaches to discussion and guidance.

Group counseling has been adopted in many schools, but whether it is as effective as individual counseling has not been established. Perhaps such a question demands research of a longitudinal nature, carefully controlled methodology, and precise criteria of effectiveness—demands that do not appear close to fulfillment, although there are efforts in these directions. For example, Thelen (1968) noted that students who were counseled individually were rated significantly higher by their counselors in growth and self-understanding than those counseled in groups but that there were no significant group differences in persistence in school, academic achievement, or goal motivation. Although students enrolled in either group or individual guidance were able to assess their educational goals more realistically than noncounseled students in a control group, neither group nor individual guidance procedures led to increased self-acceptance or the realistic assessment of vocational goals. However, in another study, where students were divided into blocks functioning as small groups, three times as many completed their junior college program as did regular liberal arts students (Chalghian, 1969).

Other questions have been raised about whether a school counselor should deal with personal and social problems or whether they should be dealt with by people specifically trained for such situations (Sensor, 1962). Whether the counselor functions best as an academic advisor or as a professional offering psychotherapeutic help with personal problems is less important than the fact that he does not have time to function in both roles. To cope with such time pressures, Meramec Community College (Missouri) (T. Jones, 1969) has developed an academic advisement program that prepares personnel with intensive in-service training to be active academic advisers, and it allows professional counselors to deal primarily with student problems of a less cognitive nature.

Since time obviously exerts a press, the adequacy of preparation and the element of paraprofessional expertise also demand consideration. Drawing from research reports in education and sociology demonstrating that students taught and/or counseled by other students will benefit from such an experience, S. Johnson (1969)' developed three models for using students as teachers and counselors. Differing from other approaches because it does not require the students who teach or counsel to be academic superiors, the greatest changes in desired behavior are predicated here for the counselor and tutor, not the counseled and tutored. Objectives, procedures, and plans for evaluation are also provided for the three models, each of which deliberately capitalizes on the influence that peers have on each other.

Other questions concern the effectiveness of counseling, in addition to questions of just what procedures should be established and who should act as counselors. In a study by McConnell and others (1965), student personnel services were found to be inadequate when measured against selected criteria. Yet, reviewing the effects of a pilot program of group counseling for prospective freshmen at Phoenix (Arizona) Junior College (Spector and Garneski, 1966), in which an experimental group of students counseled for six to eight hours were compared with a noncounseled group, the counseled groups achieved significantly higher grade-point averages and had a higher rate of peristence than did the control group. Also, despite some variation in generally favorable student reactions to preregistration counseling, one of the greatest flaws in counseling practice appears to be the short time for interviews between students and counselors (Pearce, 1967).

Issues in counseling are not limited to concerns with methodology, remedial students, or the counselors' roles, of course. Often they reflect broader questions. For example, anticipating by a few years the Woman's Liberation platform of the 1970s, a few studies have dealt with women—their perceptions and attitudes toward academia. From responses to a questionnaire for married women at Lansing (Michigan) Community College, Hunt (1966) recommended that college-going women be counseled to help them accept the fact that most of them will play a dual role for some period of their lives. For women of all ages, a need was discovered for the planning and replanning of a role neither too specific nor too short term; for mature women, it was felt that counseling should help them to plan realistic and individual educational programs. However, before such programs can be established, we must consider not only the goals of these women but also the impact on them of time pressures, of their families, and of their own motivations.

Knoell's (1969) study of high school graduates in four metropolitan areas (Dallas, Philadelphia, San Francisco, and St. Louis) has implications for counselors and developers of counseling programs as well as for other educators. Her data present a different side to the negative picture of ability from the one that was drawn by Jensen (1969) and that received so much attention. As well as IQ measures, the particular high school attended and the neighborhood in which a family resides influence issues of college attendance and persistence. Rather than continue to stress the usual paper-and-pencil tests, we should all take a different and broader look and attempt to make academic/vocational guidance efforts relevant to all students.

Reports that provide inputs to our understanding of junior college people and the institution itself are numerous. Many are repetitive in terms of the variables examined, the methodologies and the instruments employed, and the criteria established. Fortunately, others take more interesting approaches, use more pertinent material, and are founded on definitive criteria. While research in the junior college is often conducted without reference to guidance and student personnel services, it may have a greater impact on these programs than on regular curricula. However, we need to establish a certain base-line fund of standardized information. For example, data from a random, stratified sample of Florida students suggests that the "average" student attends a junior college in his own county directly after high school, takes more than two years to get his diploma, works while at college, graduates from the school first entered, enrolls in a transfer program, majors after transfer in education or abstract sciences, and feels that his junior college experience was helpful. Statewide standardized student information systems appear needed (Florida Community Junior College Inter-institutional Research Council, 1969). Another type of data bank has been developed by Harrisburg (Pennsylvania) Area Community College by compiling information on presently enrolled and former students (Snyder and Blocker, 1969a, 1969b). Both these information systems are of potential value for junior college counselors.

A slightly different focus was taken by investigators who examined guidance and placement programs in an experimental junior college sequence (College Entrance Examination Board, 1968). The purpose of this program was to provide information to aid students in making realistic decisions. Descriptions of student educational/vocational interests, special abilities (in reading, written communication, and fundamental mathematics), and other data were presented to help make decisions in areas of curriculum and future planning.

Several studies of students in single institutions focus on extrinsic influences, intrinsic needs, and special devices to cope with particular problems. In a survey conducted at Erie County (New York) Technical Institute (1968), the most influential recruitment factors were, in order of importance, the high school counselor, the college counselor, parents or other adults, friends, and, finally, brochures and leaflets available from counselors. Factors of little influence were high school and college career introduction days and such mass media devices as mailings, newspapers, and public displays.

Financial aid programs enter the student personnel picture, too. To determine the availability of financial aid, G. Jones (1969) examined the socioeconomic status of junior college students, analyzed the characteristics of students in the poverty class, and isolated factors preventing college attendance. The most likely sources of aid were not generally known to eligible student populations or were found to have built-in qualifications, restrictions, and limitations making the low-income student automatically ineligible. Perhaps so few poor people attend colleges mainly because the restrictions and complexity of financial aid programs make money unavailable to those who need it most.

No department or special function of a school can exist wholly independent of others, just as no person lives completely isolated from others. Some relationships are fairly superficial. Others, such as counseling services and remedial programs, are directly connected to school curriculum. How do remedial programs affect the student? How pertinent are they to the lives of the people they purport to serve? Some attempts to answer these questions will be described in the following section.

Remedial Students

The dedication to a curriculum designed to meet the identifiable educational needs of disadvantaged students is well documented by the statements of many who are actively involved in junior college education. Whether "disadvantaged" is defined in terms of academic handicaps or socioeconomic deprivation, most schools acknowledge a concern for these students. For schools especially geared to community development, particularly those in urban centers, the concern is immediate.

Whatever the definition of disadvantaged, reference frequently is made to the effects of deprivation on aspirations, values, motivation, and self-concept, as well as to its influence on academic progress. According to several studies, for example, Clarke (1966) and Kuusisto (1966), the student who falls under this heading needs to develop positive feelings of worth and value that are important for him individually and for society in general. He also needs to develop the social, conceptual, and manipulative skills necessary to fulfill his goals. These studies recommend that college programs attempt to develop special skills in students and to stimulate changes needed for such development by concentrating on what can be done within the context of a student's own nature and the pressures exerted upon him. For the disadvantaged student, these pressures include a lack of educational tradition, low motivation and low self-esteem, poor reading and language skills, antagonism toward school and authority figures, and, frequently, an unstable home life. To improve self-image and to reinforce motivation, a comprehensive program must give students a chance to experience enough success in learning to raise their levels of adaptation to a more generally acceptable behavioral pattern. It must not be a program whose net result is satisfaction with a status quo that is a far cry from our most humane desire for man's actualization. Disadvantaged students need options that they can see as real opportunities. Programs to create or maximize such opportunities often require variations in admission procedures to include criteria other than academic achievement.

In addition, preadmission counseling designed for disadvantaged students must be available for those who need something other than the usual liberal arts curriculum.

Several colleges have designed special readiness programs to integrate disadvantaged minority youths into both college and community. The College of San Mateo (California), for example, rejected scores on entrance examinations for disadvantaged students on the grounds that they were invalid predictors of grades (Pearce, 1967). At Foothill College (California), a program designed to help students needing remedial work included a combination of courses in English and psychology, a team-teaching approach, and block scheduling procedures. It was also recommended that key instructors be recalled to the campus at least three weeks before the beginning of the fall term to develop a program to test and diagnose students, maximize the instructors' effectiveness and, finally, provide for continuing counseling and student evaluation (Bloesser and others, 1968).

Other special programs have been instituted, either as special preschool programs or as adjuncts to or substitutes for existing curricula. At South Georgia College, a nine-week summer session was designed to provide academic help for the marginal student, equip him for college, and improve his self-concept (Lackey and Ross, 1968). Detailed daily student records netted several negative findings and, because of these, sensitivity training was recommended for the staff.

In a study that assessed career planning for low-achieving students, Roman (1969) found that such a program can be effective for the student in several ways: directing him in self-appraisal; teaching him to establish immediate, intermediate, and long-range goals; helping him to formulate alternative goals; and encouraging the adoption of positive attitudes and values. Results also suggested that career planning was effective in increasing academic persistence.

Student and faculty questionnaires are used to identify and assess programs especially designed for the disadvantaged. Looking at various methods used in California colleges, Berg and Axtell (1968) noted a pervasive money problem, lack of study time, a low degree of correspondence between expectation and reality, and a general approval of the institution. Other investigators, assessing the effectiveness or usefulness of programs in single colleges, sometimes report results worth considering in other schools. A follow-up survey of sixty-seven Project Success students at the Urban Education Center, City College of Chicago (Illinois) and of sixty-nine students receiving remedial training at other campuses in Chicago indicates that students overwhelmingly support the principle of remedial education, that personalized remedial training significantly increases their desire to persist in college, and that remedial assistance cannot be instituted as a program adjunct—that is, merely to intensify the usual curriculum of a single year (Baehr, 1969).

Other surveys evaluate different remedial programs. Opinions were obtained through questionnaires and interviews about Georgia Southwestern College's remedial program, regarding dissemination of publicity, the program's deficiencies, and potential improvements (Fisher and Lieberman, 1965). Unfortunately, the students did not regard this program as an opportunity to learn anything or to form a basis for choice between college or another activity. Therefore, certain curriculum changes were recommended to accommodate low-achieving students professing different levels of aspiration, abilities, and interests. Also pointing to inadequate guidance procedures, fairly consistent results were noted in a study conducted at Cerritos College (California) (Fitch, 1969). After being placed on probation, only 10 per cent of the students initially selecting a transfer major changed to a terminal major. Almost the same number of probationary students changed to a more difficult major as did those selecting an easier one, while the proportion of students seeking terminal majors declined over time. A major cause of high attrition rates, as well as failure to earn junior college degrees, was attributed to this reluctance on the part of students to accept more realistic goals—a failure that, according to research, probably is tied to family and social pressures, preconceived associations of certain levels of prestige with different majors, and ineffective remedial instruction and guidance programs.

Other findings are more positive. At San Diego City College, for example, 122 students in the general studies program were compared for four consecutive semesters with a control group of 128 students enrolled in other programs (Heinkel, 1970). Completion of the general studies program seemed to encourage males and minority students to reenroll in school for a second semester. Additionally, minority students who had enrolled in the program dropped fewer units for the first semester than those who did not enroll in it.

But no matter how well research is conducted, how careful the selection of criteria, or how appropriate the methodology, evaluation of any program may not help an individual who forms but one spoke in the large wheel of student populations. While there are several subcategories of the high-risk student, the stereotyping of his performance needs no documentation. We need better understanding, not more figures, and we need truly committed people to work with low-performing students. We must also understand the differential characteristics of students who are categorized as high-risk and answer such complaints as Moore's that "black students are being denied college entrance because of a white standardization measure—entrance exams and high school rank" (Moore, 1970, p. 42). What are the strengths of disadvantaged students in areas other than academic ability? What are some of the goals of under-achieving students compared with the goals of achievers and overachievers? Do the attitudes of these disadvantaged students differ from those of other students?

An allied question is whether the attitudes of remedial students to academic skills, activities, and aspirations differ from those of high-achieving students. A student's perceptions of self and of the ideal student, as well as his perceptions of his college's expectations, have been surveyed by several investigators. At Los Angeles City College, students admitted on probation because of low test scores viewed the college from a vocational orientation and saw no need for high academic skills and interests, although they did believe that the ideal student possessed such qualities. They also expressed faith in the junior college to provide what the economy and the social milieu had not offered them; faith in the junior college as an aid to a more productive economic life; a very high self-esteem as students; and an expressed willingness to subject themselves to the discipline of regular study. Further, they were confident that their values and needs were similar to those of both the college and the ideal student (Stein, 1966).

If some congruency exists among certain characteristics, how can we better understand and assist the disadvantaged student?

Like Cross (1968) and others, Knoell (1970, p. 129) argues against the use of traditional instruments to assess this type of person, pointing to "the long history of frustration and failure which has characterized the use of verbal tests to assess disadvantaged youths. Their consistently low scores belie their staying power in school. . . . There is little or no evidence of undeveloped potential for learning in their profiles of scores on the traditional tests, particularly in areas deemed appropriate to the collegiate level of education. The disadvantaged student tends to be handicapped in a variety of ways when confronted with group tests of aptitude and achievement in common use in the schools. . . . A prior handicap is his basic lack of motivation to do well on the tests, in part because of his self-concept as a loser in school competition." And Sheldon (1970a) questions all placement testing—for any group of students.

Since testing and other selection procedures usually apply to academic aptitudes and not to other qualities and, accordingly, can have negative effects on the expectations of certain students, we should look for different methods of appraisal and for alternative educational systems. Every person possesses both strengths and weaknesses. Do we honestly bother to look at both?

Studying the Students

6

In the past, most attempts to study student populations began with the premise—declared or implied—that the major characteristic differentiating one person from another was intellectual ability. From this premise, a whole line of inquiry developed—from Binet to the contemporary stress on tests and measurements for assessing individual differences. Ability—frequently represented by IQ—was considered the alpha and omega of knowledge about people in schools. It was seen as the key to understanding, the proper tool for predicting, and the basis for academic selection procedures—into classes, programs, and schools.

Gradually, different emphases arose. Intelligence was still considered basic and few researchers ignored it, but questions of motivation and goal direction entered the picture. Then a different twist emerged, and emotions came to the fore. Some people looked to them as the ultimate dimension, while others chose only to acknowledge their presence and still focused on the so-called cognitive domain. Of very recent vintage—in fact, still fermenting in the vats—is the notion that we can separate neither mind from body nor affect from cognition. Because the person comprises many parts, many variables affect his behavior.

Because we believe people may be most usefully considered as integrated wholes, this chapter does not explicitly isolate studies of academic ability or prediction from studies of characteristics. Instead, we choose to put together the many variables that make people what they are, looking at cognitive dimensions as related to the affective and at the affective or personality traits as they intertwine with the cognitive. Accordingly, we consider here a few of the research descriptions that characterize students and point out new directions for studying them.

One of the most comprehensive, definitive descriptions of the junior college student was given in 1968 by Cross. Guided by two basic purposes—to synthesize the findings of past research and to identify areas in which further research was needed—her report is directed primarily to faculty and administrators. It is not a critique of past research but a synthesis of several important studies conducted in the 1960s, with special emphasis on research that used broad samples of people from certain geographical areas and that reported appropriately comparable data.

Although Cross explicitly states that since junior college populations change so rapidly, research on their characteristics should be a continuing effort, some of her conclusions are important for any time. For example, in measures of ability, present tests are effective measures of success only insofar as they assess students in traditional educational curriculums. For the student thus oriented toward the typical liberal arts model, the scores are higher on tests oriented in the same direction.

Other investigators find measures of intellectual orientation to clearly differentiate among high school graduates who do not enter college, those who enroll in junior colleges, and those who attend four-year colleges (Medsker and Trent, 1965; Trent and Medsker, 1968). Using data obtained from Project Talent, a nationwide study of high school youth (Goldberg and Dailey, 1963), Cooley and Becker (1966) report that, on the whole, junior college students have more practical orientations to college and to life than do their more intellectually exposed counterparts in the four-year college and, further, that junior college students tend to be more like noncollege youths in terms of abilities. On measures of autonomy and nonauthoritarianism, variables frequently associated with intellectual disposition, several investigators found lower scores for the two-year students and less flexibility in thinking than in four-year college and university populations (Warren, 1966).

Junior college students generally do not consider themselves as well prepared for college as do students in four-year colleges and

universities. They have less confidence in, and are frequently critical
of, their high school courses and teachers. But, when nonacademic
areas—such as sports, cooking, manual skills, and sewing—are
assessed, junior college students express more confidence in their
abilities than do their peers in other higher educational institutions.
However, this suggests that many junior college students have different abilities that demand consideration. In fact, since the range of
scores among junior college people is so vast and since we still do not
know what the pattern of special abilities may be for students not
traditionally directed, increased flexibility in testing seems essential
for understanding this population in the 1970s.

When other variables are examined, Cross's synthesis points
to the lower socioeconomic status of parents of junior college students. This point, however, has been contested by Jencks and Riesman, who argue on the basis of limited data that "the parents of
students who enroll in community colleges are slightly richer than
the parents of students at four-year institutions" (1968, p. 425).
Whatever the status and whatever the direction of mobility—upward or downward—we need to know much more than we now do
about the home environments of junior college students, the kinds
of stimuli they encounter (and to which they do and do not respond), the degree of parental encouragement or discouragement,
and their parents' backgrounds.

Assessing the element of finances, we find that here too research findings are far from consensual. "While students attending
junior colleges say that cost and location are prime factors in their
selection of a college, few confess to major financial worries, and the
cost factor alone does not seem to prevent students from seeking
higher education" (Cross, 1968, p. 49).

When academic/vocational goals are used as the focus of
study, there appears to be widespread uncertainty among young
people about what they want to do with their futures. In high
school, many make decisions that close certain doors for them, as
indicated by the fact that approximately one-third of the students
who enter junior college have not taken a secondary school course
that would permit them to enter a four-year college. A preponderant
number of junior college students examined in the 1960s appeared
more unsettled about future plans than did either four-year college

or noncollege populations, and, consequently, a sizable number expressed interest in some kind of counseling and guidance directed toward future plans. However, a different attitude toward counseling was expressed by Cross when she described the characteristics of occupationally oriented students:

The responses that occupationally oriented students give on questionnaires present a picture of young people who know what they want and are pursuing an obvious pathway to their goal. . . . With the exception of wanting help in finding a job, occupational students express no more desire for counseling or guidance or tutoring than other community college students. In fact [as pointed out by the College Entrance Examination Board, 1968], they are less likely to indicate that they want help regarding educational and vocational plans than are transfer students [1970, p. 3].

In spite of the time that has elapsed and the vast number of studies that have been conducted since the middle 1960s, the research picture has not changed a great deal. It is indeed unfortunate that we must still report the need to develop further instruments to assess the junior college student and to explore new approaches to understanding him. The emphasis here is definitely on further and new. Penetrating tools that accurately and comprehensively describe the community college student must be developed, and we hope that these steps will lead to a sensitive awareness of him and his distinct strengths and weaknesses.

At this time, however, since "we possess only traditional measures to describe a student who does not fit the tradition" (Cross, 1968, p. 53)', the inevitable result is that the newest college student is pictured as less adequate than his peers in higher education—and less able to perform tasks developed for different types of students. Although a considerable overlap is apparent, as a group, junior college students are sharply differentiated from senior college students on the basis of intellectual dimensions. And, despite some attempts to design different assessment techniques (Knoell, 1970; Brawer, 1967, 1970)', most tests show that these students are less highly motivated toward educational success. As Cross puts it, "It hardly seems likely that we will help each student develop to his fullest potential by offering a single scheme of opportunities, rewards, and punishment. The great future task is to investigate whether, and in what ways, the junior college student differs in *kind* or in *pattern* of abilities, rather than in *degree,* from the traditional college student" (1968, p. 53). A similar plea is made by Knoell in her report about urban populations and their educational needs:

Community college counselors and faculty members have long felt that the [available] college admissions tests from the several national programs . . . are not particularly useful in counseling and placing junior college students. Results from the American College Testing Program battery and the College Entrance Examination Board's Scholastic Aptitude Test are of course used by the two-year colleges to advise students about their probable success in university-parallel programs, and to assign them to remedial or developmental courses. The appropriateness of the tests may be questioned for students who have not pursued a college preparatory program in high school and who then attend a community college which does not require such preparation. The validity of the tests for students planning to enroll in occupational programs requiring only a minimum amount of general education and other verbal content is also, of course, open to serious question.

[Needed are] useful instruments to assess the possible strengths and weaknesses of disadvantaged youth . . . [and high school students] . . . who might be recruited to a community college. . . . [Also needed is] information from such tests as a basis for planning new programs and services for those who are attracted to college [1970, p. 130].

Other broad-scaled investigations focus on different variables in attempting to draw general profiles of the junior college student. A sizable number of investigations have been conducted by people involved with the American College Testing (ACT)' Program. Among these, Richards and Braskamp (1969) used questionnaires, checklists, and especially designed procedures to express in quantitative terms the characteristics of students and the colleges they attend. Since correlations among student and college characteristics ranged from low to moderate, only broad conclusions can be drawn. For example, two-year colleges rating high in conventionalism, cost, and private control tend to attract more talented and intellectually oriented students than do those schools with predominant tendencies toward the vocational. Typically, large colleges corral a broader range of people than do small colleges, and colleges scoring high on transfer emphasis tend to attract more students with academic potential than do nontransfer-oriented schools. Variations among students in these high-transfer colleges suggest that the college experience may be more important in determining transfer rates than are the characteristics of entering students. Also using ACT data (American College Testing Program, 1966), Baird (1967) examined specific differences between students who had and those who had not decided on a vocation. Reports of several thousand students from thirty-one institutions who selected from among eighty-nine vocational fields indicated that the only sizable difference concerning college goals was that undecided groups tend to stress intellectual abilities whereas the decided students do not. Such items as academic aptitude, self-confidence, and aspiration showed no noticeable differences—results suggesting to Baird that vocational indecision should be expected at the age when most people enter college.

Again from these same ACT data, the contentions were reaffirmed that diversity characterizes American higher education and that this diversity invalidates generalization about the standards and purposes of higher education as a whole. In any attempt to reconcile institutional offerings and activities with the needs of college-going populations, it is important to understand these differences. In this sense, the college that offers a buffet lunch of courses and activities seems to be on the right track.

Let us look now at some less general relationships among other important dimensions of junior college students. Many questions have been raised about the particular personality characteristics that lead to specific kinds of behavior. Although one may suggest that almost all are important, some variables—for example, feelings of security and insecurity—appear more valuable than others in predicting certain student behaviors. In some cases, students who enroll in a certain program or who designate one kind of major may conceivably demonstrate special characteristics. At Illinois Central College, however, no significant differences were found among students in business, health, technical programs, and agriculture, or between transfer and terminal students, although regular

day students differed from night students at an extremely high level
of significance. Day students showed less confidence, less stability,
and a greater concern with self-identity in relation to present and
future; further, they tended to be more dogmatic, less effective in
critical thinking, and less creative than the night students (Grout,
1969). Do night students tend to be more secure because they differ
in other characteristics? Because they hold regular daytime jobs and
thus indicate some vocational direction? If answers to such questions
can be found, we can perhaps help regular day students develop
greater feelings of security.

Still other questions may be asked about students' perceptions of themselves, of others, and of their institutional environments.
Do, for example, the individual needs and/or environmental perceptions of junior college students differ from those of university students? Using Stern's *Activity Index* (1950–1963) and Stern and
Pace's *College Characteristics Index* (1963), Butler (1968) found
that although both student groups have generally comparable personalities, junior college students appear more objective toward life
and favor less self-indulgent experiences than do university students,
who prefer sensory gratification and involvement in a typically collegiate atmosphere. From an environmental perspective, the junior
college academic climate provides less encouragement for leadership
and self-assurance and less exposure to diversity in terms of faculty,
public discussion, and innovation than does the university.

Does a particular course have any effect on student self-
concept, acceptance of self, personal adjustment, and attitudes toward self and others? Introductory psychology classes at Rio Hondo
(California) Junior College (Corey, 1967) were divided into five
comparison groups. No differences were found in self-concept, self-
acceptance, or ideal of self-concept, but certain classes did influence
student adjustment.

Are there identifiable differences in motivation between low
socioeconomic students and students from the middle class? Are
there personality factors that distinguish nonachievers from different
socioeconomic backgrounds, and are there discrete measures of
motivation that distinguish between academically achieving and
nonachieving students? Using several instruments—paper-and-pencil and projective—Hall (1968) found that achieving lower-class

students have higher needs to achieve high scores than do achieving middle-class students. Other variables seem to discriminate between high and low achievers. In a study conducted by Fox (1967), for example, high achievers responded positively to adult approval, school experiences, relations to authority figures, and self-concept, whereas low achievers responded positively to academic associations, success patterns, social relationships, and goal directions.

What about student perceptions of their education and of how it fits their academic and vocational goals? Baird, Richards, and Shevel (1969) analyzed replies to such questions as: What are the personal and educational goals of college students? How do they evaluate their college teachers? What are their educational and vocational plans? To what degree are they satisfied with their education? To what extent do they have a sense of their own progress? The resulting composite picture of the "typical" student suggests a commuter who attended high school just before entering college, is financing his education by working, sees vocational training as the most important goal of college attendance, and generally responds favorably to college teachers.

How does academic potential affect student perceptions of their education? Students entering a two-year college acknowledge fewer nonacademic high school accomplishments than do their counterparts in four-year colleges. Too, they generally choose their institutions for practical reasons, select such courses as business and agriculture, and tend "to aspire more often than their counterparts in four-year colleges to less than a bachelor's degree" (Baird, Richards, and Shevel, 1969, p. 44).

This tendency of junior college students to be influenced by practical considerations rather than by intellectual and social ones also leads them to see the worth of a college in terms of its ability to prepare them to attain higher incomes than they would otherwise be able to command. They are less concerned with personal and intellectual development than are their four-year counterparts and less inclined to look to graduate training as a goal (Richards and Braskamp, 1969). In general, these students can be described as pragmatic individuals who seek vocational training; they are not usually talented students with intellectual and academic orientations and are generally the first in their families to attend college. In this sense, the college is still in a position to function as a prime agent of social mobility.

Students make decisions not only in terms of their perceptions but also in terms of their value systems. Some efforts at assessment are built on the rationale that if values constitute an essential part of the individual's makeup, we can better understand the person through assessing these values. Since the schools have always been a means by which a culture transmits its values from one generation to the next, it seems perfectly appropriate for such institutions to gather information about their students' value and belief systems. However, not until Jacob issued his report in 1957 was the investigation of values among college students either seriously or systematically considered. And, in the many years since then, relatively little has been done toward carefully assessing the values of college students, particularly those at the junior college level.

One part of a study coordinated by the Clearinghouse assesses the value systems of faculties, entering students, and staffs in three California junior colleges. Using data compiled in this project, Park (1970, 1971) discusses the institutional personality of junior colleges according to the values held by faculty and staff members. A monograph by Brawer (1971b) assesses the values and belief systems of these same populations in terms of the so-called generation gap, student activism, and distinguishable points of congruence. Some of the major findings suggest that the greatest differences in values are those between students and faculty members—that is, age and role play the major part in determining incongruence in values. This finding obtains even when students majoring in one subject area are compared with instructors in the same subject field. This seems a fruitful area of study.

One of the few studies of attitudes and beliefs among junior college personnel was conducted by Sogomonion (1965), who questioned students enrolled in political science courses about such issues as the United States' intervention in disputes of other countries, freedom of speech on campus, and civil rights. In response to whether students were justified in demonstrating during the Free Speech Movement on the University of California campus, most agreement was found among those in the oldest age group, who denounced the "activists." The nineteen- through twenty-one-year-old group was second highest in condemning the Berkeley "rioters." The authority and disciplinary attitudes of parents and elders were seen as having a restraining influence on the younger students, who generally tended toward noncommitment.

Examining the interpersonal values of forty junior college students enrolled in a terminal course, 116 junior college students in a transfer course, and 93 university students, Abbas (1968) measured qualities of support, independence, conformity, benevolence, recognition, and leadership. On the value of conformity, a significant difference was found between the low scores of university students and the high scores of each of the two samples of junior college students; on the leadership scale, university students scored higher than did transfer students. No significant differences were found on other values. Although junior college students may have scored higher on conformity because they live at home, it may well be that the differentiating characteristic is nonconformity itself. Perhaps the university attracts the nonconformist.

Another comparison between value systems used a questionnaire that had been adapted from a larger survey (Hadden, 1969). Forty-two of ninety-five attitude items were shared by a majority of the junior college students and the four-year college population. However, contradictory views were expressed by the junior college group and college seniors and by the junior college students and the faculty groups studied by Blai (1970b).

Attempting to determine the extent of agreement on educational values among students, parents, and faculty, Paetz (1966) analyzed data regarding perceptions of junior college values, the value of a college education, and the value of a particular college. Students appeared to be realistic in their value rankings and in their career choices and to be closer to their parents' than to the faculty's values.

Peer groups and faculty are in powerful positions to facilitate academic and intellectual goals (Newcomb, 1962) and thus to encourage certain value systems (Sanford, 1962). Some data comparing attitudes and opinions of students and faculty are tabulated in the second volume of Feldman and Newcomb (1969). None, however, deals specifically with values at the junior college level.

While such material as we have been discussing here may

help us understand college-going populations on the basis of their belief systems, they fall short in helping us plan programs, choose curriculums, and devise goals for the junior colleges. In light of this inadequacy, are we justified in continuing to examine student characteristics, values, and perceptions while ignoring information we already have that may help us understand how we are affecting these people?

Until recently, this dilemma was not so pronounced because we could look at the junior college student only in comparison with students in either high school or four-year colleges and universities. Pictures of the student attending the two-year college, either public or private, were pictures by inference only. We were aware of certain characteristics—and many stereotypes—of the college student at such-and-such a university, and, from this information, we attempted to draw profiles of his counterpart in the two-year college, however inaccurate they may have been.

Several people have been instrumental in changing this research outlook. Medsker's work concentrated on people at the junior college level, and, with Knoell (1965), with Tillery (1971), with Trent (1968), and with others working at the Center for Research and Development in Higher Education, Berkeley, he has drawn portraits of this newer student in this newer form of higher education. In 1968, however, despite this new-found emphasis, Cross could still plead for studies that would employ different forms of assessment to examine the nontraditional student.

Whether others heeded Cross's pleas directly or whether they also felt the need to look at the junior college student in a specialized way, the late 1960s saw some changes in the approaches to understanding this person. More and more attempts were made to look at the junior college student separately from his counterparts at other educational levels, and while many of these studies were indigenous to the institutions where they were made, others were broader based. Whether the information we need—or think we need—is obtained on a regional or national basis, however, by the mid-1970s we certainly should possess sufficient data about junior college students to make sound decisions regarding appropriate alternative educational forms.

We still, nevertheless, need different approaches to understanding this growing population. Knoell's (1970) report on students who must yet be served—disadvantaged youths—initiates some nontraditional approaches to assessment. This is an important beginning. Brawer's (1970) conceptual model presents yet another approach that is definitely not traditional, albeit rooted in comparatively well established psychological theories. Again we see beginnings and new directions, but where are we going?

Today we know more about people than we did before, yet, because our society is changing so rapidly, we also know less. How can we merge our knowledge of people with education and educational practices? Can we justify an educational system that, even at the college level, still places desks row upon row, still looks to techniques that were antiquated years ago? If higher education is truly to "meet needs" rather than to exist as an obstacle course to exclude certain people from further education, we not only must have accurate pictures of our students but also we must know how to relate college programs closely to their daily lives. By defining and following educational objectives that are both realistic and relevant, we can be in a position to fulfill contemporary expectations of individual development.

We perhaps know more than we need to know about college students today. What do we do with this knowledge? Our questions have not been easy to formulate. The answers may be even less precise. One thing we do know now: "The formal, artificial social order of the school does not furnish a proper milieu for the development of normal personalities; that is why students are rebellious: they want to live" (Waller, 1967, pp. 445–446, written in 1932).

These two chapters have reviewed a mere fraction of the hundreds of studies of junior college students. Taken individually or as a group, the reports are like descriptions of a bed of pebbles. They tell us much about a few general characteristics but little that delineates a single pebble or an individual student. There are few anecdotal reports; almost nothing tells what college has meant to one student or to one type of student. One way to cope with this mass of literature on students is to look at people as pebbles—how they appear on the surface and then how they look under close scrutiny. To talk about characteristics of either pebbles or people and to come up with an approximate picture of the average are not at all difficult tasks. It is infinitely more difficult, however—and vastly more interesting—to describe unique traits of a single pebble or an individual and, eventually, to arrive at the conclusion that no pebble—and no person—is exactly like any other. If we cherish our differences—as so many of us do—let them live by incorporating them into our understanding of man.

What Is Good Teaching?

 7

The importance of *good teaching* is shouted from the podiums at national conferences, iterated at otiose faculty meetings, and intoned by every school principal and president. At any gathering of educators, soon after everyone has had his say about finances (how to get more)' and student activism (how to have less), changed instructional practice comes to the fore. Teaching is a perennially timely topic.

Public schools provide a variety of incentives for good teaching, including advanced pay for extra course credits and frequent workshops on instructional techniques. Universities try to interest professors in instruction and offer everything from a national Project to Improve College Teaching to campus centers that help instructional planning and test construction. However, in-service education of public school teachers remains the slum of American education; and university professors, operating within their own role definitions and with an inertia born of decades, wait patiently for the latest wave of demands to pass by.

Community college teaching is not quite the same as teaching at other levels of education, although it is modeled partly by teaching in the secondary school and partly on the four-year college image. Hence, comparisons with the university—although frequently made—are inappropriate. The differences are obvious. Junior college instructors are aware that they are not expected to conduct research or publish. A variety of intramural procedures is more likely to influence their instruction. And, perhaps most important, for

99

years they have been involved in attempts to teach untraditional students—a task that university professors are first beginning to be aware of.

Too, the upheavals that have plagued university campuses, distracting faculty members from their productive or contemplative activities, have bypassed the junior college campuses for the most part. Junior college instructors are well aware of the rhetoric that has ascribed the relative calm on their campuses to their interest in teaching, their dedication to students, and their superior interpersonal skills. Although these statements are only half true, they help to isolate the community college instructor from his counterpart in the university. For better or for worse, and regardless of the variation in definitions of good teaching, the junior college is wedded to the practice. It has no other defensible raison d'être; in Thornton's oft-quoted words, "either it teaches excellently, or it fails completely" (1966, p. 21).

This chapter offers a commentary on good teaching—what it means and what it might be. Teaching as *causing learning* is the definition used here. It thus represents the value position, the filter through which present teaching practices and summary statements are viewed.

Objectives

The concept of defining specific, measurable objectives in instructional programs has gained many adherents. In Mager's (1962) terms, a specific—or "behavioral"—objective delineates the task that a student shall be able to perform at the end of an instructional sequence, the conditions or circumstances under which he will perform this task, and the criterion level or degree of accuracy he will manifest. This is the heart of defining instructional objectives; the rest is commentary. However, the commentary has attained formidable proportions with volumes being written about the subject—how to do it, why it should or should not be done, what the consequences of specifying objectives are or will be, and the relationships between the use of objectives and the various theories of learning and philosophies of education.

Specifying objectives has an immediate relevance to the junior college because of its acknowledged commitment to teaching.

Many junior college instructors and supervisors of instruction are aware of current methods, media, materials, and techniques of instruction—in fact, in many junior college districts, "innovation in instruction" has become a catchphrase. Some advocates of changed instructional practices seize on the concept of specific objectives and, with some success, manage to move it into the realm of junior college instruction. B. L. Johnson (1969) refers to contemporary uses of objectives, finding them in several junior colleges where television, autotutorial programs, and a variety of multimedia instructional systems are favored. Cohen (1969) applied the concept to the institution as a whole in his hypothetical college of 1979. In this scheme, each course and, indeed, the entire curriculum would be built and revised on the basis of the specific objectives attained by students. And, beginning in 1969, a concerted effort was launched to have junior college instructors in three states write objectives (Regional Education Laboratory for the Carolinas and Virginia, 1970).

Accordingly, it seems appropriate here to review a few of the many books that describe the process of writing objectives and offer a rationale for so doing. In 1970–1971, over a dozen books on how to write objectives were published in paperback form. Many of these texts should be avoided by junior college instructional supervisors or faculty members who wish to learn the process, primarily because they are too elementary. The reaction then becomes one of "this process is suitable for grade school or for those instructors who desire only that their students memorize data, but it does not fit my own academic work." Other texts are of dubious value because they are so jargon-ridden that the reader must learn an entire new terminology merely to understand the process. In addition, many are uninteresting. These can be avoided, considering the number of useful texts on the market. Books that are worthy of favorable attention include works by Tyler, Mager, Kibler and others, Cohen, Popham and Baker, and Johnson and Johnson.

A seminal work is Tyler's *Basic Principles of Curriculum and Instruction* (1950). Tyler's rationale is that any curriculum or plan of instruction may be structured best if questions of how purpose, appropriate learning experiences, and determination of outcomes will be assessed are answered in advance. Obviously, this view requires a clear-cut statement of the specific objectives to be attained by students who complete the programs. Tyler worked on the philosophical and psychological bases of curriculum and instruction for twenty years before publication of his book. And now, his rationale still remains the cornerstone of the process of objectives writing.

Mager set down specific guidelines for writing what he called "behavioral objectives" in *Preparing Instructional Objectives* (1962). Dividing the objectives into three parts—task, conditions, and criterion—he prepared a manual of instruction in how to write them. The book is demonstrably effective in teaching the elements of objective writing, but the examples Mager uses are elementary behaviors—tasks that require little more than memorization or direct recall of information. For this reason, the work has been criticized by writers who feel the concept of specifying objectives can be applied to complex behavior, and, because he used pedestrian examples, Mager debased it. Nevertheless, he did stabilize the criteria for objectives and, for years, instructors at all levels of education have applied his three-part scheme in building objectives in their own courses.

Mager prepared a second book, *Developing Vocational Instruction* (co-authored with Beach, 1967), listing specifically the manner of analyzing the behaviors to be attained at the end of vocational courses. And he extended his work into the area of affect or the demonstration of attitude in a third book, *Developing Attitudes Toward Learning* (1968). In this work, he used narrative form to point out how to write objectives so that students' attitudes toward a course, topic, or subject can be assessed. The three Mager books can be used as basic works in the library of any junior college staff member who is interested in the details of instructional planning.

One of the most thorough books on writing objectives was prepared by Kibler, Barker, and Miles (1970). The authors discuss different types of objectives and ways of planning instruction around them, and they cite a number of pro and con arguments regarding the process. In addition, they relate objectives to the various levels of the cognitive and affective domains of knowledge as postulated by Bloom (1956) and Krathwohl (1964). They offer programed practice in writing objectives and provide several samples of objectives drawn from various secondary school and college courses.

The concept of specific objectives was applied directly to junior college instruction by Cohen, whose *Objectives for College Courses* (1970) includes a statement of the rationale for writing objectives, a programed lesson in how to write them, and examples of objectives used in junior college courses. In addition, he lists in question-and-answer format a number of frequently raised arguments about the process.

No discussion of the writing of instructional objectives can be complete without mentioning the work of Popham, who extended the concept into programs of teacher preparation. His book, *The Teacher Empiricist* (1970), offers a rationale for the use of objectives, along with sample objectives, test items, practice exercises, and a variety of specimen objectives. His *Establishing Instructional Goals* (1970), co-authored with Baker, is a programed lesson in selecting and preparing objectives. S. and R. Johnson have also done much work in this field. They prepared a useful set of programed materials in which instructors are led through the process of specifying and analyzing objectives, arranging appropriate instructional activities, and defining their instruction on the basis of results (Johnson and Johnson, 1970).

Also recommended for the junior college instructor are thirty-nine sets of specific objectives for various junior college courses that may be obtained from the ERIC Document Reproduction Service (Capper, 1969). They represent the culling of useful objectives from hundreds of junior college course outlines collected from instructors in all parts of the United States. Instructors who wish to see other samples of objectives before writing their own can obtain specimen sets from the Instructional Objectives Exchange (Box 24095, Los Angeles). A catalog listing the thirty-six sets of objectives that can be obtained from the Exchange also is available.

Thus, there is no dearth of information regarding the process of writing objectives. Various educational leaders have extended the concept to the junior college level and much work on objectives is being done by junior college instructors. The concept has become the core of several instructional programs and is, in fact, used as a basis for instructor evaluation in at least one institution (Cohen and Shawl, 1970). These efforts point to a firm future for the use of objectives in junior college instruction.

However, not all the commentary on objectives as a core concept in instruction has been favorable. The National Council of Teachers of English passed a resolution at its 1969 annual meeting urging "caution in the use of behavioral objectives in the teaching of English" and amplified its misgivings with another, more detailed resolution in 1970. The extent of the controversy regarding objectives in English instruction is revealed in *On Writing Behavioral Objectives for English* (Maxwell and Tovatt, 1970). Several papers in the volume suggest a deep concern that finite objectives may prove antagonistic to the spirit of the English curriculum. In this book, in addition to arguments for and against objectives, the Tri-University Behavioral Objectives for English project is described, a project that represents a serious effort to determine appropriate objectives for English.

Other subject-field representatives are groping for appropriate ways to introduce objectives into their own teaching. And, with the emphases on "performance contracting"—the awarding of money based on the specific outcomes of instructional programs—and "accountability"—the holding of someone in addition to the student responsible for his learning—it is clear that the concept will receive considerable attention. No instructor in the junior college, then, can afford to ignore the writing of objectives. The practice should be tried. If it is to be rejected, let it be on the grounds that it is demonstrably unsuitable to junior college instruction or that it is philosophically incompatible with the open-door college, not on the whim of instructors who identify objectives with educational technologists and accordingly reject the process without giving it a try.

Media

The writings about the media of instruction in the junior college fall into two categories: exhortations and summary statements regarding the benefits of reproducible media, and assessments of the effects of the various media employed in actual teaching situations. Most polemical and state-of-the-art commentary falls under the heading "instructional innovation"—a term used to cover reports of any practice other than the "stand-up-live-lecture."

Instructional innovation in the community college has been

well covered. In 1963, B. L. Johnson visited or corresponded with top administrators in nearly 100 colleges, asking about the number of innovative techniques in their institutions (1964). Again, in 1967, he spoke with people in more than 250 institutions asking the same questions and summarizing his findings in *Islands of Innovation Expanding* (1969). Other investigators also have surveyed innovations in the community college. Reitan and Lander (1968), for example, obtained information on instructional practices in forty-five colleges in the northwestern United States during 1968.

Innovations in junior college education are usually listed under kinds of media employed or under main categories such as course and program planning, technological aids, facilities use, and scheduling arrangements. B. L. Johnson (1969) found that junior colleges lead in using programed instruction, autotutorial teaching, television, and other mechanical devices. In addition, he reported the use of a variety of innovative techniques that were not "hardware based"—for example, simulation exercises, independent study, and the use of students as teachers. He concluded that the junior college as an institution is receptive to the use of different forms of instruction—in fact, the segment of higher education most responsive to new instructional techniques. The Reitan and Lander study also includes a list of curriculum and instructional innovations and useful information on how to obtain this type of data from other colleges.

Many indigenous reports of new efforts in curriculum and instruction emanate from the colleges and from the reports of conferences where junior college staff members get together to compare notes on what they are doing. A set of short monographs reports on innovative courses of study at one college and the methods of instruction used in them (Harrisburg Area Community College, 1970a, 1970b). The so-called "systems approach," used in developing courses in chemistry, psychology, and English at Meramec Community College (Missouri) has been described in a paper prepared by St. Louis Junior College District (Hunter, 1970). Many similar parochial reports may be found in *Research in Education* and in the *Junior College Journal;* hardly an issue passes without a report of some changed form of curriculum, new course, or different instructional pattern.

Conference proceedings yield a variety of anecdotal material on instructional techniques. William Rainey Harper College (Illinois) reported the information discussed at a six-week summer workshop on instructional development at that institution (Voegel, 1970). The role of the dean of instruction in leading his faculty toward the use of new instructional techniques was examined at a workshop at UCLA (Chadbourne, 1969). The 1969 Minnesota Junior College Faculty Conference yielded suggestions on uses of grading systems, alternatives to traditional course requirements, and the uses of various instructional media (Moen and others, 1969). An Appalachian State University (North Carolina) conference on improving instruction in junior colleges resulted in a paper on the need for clearly stated objectives, the uses of various media, and commentary on characteristics of students (Appalachian State University, 1969).

As a teaching institution, then, the junior college is ready to take on different instructional forms. It will try anything and, just as quickly, discard it in favor of something else. The criteria on which new instructional techniques are introduced and/or rejected fall far short of those the true disciplinarian in instruction would find valid. Nevertheless, "teaching" is the watchword and, if anything is happening in instruction anywhere, some junior college is doing it.

Reproducible Media. In common with some secondary schools and a few universities, many junior colleges have stressed the introduction and use of reproducible media. In fact, the 1960s were characterized by vast claims for—and often equally vast disillusionment with—new media. A medium would be invented, modified, or applied to the instructional process. Journalists, hardware salesmen, and educators (those one might call "professional innovators") proclaimed the millennium by claiming that television (autoinstructional programing, dial-access information systems, audiotape) would release teachers for creative interactions with students. Researchers found that the medium could instruct as well (or as poorly) as a live instructor. Institutions obtained funds to purchase hardware and install the new techniques. And then, as initial enthusiasm wore off, or the innovator left the campus, or the funds ran out, disillusionment set in with attendant abandonment of a particular medium.

This pattern recurred in many colleges and with a variety of new media. Television alone was the subject of much debate. Gross and Murphy (1966) documented problems associated with the introduction and continued use of instructional television, difficulties ranging from faculty antagonism to improper use of the medium. Evans and Leppman (1968) traced faculty resistance to television in a well documented study of ten universities and found numerous maintenance problems. Using survey forms and interview schedules within a research design stemming from sociopsychological theory, they found resistance based on both the personal characteristics of faculty members and the characteristics of the traditional college as a social system. They concluded that the reasons for terminating an innovation are extremely varied, but that most relate to the idiosyncrasies of instructors and the basic tendency to resist change inherent in most social structures. Whatever the reason, some schools have closets full of unused hardware.

Brown and Thornton (1963b, pp. 6–7)' anticipated the problems of introducing and maintaining reproducible media in higher education when they pointed out that "difficult decisions will be required in the cases of proposed uses that are viewed favorably by trustees and administrators, but with suspicion by professors who fear their effects on job security, individual freedom, or rewards or conditions of work." Studies comparing various media on the basis of costs or learning effect thus missed a crucial point. Faced with a new medium, a professor may wonder what its adoption will mean to him. Believing that instructors will use a medium because of its demonstrated efficacy in causing learning is awarding a selflessness to them that few possess. Nor are administrators blameless. They frequently accept the promises of every media promoter at face value and then seem surprised when a device fails to solve all their campus problems.

Why junior college staff members accept or reject new media has never been studied in depth, perhaps because such inquiry requires combining elements of psychological, organizational, and sociological theory. Stemming from investigations conducted at other levels of education and stressing other concepts, some evidence is available, however, and extrapolations to the junior college can be made. For example, Dubin and Taveggia (1968) reanalyzed data from ninety-six investigations done over the previous forty years in which media were compared, and they found that the studies canceled each other out. That is, for each study that identified a learning advantage in "lecture" over "discussion," another found the reverse. Faced with these results, any instructor may conclude that whatever teaching method he uses will be beneficial to some students but not to others—so he may as well not try out anything new. Or as Dubin and Taveggia conclude, "the net effect of the inconclusive data was to permit each person to hold his private preference concerning a given teaching method without the data demanding its alteration."

Rapidly expanding student enrollment provides another excuse for avoiding change, supporting a belief that students thrive on what is offered. Such reasoning is used in many articles and speeches, but it is easily rebutted. Schwab (1969, p. 4) comments: "If the first principle of education is to expend the minimum energy necessary to satisfy the ignorant client, so be it. It would be a mistake, however, to assume that 'to tolerate' means 'to be satisfied with, to be pleased by.'" Or, as Cohen (1970b, pp. 129–130) put it, "Answering criticism by citing enrollment figures . . . is fatuous; a counterargument can be raised that young people in America have few other socially acceptable places to *be*."

Lack of energy and time—a phenomenon noted by many authors, Garrison (1967) in particular—is a compelling reason for maintaining old forms. Instructors must revise courses, select new media, and rewrite objectives. And many junior college instructors meet 200 students per week. Maintaining records alone for 200 people is a huge chore. If an instructor gives an assignment to his students, and if, when the papers come in, he spends only three minutes in reading and reacting to one paper and recording the results, ten hours have been used, leaving little time for anything else. Unfortunately student assistants or paraprofessional aides are not widely used in two-year colleges.

One more phenomenon is worthy of note here: perhaps instructors perceive reproducible media as substantialities that take them away from the students. For example, in a study of students and staff members at three southern California junior colleges (Cohen, 1970d), the 238 instructors were asked, "What do you think students look for when they enter a class for the first time?" The overwhelming first choice was "instructor's personality." When asked what they thought students would most like them to do, their most frequent response was "be available for individual conferences." In other words, the instructors invariably put themselves at the center of the enterprise and saw the college as only a housing that would bring students into proximity with them. Their attitude is all right superficially, but such instructors may never allow an audio- or video-tape recorder to take their students away from them. Incidentally, in this same study, when the nearly 2,000 students were asked what *they* first looked for, the first choice was "specific learning objectives." As Bright (1967) noted, it is unfortunate that the question of the role and status of the professor rarely is studied when the subject is presented by a medium other than by the professor himself.

In the junior college field, most indigenous reports and most conference proceedings focus on straight reportage that can be best characterized under the heading, "here's the way we do it at our place." Attempts at evaluating the effects of newly introduced techniques are very rare. Accordingly, carefully designed experiments are worthy of particular attention if the programs are evaluated for their effects on teachers, students, or parent communities.

The Florida College Teaching Project (French and Cooper, 1967) was a two-year study in which teachers of biology, English, humanities, mathematics, physical sciences and social sciences at the university and at various junior colleges in Florida tested the value of orienting courses toward student participation and away from lectures. Each instructor conducted one conventional course and one experimental, less-structured course covering the same material. Although there was little difference in the mean achievement of experimental and control groups, more able students did better under experimental conditions, while less able students did better under conventional conditions. Teachers felt that students in the experimental sections learned more about matters related to but not actually a part of the course material. Comparing experimental and regular classes, students felt that they did more work in the experimental situations, were more independent in them, and were more comfortable (but less secure) in them. In the first year of the program, student reaction to the experimental courses was generally negative; in the second year, it was more positive.

An example of an indigenous experiment is afforded by a study conducted at Miami-Dade Junior College (Florida). During the spring semester 1970, an experimental group of fifty-four students was provided with objectives each week and with five media options. The objectives specifically indicated the work required to obtain a particular letter grade. The student then could suggest both the objectives he wished to pursue and the media form in which he wanted to learn them. Although the experimental group students earned higher grades than did the control group in English and social science classes, pre- and post-testing on the Cooperative English Test did not reveal significant differences in learning (Greenberg, 1970). Similar studies are in the ERIC files, but they are infrequent.

Multimedia. Nevertheless, inconclusive and nonexistent research reports do not delay the construction of various types of instructional programs that are based predominantly on reproducible media. "Multimedia"—a generic term used for courses or programs in which various autoinstructional devices are used in combination—is popular. Frequently employed components include programed workbooks, audiotapes alone or along with filmstrips, TV presentations, and laboratory exercises. Occasionally, institutions in which multimedia instruction has been introduced use the term "instructional systems"—a misnomer, however, because systematic controls, feedback mechanisms, and evaluative devices usually are lacking.

Much has been written about multimedia. Rationales for developing multimedia instructional sequences have been presented by many people, including Briggs and others (1967). Multimedia programs are described by Brown and Thornton (1963b) and B. L. Johnson (1969). Banister (1970) and Postlethwait and others (1969) explain procedures for constructing the sequences. Add to these the reports on instructional "systems" (Banathy, 1968;

Trzebiatowski, 1968), and the outlines of a formidable literature emerge.

Implementation of multimedia instruction on a college-wide basis rarely is found, although some institutions are heavily committed to the process. St. Louis (Missouri) Junior College District introduced a multimedia instructional approach in English, chemistry, and psychology at one of its campuses, developing the program in four phases: planning, preparing the components of the system, demonstration, and evaluation. Components included a variety of individually paced learning activities built around several different media forms (Hunter, 1970). Preliminary evaluations showed a significant increase in student achievement; the rate of failure in the chemistry course dropped 10 per cent, and dropout rates were lower than before in English and psychology.

In the late 1960s, Mt. San Jacinto College (California) and Harrisburg (Pennsylvania) Area Community College began using taped lessons and programed workbooks to teach shorthand and typing. The instructors at Fullerton (California) Junior College built tapes, filmstrips, and worksheets into seminars in several mathematics courses. Golden West College (California) adopted Postlethwait's (1964) audio-tutorial system for teaching its biology courses and prepared slides and tapes for remedial English. In most of these installations the instructors put together the multimedia sequences themselves, taking ideas from various sources, making local adaptations, and preparing the requisite materials.

The instructors usually allow multimedia evaluations to be made by institutional research offices, for they are less concerned with evaluating the effects of their efforts than with maintaining and revising their projects. Hence, the level of sophistication of program evaluation depends on whether a college has a knowledgeable research director or a liaison with a neighboring research group. Some colleges collect information on students' affinity for the instructional forms. Others compare costs, and a few assess student learning against the objectives set up by the program directors.

For example, two industrial arts classes in beginning electronics were compared with each other (a total of 244 students in both) to assess the effects of multimedia. The study concluded that the system is not suitable for all learners (Harmon, 1969). General science and physical science students took part in studies that respectively investigated lecture/demonstration and an autotutorial laboratory. Eighty students who experienced lecture/demonstrations were compared with eighty-two who completed their laboratory work on their own (Bradley, 1965). Class examinations and final grades reflected no difference. In another study, final examinations and a standardized test of science reasoning and understanding were administered to evaluate the effects of an autotutorial laboratory that allowed students to come and go of their own volition. The autotutorial method had been introduced to replace the traditional laboratory for physical science students. Although no significant difference was found, the author noted that lower-ability students did better with the autotutorial laboratory (Rowbotham, 1969). Beyond this type of generalized study, research on the effects or influence of multimedia instruction per se rarely is found. Researchers assess the media forms separately, while colleges put them together in various ad hoc combinations.

The Indefinable Art

To coin an oxymoron, the evaluation of instruction in the two-year college is a consistently haphazard exercise. All students pass judgment on their courses, sometimes responding to questionnaires regarding the quality of the instruction they have received and, whenever possible, flocking to favored instructors' classes while shunning others. Instructors appraise their work, chatting with each other about the way a particular class "felt," or by viewing students' papers and wondering where they went wrong (or right). Administrators visit classes, collect collegial remarks, compare grade marks issued at their own and neighboring transfer institutions. Even townspeople judge the courses and the instructors, using hearsay as their chief source of information. All these processes occur simultaneously but none can be rightfully called "evaluation of instruction." Many reasons for the colleges' failure to institute valid evaluation processes may be cited, but one—the inconsistent, invalid, definition of "teaching" that pervades the field—underlies them all. Not the problems associated with defining "good teaching"—but with defining teaching at all.

To illustrate: The Project to Improve College Teaching, jointly sponsored by the American Association of University Professors and the Association of American Colleges—two prestigious organizations—published a well written monograph on the subject of college teacher evaluation (Eble, 1970). The monograph reviewed evaluation procedures in many universities, examining the variety of practices in use and suggesting combinations of alternatives. The monograph is typical of many that emanate from projects, conferences, and professional associations that purport to address college teaching—in fact, it is better than most. But there is the same serious flaw in this monograph as in others of the type. Nowhere in the discussion of evaluating teaching is the term "teaching" defined. It assumes that everyone knows what teaching is; and it assumes that teaching is what people called "teachers" typically do, usually in classrooms, and that some do it better than others.

The monograph—and we are not criticizing the Project to Improve College Teaching per se—proceeds to discuss teaching from the point of view of giving recognition to it, improving it, evaluating it, supporting it, collecting evidence of it, and so on, never once acknowledging that "it" is so variously defined that a common ground for discourse is entirely lacking. The author gives some recognition to this problem by stating that, at the university level, "teaching is likely to be less well defined and judged than research or service," but he fails to acknowledge the impossibility of validly measuring something not reliably defined.

The definition of teaching as an ill-defined art form pervades the field. Invariably articles, books, and monographs written about instruction in higher education address teaching in these terms. Highet called his book *The Art of Teaching* because he "believe[s] that teaching is an art, not a science" (1950, p. vii). *Effective College Teaching* includes the statement, "Teaching is an art. There is little that is scientific about it. . . ." (Morris, 1970, p. 82). Written for prospective college instructors, *Do You Teach?* begins: "Although teaching is an art—an art that must be developed by each teacher in the light of his own experience. . . ." (Skilling, 1969, p. iii). Kelley and Wilbur, who address their book directly to junior college instructors, discuss "the art of teaching," admitting that "the word 'art' to describe junior college instruction was chosen carefully" (1970, p. 135).

The list is long and other examples could be cited. Teaching is an art form. Well and good. But the field of instruction cannot progress at all as long as teaching is regarded primarily as an indefinable art. Nor can instruction be modified, manipulated, or evaluated. If teaching is an art, all we can do to improve patterns of instruction is to find artists with a different vision—a haphazard exercise at best. Or perhaps we can reward some artists differently from others, set higher prices on their work and hope that lesser artists will copy them—an exercise that leads to those ugly words, "merit pay." Evaluating teaching comes to naught as long as teaching remains poorly defined; and it is ludicrous to continue attempting to find better ways of evaluating the unmeasurable. Measuring art eventually comes down to standards of critical judgment, and, although these may be well applied to the art of teaching, they do nothing to advance the process of instruction.

Toward a Coherent Philosophy. Singular, consistent definitions are a first requisite, and much depends on institutional intent. For example, the institution that holds student learning as its prime value will define teaching as "the process of causing learning" and will devise an instructional supervision scheme, not one of faculty or course evaluation. The college staff that accepts this definition and acts accordingly has already "evaluated" itself. By focusing on student learning, it has played down other functions that readily may be assigned to it—for example, sorting and certifying young people for advancement to employment opportunities and/or further education, acting as the prime custodial agent for young people with few other socially acceptable places to be, and indoctrinating young men and women with the belief that those with more college credits are better than those with fewer.

This focus on learning and the processes of instruction (defined as "causing learning") has been accepted by some two-year colleges and, where it has, certain distinct modifications in institutional practices have followed. Instructional supervision based on specific course objectives has supplanted "teacher evaluation," and the adoption of media forms in accordance with their demonstrated efficacy in enhancing student learning has replaced the purchase of hardware according to the whim of an influential staff member or the exigency of an extramural funding agency.

One college's attention to instructional processes has produced results that are worthy of particular note in this context. Golden West College (California) was opened in 1966 as the self-styled "innovative campus" in a two-college district. In the intervening years, its instructors have instituted programs to teach biology in autotutorial format, English through a variety of reproducible media including audiotaped/slide presentations and computer-assisted tutorials, and they have constructed a number of televised courses. In addition, half the faculty is participating in a "supervision by objectives" scheme in which their course objectives and instructional plans are reviewed by their department chairman and the dean at least twice a year. Add a variety of other instructional innovations, including modular courses and a large group of multimedia sequences in the social sciences, and the outlines of an institution built on the best principles of instructional planning emerge. Details of some of the Golden West instructional processes have been reported, but not the entire story of how this college was built on firm instructional processes. Significantly, what has happened at Golden West is not innovation for innovation's sake. It is multifaceted instruction arranged and modified deliberately around defined outcomes.

How does a college adopt a coherent philosophy or set itself on a consistent path? No single practice or technique of leadership, no one pattern of finance can create the "climate for innovation" so frequently called for by those who speak for improved instruction in the community college. It takes a combination of charismatic leadership at the local level, support from the district administration, association with proximate institutions, dedication to the outcomes of instruction rather than to the processes themselves, and a variety of subtle factors that cannot be enumerated, let alone picked apart for their separate influences. It does not happen overnight—a continuing commitment on the part of the natural and titular leaders of an institution is essential. The college administrator who would seek the "key factor" to set his college on the road to the best instructional practices is engaging in a bit of self-delusion. There is no one key factor; there is a combination of subtle and overt, carefully considered actions and individuals that work together to create the appropriate "climate." Not the least of these is the chief administrator himself, who must have a clear vision of what he wants his college to become.

Whether a college can be proficient in all its functions is open to question. Golden West College is outstanding in instruction, but its community service and student activities programs are poorly developed. Another college may be intensely responsive to its community, taking leadership in arranging cultural activities and promoting coordination among community service agencies, yet it may be quite archaic when it comes to the teaching function. Still a third institution may have a full range of student personnel services, a campus that offers its students a home away from home, a full complement of situations in which they interact with peers and staff members, join clubs, and engage in recreational activities, without doing much for the surrounding community or for the discipline of instruction. The vision of the ideal institution must be tempered by the reality that a college cannot be outstanding in all its designated functions.

Perhaps the coherent philosophy and vision come first; perhaps they arise post hoc. Regardless, well defined curriculum and instruction go together along with specific objectives, innovative media, and assessment of institutional effect. The junior college as a "teaching institution"? "A motley but uncoordinated array of good teachers," to quote Dressel and DeLisle, "does not yield a sound . . . experience. A well-planned curriculum, of which an essential part is a statement of objectives and a rationale for the experiences provided, is a necessary structure in which instruction can be appropriately defined in relation to the learnings desired. If a faculty cannot or has not been able to agree on a comprehensive curricular design, good instruction will surely be fortuitous" (1969, p. 77).

What is in the offing for junior college instruction? The concept of "instructional accountability" that is bruited by legislators, educators, and journalists—all of whom seem to have different perceptions of the meaning of the term—may have a favorable impact. The traditional pattern of sorting and grade-marking students, unsuited to the community college, has been mitigated in many institutions where the "F" grade has been supplanted by a "W" (withdrawn)'. The "cooling out" function (letting the student know he does not belong in college) is outmoded, but it dies hard; program standards are maintained under a hundred different guises. Nevertheless, the issue of accountability raised by many community groups says in effect, "We want more than equality of educational opportunities; we want some degree of equality of educational results."

This can prove a boon to junior college educators who have a marked concern with instruction. Current knowledge of learning processes combined with a pedagogy directed toward teaching, not judging, can serve to undergird curriculums that are accountable for the learning achieved by students. Abolishing the penalties for dropping out, setting specific objectives, offering a variety of instructional media in all courses, abandoning grades in favor of statements of defined accomplishments, evaluating faculty on the basis of student learning—all are found in various institutions. Putting them together in a single program that accepts all students and teaches them at their own rates of learning is a definite possibility. This would indeed be a new form of post-secondary education, a form distinctly identified with the two-year college.

Challenging Traditional Concepts in Curriculum

 8

Open-door college, open-end curriculum. By its own admission, the two-year college will offer any course for which fifteen students and a qualified instructor can be found. How then characterize the curriculum? Something for everyone? A supermarket? A set of experiences to be suffered by every registrant?

There is ample information on the general aspects of junior college curriculum. Reynolds' *The Comprehensive Junior College Curriculum* (1969) covers well the variety of program offerings and organizational patterns from which a picture of junior college curriculum can be drawn. The ERIC collection includes several sets of conference proceedings in which sweeping statements declare the pressing need for this or that curriculum sequence, the role of various categories of personnel in curriculum change, and/or descriptions of different programs. Views of curriculum in the form of sets of exhortations or statements about the way it is done at one or another institution are well covered in the many conferences and workshops addressed to junior college educators. Accordingly, these aspects of curriculum will not be considered here. The reader who seeks information on course offerings at various institutions is advised to peruse Reynolds' book, a set of college catalogs, or *Research in Education* and *Current Index to Journals in Education*, using such descriptors as "program development," "curriculum development," "experimental curriculum," and "experimental programs."

Rather than recapitulate the descriptions of "transfer," "general education," "vocational," and "community service" courses, here we stress the rationale underlying curriculum development and evaluation in the community college. We point to four major thrusts —the rationale behind definitions, current emphases, transitional trends, and future directions. The literature dealing with junior college curriculum is perceived in terms of the recurrent issues in innovation and curriculum integration. And while "general education" "transfer" and "remedial" curriculums are discussed, vocational-technical programs are accorded separate treatment in Chapter Nine.

Particular emphasis is given to courses and programs especially devised for students variously identified as "marginal," "remedial," "under-educated," and "new"—to name a few of the euphemisms in vogue. Rather than attempt to sort out the inconsistent usages and varied meanings of these terms, we have chosen to use one word—"untraditional"—for all students who, for whatever reason, do not fit the image of the curious, eager college student of blessed memory. Perhaps, "untraditional" is—or should be—the one theme consistently running through any examination of the community college—whether in terms of curriculum, instruction, people, or institutional structures. In concept, the community college is really a phenomenon of twentieth-century America. It is gradually developing a tradition than can best be described as "nontraditional."

What Is a Curriculum?

Curriculum may be defined in several ways. In typical parlance, the curriculum is simply all the courses offered by an institution. Or, more carefully stated, a sequential arrangement of courses. Reynolds offers one more definition: "the total of all the learning experiences the learner has under the supervision of the school" (1969, p. 1)'. These definitions are generally accepted, but they do not cover a wide enough range. For example, along with many other curriculum theorists, Goodlad (1966) sees curriculum as "a set of intended learnings." Mere semantic games? Quite the contrary. Each definition reflects the user's philosophy, value structure, and basic intent.

The usual definition of curriculum employed in the junior

college is "a set of courses"—and it is easy to see why. When curriculum is so viewed, it becomes readily understandable and amenable to manipulation. One knows what the curriculum is merely by counting the courses in a catalog. One can tell how many students have been touched by the curriculum by counting course registrations. The curriculum can be judged more-or-less successful by noting the numbers of its graduates. It can be classified as well; it is "transfer" if a university will give full credit to students who have attended the classes; "occupational" if an employer will grant jobs to its graduates; or "community service" if it falls neatly into neither of the first-mentioned categories.

Other institutional needs are well served by the definition of curriculum as "a set of courses." Must we change curriculum in order to be considered up-to-date? Add a new course, merge some preexisting courses, rearrange a sequence of courses. Must some special groups be satisfied? Does the English department feel it needs a new subremedial course? Is a group of students clamoring for group-process experiences? The decisions can be made on the basis of political accommodation. All can be managed within the framework of the curriculum as a set of courses.

The curriculum as Reynolds' "total of all the learning experiences the student has under the supervision of the school" is another matter. To examine curriculum under this definition demands assessing counseling services, student activities, and the entire range of planned programs with reference to the ways they affect the students. Curriculum as "a set of intended learnings" is even more different and much less easily understood. Assessing curriculum as a set of intended learnings requires that specific objectives be enumerated, that data be collected on whether or not—and the extent to which—anyone has learned anything. It demands an institutional research effort of a magnitude rarely seen on any college campus. It is the view of curriculum as *process* that is effectual only to the extent that it develops *product* (human change). The course titles become relatively meaningless; the number of times per week that courses meet is incidental. The object of attention is the student —particularly, how he thinks, feels, and acts—when he leaves the institution as compared with when he arrived.

To state that few junior college instructors or administrators view curriculum in terms of process and product is not to slander them. Educational theorists—university-based and elsewhere—have done little to relate their work to quotidian issues. It is quite possible for a graduate degree candidate to take courses in the philosophy of education, the theory of curriculum, and the idea and practice of instruction without once hearing how these philosophies, theories, and idealized practices bear on the realities of the schools. Accordingly, when Reynolds writes about junior college curriculum and uses the definition of curriculum as an arrangement of courses, he is only commenting on what is, not what might be. Similarly, when B. L. Johnson (1969) tabulates innovations in curriculum, he is listing the realities with only a minimal attempt to relate them to theory and philosophy. The theorist who would connect junior college curriculum to theories of curriculum development has not appeared—a point deserving reiteration. With 100,000 staff members and nearly one-fourth of all the college students, with a charge unique among institutions of higher education, the junior college has no curriculum theorist. No one is addressing himself to rational curriculum planning for the institutions as a whole and, indeed, few single institutions are blessed with people who address curriculum in rational terms.

Can the smorgasbord of courses offered by the community junior college reasonably be called a curriculum? It depends on the definition of curriculum to which one subscribes. As Quimby points out: "A definition of *curriculum* appropriate for rational planning is not easy to come by. Contemporary usage of the term, for example, emphasizes descriptively what schools and colleges offer students in the form of subject matter courses, activities, and the great catchall—experiences. . . . This notion that courses, activities, and experiences constitute a curriculum lack[s] the necessary precision required for thoughtful planning" (1970, p. 2). The multiplicity of institutional purposes that have been accepted by the community college in its drive for status as a full partner in the American educational enterprise seems to preclude its spokesmen attending to a rational definition of curriculum. Even so, it moves.

Special People, Special Services

Except in a few institutions where a truly integrated curriculum has been introduced, the transfer curriculum remains the core of the program in the two-year college, despite much discussion of general education and programs for untraditional students. The reasons are many, for example: prestige—junior college status as a "college" demands it; instructors think they know how to organize a transfer curriculum—many, as recent graduates, clearly remember their own progression through one; the per-student cost is less than the cost for programs that demand special equipment—such as most vocational-technical courses; and not least, the students, their parents, and the accrediting agencies feel comfortable with a transfer curriculum because it fits into their idea of a college. However, attempts to fit a traditional curriculum to untraditional students give rise to basic difficulties. Confrontation of these difficulties has led the colleges in various directions.

The Untraditional.   The untraditional student in the community college is treated as a special case. A variety of types of courses are considered right for him because he rarely survives the usual pattern. And, generally, he gets both untraditional courses and much extra attention. A study of special programs in California community colleges (Berg and Axtell, 1968) found that the most common pattern is a series of remedial courses—usually traditional courses with watered-down content. A second popular approach is to provide special services such as tutoring, extra counseling, and a variety of financial aids. Whereas the intent of special courses is to keep the student from flunking out of school, special financial aid intends to keep him from dropping out to go to work. A third method identified in the California study includes complete revision of registration, grading, probation, and suspension practices. All aim to keep the students on the roll books. It is as though the colleges are saying collectively, "If only we can keep them in school, we know that something of positive value will accrue to them."

Special summer programs that offer help to untraditional students have received much attention. Because they deal with readily identifiable populations and specially devised sequences, institutional researchers seem to prefer studying such programs—for example, Los Angeles City College examined the effects of a special summer program on three groups of students: some with low high school grades, some from bilingual homes and also with low grades, and some who had been unable to maintain a C average at the college (Gold, 1968b). A special summer program was devised with members of all three groups taking experimental classes and tutorial sessions. Pre- and post-tests determined that students' reading abilities improved along with certain of their attitudes. Eighty-three per cent of the students stayed in school through the summer program, and about two-thirds of them enrolled in college for the fall term.

A similar program at Spartanburg Junior College (South Carolina) was assessed to determine if special study in English, science, and group processes would enable students to compete academically with regularly admitted students (Couch, 1969). Pairs of students matched by College Board scores were used, with one student enrolling in the summer program, the other taking no additional work. As a result, the experimental group surpassed the group that did not have the additional summer work—but not to a significant degree.

A study conducted by Bean and Hendrix at El Centro College (Texas) (1968) reported the results of an experimental "mini college" in which five teachers shared responsibility for the same students in a core program of courses. The program objectives were to increase student identity with the college and to increase student learning. In addition, the program intended to enhance the use of team-teaching concepts and reproducible instructional media. A battery of learning and attitude scales was administered to the students, but no abnormal gains were noted. In common with reports emanating from other experimental programs, it was found that students and instructors held positive attitudes toward the experience. This is the Hawthorne effect in action: offer something different and the people thrive on it—at least initially.

These illustrate only a few of the many attempts to assess the effects of course work and special studies for students who have been identified as deficient in ability to deal with the usual course work. The summer supplemental programs have become quite popular and are evidence of the community college's attempt to enhance the educational experiences of the untraditional student. The "basic studies" program is known in nearly every college. Some of these programs are imaginative, offering a wide range of activities not previously found in college curriculum; others are traditional, offering only recurring patterns of the same classroom-bound experi-

ences. Still, the colleges are trying because they are taking the brunt
of the ever-growing enrollment of untraditional students.

Other colleges have excelled in constructing special programs—for example, Malcolm X Community College in the Chicago city system, where full-scale "black education" is being tried
(see Chapter Ten). One imaginative plan for breaking the traditional pattern of college work for untraditional students was studied
by Felty (1969), who concluded that an upstate New York, rurally-
based, residential college for untraditional students—especially those
from the inner city—would be feasible and would offer significant
advantages to untraditional students. However, the high cost would
require financial support from outside the college's locale. Whether
it takes the form of an emphatic break with tradition or merely a
minimal tinkering with course prerequisites, the big story in the
junior college curriculum is the attempt to build untraditional programs and courses for untraditional students.

Community Services. Another promising development in
the junior college curriculum is in the broad area that falls under
the heading of "community services." The community service function of the community college is very important, overshadowing in
many cases the traditional academic transfer curriculum. In the
early 1950s, when community services were first being acknowledged
as an important role for the colleges to play, the term was a catchall
for every course that fell outside the category "for credit" but now
the community service area has its own goals, separate funding
channels, and specially trained personnel. Accordingly, community
service receives much attention. The American Association of Junior
Colleges has sponsored many community service studies and developmental projects, some with the aid of such organizations as the
W. K. Kellogg Foundation.

Ideally, in a community service program, a plan for community involvement is developed where community resources and
needs are identified, operational objectives defined, various alternative courses of action plotted, and programs of action initiated
(Raines and Myran, 1970). The number of community needs that
can be identified is almost endless. Community service efforts have
attempted to deal with special training needs, leisure time courses,

the counseling and redirection of adults, programs to make up for the absence of cultural activities, and coordinating the efforts of other community agencies. Harlacher's *The Community Dimension of the Community College* (1969) is an extensive summary of the variety of objectives, staffing practices, and patterns of organization manifest by community service activities among the colleges. It must be considered basic for anyone interested in this aspect of community college work.

Other reports on community services also consider the rationale and procedures of these activities. The ERIC collection includes several (Myran, 1969; Traicoff, 1969; Distasio and Greenberg, 1969; Fightmaster, 1969). The program models are described along with modes of assessing the relevancy of new programs. Administrative procedures and means of promoting and publicizing the programs are also detailed. But carefully designed and conducted attempts to assess the impact of the college in the community are lacking. Such research is difficult to arrange, and reports of the impact of community services are unlikely. In common with their counterparts in other areas of the educational enterprise, community service people tend to build their programs first, get them running well, and assess effects later, if at all. The idea of building in genuine program assessment procedures when the program is launched is simply not considered.

General Education. The need for general education—that is, for programs that try "to provide students with the broad outlines of human knowledge" (Mayhew, 1960, p. 6)—pervades discussions of the two-year college curriculum. General education has a long history in American higher education, occurring in cycles and becoming more or less emphasized depending on the apparent social needs for specialization. That is, calls for a return to "basic values" create drives for general education, whereas traumatic events such as the Soviet launching of Sputnik stimulate demands for specialized science and technological curriculums. General education reached a high point in the 1940s and early in the following decade, touched bottom in the early 1960s and, riding a wave of student protest against premature overspecialization, swung rapidly upward in the late 1960s. Still, most present spokesmen for the community colleges argue for expanded vocational-technical programs and, if widespread unemployment among youth is a reality of the 1970s, general education again will take a back seat.

Many of the old questions about general education in the four-year institutions recur in contemporary arguments about junior college curriculums. What percentage of a student's program should be general education and what percentage should be specialized? How can a junior college require that a matriculant go through the general education sequence when he wants training in secretarial or medical skills so that he can obtain immediate employment? The proprietary schools that do not require general education offer attractive competition. What is the place of student activities in general education? Student activity programs, as they influence student values and enhance their skills, have always been a weakness of the curriculum: being at an institution for two years at most, students tend not to participate in organized college activities. Thus, what is the place of general education in a community institution where the total environmental effect has little chance to operate? Most students live off campus and a sizeable percentage is gainfully employed away from the college. What effect can the college have in only the few hours the student is on campus?

A major and continuing question in general education—not only at the junior college—is whether courses that are introductory to academic disciplines can serve general education requirements. Mayhew takes a negative position: "To suggest that Introduction to Business, Economics, Principles of Sociology, and Social Psychology are of equal value in achieving social science outcomes of general education strains even the most flexible of logics" (1969, p. 200). Although it seems that general education as a set of distribution requirements is becoming passé, the concept does linger.

Another issue is whether or not a university will give credit for general studies. The community colleges that have interdisciplinary courses usually construct them for terminal students outside the transfer or regular curriculum. The excuse is that the senior institutions will not accept interdisciplinary courses for transfer. Yet, as Reynolds points out, the argument "does not permit inquiry on the four-year college campus [about] the acceptability of the suggested curriculum alteration. The unwritten law of tradition stipulates instant rejection without any effort to test the situation" (1969, p. 149). Everyone seems to forget that, as B. L. Johnson noted years ago (1952), when junior colleges vigorously pursue the issue, the universities usually acquiesce.

Students are the one group that could create a resurgence in general education. The growth of "experimental" colleges and "free" universities in and around four-year college campuses suggests what students can do when they try. However, the fact that these efforts have not been made by two-year college students indicates either that the colleges are fully satisfying the students' needs for general education or, more likely, that students fatalistically accept the idea that, like high school, college is not relevant to questions of feeling, attitude, value, and genuine experience. College is an experience to be endured.

General education has been recommended as the core of the two-year college curriculum by such diverse writers as Cohen (1969), Hutchins (1968), Cosand (1968), and Wiegman (1969). Will they be heeded? Cohen's proposed college would have all but general education relegated to institutions other than the community college—an idea too visionary to be accepted by the politically-sensitive community college administrators. Hutchins ties his vision of general education to the liberal education that was offered to the elitist groups of an earlier era—too aristocratic for the community college in its role as an institution for the common man. Cosand's anticipation of general education in the community college of 1980 is diluted with his notion that the colleges will become ever more comprehensive. But in the Gresham's Law-in-reverse that propels the institutions, the hard transfer and technical programs will probably drive out the soft liberal studies. And Wiegman's recommendation that college departments should incorporate both transfer and occupational programs in singular divisions of "Communications and related technologies," "Behavioral science and related technologies," and the like, must yet face the well-known wall that separates the two curricular blocks.

If general education is on the upswing—and many indicators suggest it is—it is less a result of the two-year college educators' attending to arguments tendered by the aforementioned authors than because they realize they are expected to do something—any-thing—for the untraditional students who are flocking to their doors. Under the impact of the vast numbers of uncommitted stu-dents—that is, students who are not directly slated for either voca-tional programs or baccalaureate degrees—a variety of subdiscipli-nary courses have been constructed. No longer viewed as remedial (the nature and extent of their remedies is open to question any-way), they are beginning to be seen as self-contained experi-ences that may aid students in obtaining greater self-awareness, enhanced self-images, and clearer pictures of themselves in relation to their fellows. Many of these courses do not teach skills but offer experiences rather pointedly directed toward changing attitudes—attitudes toward self and the world, not toward literature or science per se.

It is difficult to assess the magnitude of this change toward the "personal" in curriculum. The catalogs may still show the courses listed under the old titles and assigned to the traditional departments, but viewing the course outlines or chatting with the teachers and students makes it apparent that what is being called "communications 101" is not a course in grammar and rhetoric as it might have been formerly. The students are bumping and touch-ing each other, listening to and speaking about avant-garde poetry, and engaging in, to use the idiom, "rap" sessions. This type of course represents more than a change in instructional technique. The intent has shifted from the students' learning how to manipu-late the tools of the academic disciplines to their learning about themselves. Is it not, as Jerome (1970) calls it, the liberal education of the twentieth century?

What is happening is apparent to students of American ed-ucation—general education is having a resurgence, albeit under a different name. This is not the first time general education has in-vaded the two-year college curriculum—but now it is backing in through the "not-for-transfer" and the "not-for-immediate-employ-ment" doors. Whether or not it is again a passing fad remains to be seen. Still, regardless of the impetus, the ghost of general education continues to flit about the corridors of the junior colleges, jumping out at vocational and technical teachers, swinging in the rafters at every meeting of the curriculum committees, standing nobly beside the president each time he attends a convocation.

Trends

Some interesting trends in curriculum may be discerned from the literature. Before 1969, changes were pending, as suggested by the very titles of the articles and books about junior college curriculum. B. L. Johnson's *Islands of Innovation* (1964) is more a call for new curriculum development than a report of actual curriculum innovation. The ERIC report literature for 1968 includes several articles with titles such as, "Creating a Climate for Innovation . . ." (Teter and Pate, 1967); and "Setting the Stage for Change . . ." (Banister, 1968). By the end of the decade, change became acceptable—at least change in curriculum for the untraditional student.

Although the patterns of curricular change in the two-year college may be traced in retrospect, any attempt to extrapolate from them is a precarious exercise. What appears to be a trend frequently is a fad. There is much copying of curriculum between institutions, but little disciplined, rational curriculum planning within institutions. One school will develop a different course or combination of curricular activities and publicize how well this pattern meets the needs of its students; others will then attempt to build similar patterns. According to Dressel and DeLisle, who address curriculum in the four-year colleges, some of these "new" developments "reappear on almost a cyclical basis" (1969, p. 2). Little is really new—not even the desire to appear innovative.

Are there apparent trends in curriculum? In 1967, Smith (1969) surveyed course patterns in 758 junior colleges and compared the data with similar information obtained in a 1962 study of 639 schools. The major difference was that, although the number of junior colleges offering vocational programs had not increased substantially, the actual number and types of courses had grown dramatically. Above all, the increase reflected the availability of funding and the fact that vocational education had become the darling of state and federal agencies during the 1960s.

Will the trend to increased occupational offerings continue? Little stands in its way. For more than four decades, junior colleges have offered vocational and technical courses, and, although many writers question the advisability of separating academic from vocational offerings, with the notable exception of the human services curriculums (Burns, 1971), few successful efforts at effecting a merger are apparent. The trend toward courses that are of immediate value in gaining employment shows no sign of abating.

Except for the certainty that occupational curriculums will continue to expand, it is difficult to plot curricular trends. Reynolds (1969) sees more and more of the advanced subject matter offerings moving into secondary schools, with two-year colleges picking up some of the courses presently offered in the upper division of the university. He also anticipates enhanced articulation between high school and junior college with more junior college courses requiring high school courses as prerequisites. That is, he foresees a four-year segment of education that affords general education, specialized work in an academic discipline, and/or preparation for full-time employment—the four years encompassing the last two years of high school and the first two years of college. The junior college curriculum would "occupy a sharply different place in the educational hierarchy than that customarily accorded to it. Instead of its traditionally assigned location at the beginning of collegiate education, it is more accurately located at the top two years of the secondary division" (1969, p. 19). Nonetheless, he is aware that "popular stereotyping" assigns the first two years of college to "higher education."

Reynolds' predictions may turn out to be accurate, but they are more in the nature of conjecture than soundly based expectations. Logically, the close coordination of secondary school and junior college curriculum should be developed, but curriculum construction rarely proceeds logically. Forces external to the institution—such as the aforementioned levels of funding available for the development of occupational programs—exercise a major influence on curriculum. The fact that at least a sizeable minority of the junior college staff holds the four-year college faculty as its main reference group also helps move the idea of articulation with the secondary schools into the realm of conjecture. As Reynolds himself points out, "One needs only to make suggestions to the instructional staff of the junior college concerning new departures in curriculum content or organization to learn that . . . all such suggestions [are evaluated] in terms of the reaction of the four-year college to which the students will transfer. . . . Tradition dictates that all efforts to articulate the junior college curriculum with that of other educational levels must look to the level above. . . . Suggestions that efforts directed toward the high schools might result in more fruitful outcomes usually evoke little or no interest" (Ibid., pp. 148–149).

In any discussion of curriculum trends, it is impossible to overemphasize their cyclical nature. Dressel and DeLisle point out that institutions of higher education are more-or-less autonomous and do not all move at the same speed in the same direction. "Some experimental institutions exhibit or accept change much earlier than others. By the time changes have been introduced in some colleges and universities, they may have been abandoned, modified, or so integrated that they are no longer apparent in others. . . . The full range of educational philosophies and complete array of practices may be found, at any given time, in a collective summary of American education" (1969, pp. 1–2).

Why fluctuation but not trend? Part of the answer is related to the problem of assessing what is good or useful in curriculum. The curriculum swings back and forth like a pendulum—from groups of specialized courses to integrated courses, from remedial, subremedial, and honors courses to single-course patterns. Cohen notes, "The vacillation seems to relate to the fact that no one knows whether or not students learn more or better," no matter which course pattern is adopted. "The fluctuations themselves are clearly the result of constant dissatisfaction; one curriculum paradigm is followed until . . . 'aesthetic nausea' sets in, whereupon another is adopted" (1969, p. ix).

The persistent failure to assess the worth of curriculum on any model of coherent, theoretically defensible, curriculum study makes it impossible for curriculum planners to argue the merits of any sequence on logical bases. If no one provides evidence that one curriculum pattern is more closely related to curriculum theory than another, or that one has had a greater measured impact on the students' lives than another, then decisions must be made on the basis of hunch, feel, or political persuasion. The person who would examine curriculum in the two-year college and at the same time neglect the influence of the administrator who, when faced with a curriculum decision, calls and asks a colleague in a neighboring institution how he "does" it is doomed to frustration in his understanding of the way curriculum changes. Schwab can postulate curriculum theory; the college decides on the basis of the predilections of its instructors. Tyler can propose a rationale for curriculum development; the college attends to the whims of the legislators who offer augmented funding if certain courses are offered. Goodlad can talk about rational curriculum planning; in effect, any vociferous taxpayer at a board meeting can shout him down. The public junior college lives in a political sphere—and politics is among the more irrational of human enterprises.

Making Changes. The old adage that it is easier to move a cemetery than to change a college curriculum has little application to the community college. In fact, if "new curriculum" is defined as "one or more new courses," the adage should be completely revised. The community college curriculum is like the sands of the Sahara, shifting with every gust of wind. The colleges readily adopt new courses, responding to every perceived social need. The environmental "crisis" offers a case in point. No sooner was the situation identified than the junior colleges responded with curriculums in environmental ecological education. (The entire December-January, 1970–1971, issue of *Junior College Journal* is devoted to descriptions of courses and programs that have been developed in response to this "crisis.") The response is typical: Having a problem? Build a set of courses around it, and, although the problem may not be solved, at least everyone feels more comfortable with the knowledge that young people are being made aware of it.

The instant creation of courses is a phenomenon with both strength and weakness; strength because the colleges remain readily adaptable to changing individual and social needs; weakness because the students are denied the model of an institution with a coherent philosophy. Schwab notes, "Single courses are sometimes the outcome of single happy thoughts but are rarely accorded . . . reflexive, critical scrutiny. . . . Their origins are left obscure and their outcomes only occasionally examined. . . . Least of all do we worry about our sins of omission, the courses we do not give, the outcomes we do not seek" (1969, p. 246).

"Innovation is relative," say Dressel and DeLisle. "One institution claims as innovation what others are discarding." Little actual change has taken place in curriculum "excepting only the use of the electronic and mechanical equipment of educational technology" (1969, pp. 75–76). Nevertheless, among spokesmen for the two-year college—institutional leaders, professional association heads, and some university professors with a particular interest in the junior college—innovation in curriculum and instruction is tantamount to universal benevolence. The League for Innovation in the Community College—as its name implies—coordinates conferences and workshops dedicated to stirring things up. Other consortia, and individual colleges as well, obtain foundation and governmental funds for so-called "experimental programs" that usually turn out to be more of the same offerings packaged differently.

Why? What are the ultimate aims of innovation? Several possible answers may be discerned. The most widely heard—probably because it is the most noble—is that innovation leads to greater learning attainment for the students. That is, new instructional variations will perforce result in each student learning more concepts and skills. There may be some truth in this viewpoint, because varied instructional techniques do tend to enhance sensory input. Also, much evidence suggests that different people learn better in different ways. Hence, the more ways information is presented, the more likely a greater number of students will be affected—theoretically, that is.

Another socially acceptable reason for innovation is that pervasive archaisms in curriculum and instruction are past due for overhaul. Thus, anything that will break the recurrent cycle of lectures, recitals, and similar frequently stultifying classroom procedures is good. The student, bored by year after year of passive attendance, will find his attention stimulated by the activities associated with autotutorial biology. Introduction to Sociology has turned him off; turn him back on with Social Living for Modern Man. What we have done has not worked well; let's try something—anything—new.

A less frequently iterated reason for innovation is that more students will receive more credit hours for less money—the "bigger bang for a buck" syndrome. "Enrollments are getting larger," pro-

ponents argue, "and available funds are not being increased com-
mensurately. We must find ways to process greater numbers of students for the same money." Quick to capitalize on this reasoning,
the professional innovators—a new breed of educators and media
salesman—put cost-per-student figures into their program layouts
and speak of the money to be saved if their operations are adopted.
(Did an innovator ever take pains to point out that his recommended procedure would cost *more?*) And the will o' the wisp of
saved money leads curriculum and instruction planners onward.

Simply stated, the need to bring excitement into what may
otherwise be a stodgy occupation is the most pervasive reason of all.
For innovation—like strikes and student activism—is exciting, something to break the chains of monotony that bind the professional
educator's life. A teachers' walkout meeting is titillating; it allows
the faculty to drag out the old labor movement slogans, proclaim
"Solidarity forever!" and worry covertly about its effect on their
self-image. Twenty students crowded into the president's office make
him feel like Horatio at the bridge; a student protest rally can bring
out the World War I Flying Ace in any administrator. Short of
these potentially destructive activities, what else is there? Why, innovation, of course! A good argument over a proposition to offer a
class only twice a week instead of three times, a proposal to buy a
dial-access, closed-circuit television system—this is the stuff of which
excitement is made. And note how up-to-date we look to the students
and their parents!

Toward a Coherent Philosophy.   Contemporary thinking in
the two-year college is toward innovation, away from controlled
experimentation, toward unreasoned change, away from rational
planning. Dressel and DeLisle's comments, based on a study of a
random sample of four-year liberal arts colleges ($N = 371$), are
applicable to the junior college:

*Much of what passes as innovation is but the hasty adoption of
fads. Most educational ideas are not new, though they may seem so
to the individual or the institution. Sound innovation comes about
when ideas and practices are organized, in new and creative ways,
into a coherent whole which promotes student learning. Change on
this fundamental base is rare. . . . Administrators and curriculum*

committees want to know how extensively a particular practice is in
evidence, as a basis for judging whether it is respectable [1969, p.
2].

What next for the curriculum? It is impossible to predict.
Will innovation persist? Probably, because it has become its own
end. Even reductions in the rate of expansion in funding cannot stop
the haphazard proliferation of programs. And, although the community college should come to grips with assessing its effects on its
students and its parent community, it is not likely to do so. Perhaps
it is time to stop attempting to manipulate, appraise, evaluate, or
even examine curriculum in the community college. The traditional
tools and concepts simply do not apply. Curriculum evaluation that
focuses on aspects of the environment or on the processes which presumably effect changes in students does not fit an institution in
which fewer than 20 per cent of the students complete a designated
program within the allotted time. New modes of appraisal are indicated.

What of the needed coherence in curriculum? The classical
curriculum theorist sees it as essential. Dressel stresses "the importance of unity and integration in any curriculum" (1968, p.
227). He speaks of curriculum organization and assessment within
the framework of his belief that "the college graduate should see his
total college experience as coherent, cumulative and unified" (Ibid.,
p. 212). Contending that there must be a coherent basis for making
curriculum decisions, he insists that "no profound reconstruction of
curriculum emerges from leaping from vague objectives to decisions
about facilitating agents" (Ibid., p. 25). Nevertheless, he notes that
"with the exception of a few small colleges consciously committed to
a particular position, institutions will not determine their educational programs by first agreeing on a philosophy" (Ibid., p. 29).

The principles of rational curriculum development hold that
neutral structures, "based on the fundamental educational concept
of the institution, be used to analyze and describe the curriculum;
second, that the desired learning environment be determined in detail before methods are selected to achieve it" (Ibid., p. 25). This
statement is beautiful on paper, but is unrealistic in light of the community college experience. In the world of the rational, curriculum

choices imply philosophical commitment. On what is the community college curriculum based? Does it emphasize the interests of the individual or the needs of society? Is it abstract or does it confront contemporary problems directly? Is it structured on organized disciplines of knowledge? On unified learning theory? In the context of the community college, the philosophy is discernible post hoc, if at all.

Classical curriculum theory does not fit the contemporary community college and must be modified if it is to explain curriculum development in this fast-growing enterprise. The situation cries out for new curriculum theory. Can the community junior college ever attend to curriculum as a set of intended learnings or even as a set of integrated, planned experiences when, for most of its matriculants, it is in fact not a two-year college but a place where they drop in and out, taking courses at their own whim or at the fancy of a staff adviser? How does a set of courses relate to the lives of untraditional students?

Traditional thinking about curriculum as something that is supposed to take a learner from one place to another (the very word is from the Latin "racecourse" or "running") is inappropriate. A new term is needed, a new concept—one that acknowledges the nonlinearity of the educational experiences offered by the community college. When we stop talking about the college's offerings as a "curriculum," we can abandon the futile practice of attempting to manipulate them as though they were a set of deliberate sequences, which in fact they are not. Who will coin the term?

Vocational Education

 9

Of the three traditional community college curriculum functions—
vocational, transfer, and general education—the vocational function
receives the most attention from administrators. Community college
educators expend more energy on developing and promoting this
field than they do the other two, and it is easy to see why. This function is the outstanding characteristic of the community college in its
role as an institution of higher education. Here the junior college
stands alone; it does not parallel or imitate the lower-division function of four-year institutions.

Vocational education is a generic term for all programs
whose major goal is that the student shall attain gainful employment
after a course of study requiring no longer than two years for completion. Various terms are used, often interchangeably. "Vocational
education," "technical education," "occupational education," "semiprofessional education," and "trade education" are all used in describing two-year (or shorter) programs preparing technicians and
subprofessionals, semiskilled and skilled workers. At various times
"vocational," "occupational," and "technical-vocational" have been
used to distinguish this function from "transfer" and "general"
education. "Technical" enjoys universal favor among community
college educators, although "vocational" or "technical-vocational"
has more acceptance than in the 1950s when "occupational" was
the most popular term. Before World War II, "semiprofessional"
was in wide use, since it distinguished between the "trade" education of the secondary schools and the "professional" education of the

137

four-year colleges and universities. "Trade education" has not en-
joyed favor among community college educators because of its
association with high schools and with semiskilled programs. Many
colleges offer trade programs—but only one community college uses
"trade" in its name. Here, we use "vocational" and "occupational"
interchangeably.

Occupational curriculums are less stable than college transfer programs because they reflect rapid technological and sociological changes. Although drafting, machine tooling, automotive
technology, and agriculture remain in vogue, their primacy is giving
way to curriculums in electronics, computers, space exploration,
numerical control, metrology, agribusiness, and horticulture. Paramedical programs are popular, with enrollments second only to
secretarial science and business administration. Public and human
services career occupations take up a large part of the curriculum.
Interest in reviving the city and preserving the environment are new
fields which stimulate courses in urban affairs, urban ecology, city
planning, air pollution control, traffic control, and others in the
environmental technology area. However, these courses will undergo
change as new industries and recreational outlets are created. And,
as the idea of the four-day week spreads the colleges probably will be
concerned as much with education for leisure as with education for
work. Accordingly, continuing education and community service
programs will be expanded.

Contributing to this dynamic situation are the four-year institutions which continually upgrade two-year occupational curriculums. This upgrading process, common among technical and
semiprofessional programs, is part of the upward mobility of occupations at all levels. Technical engineering, broadcasting, journalism,
and public accounting have been, or are in the process of being,
upgraded to four-year status. Balancing this situation is the accre-
tion of programs from high schools and technical institutes. In some
communities all tax-supported vocational education is conducted by
community colleges.

Fiscal Support

Much support for vocational programs derives from extramural groups—particularly government officials and community

leaders. This support is reflected in federal and state legislation and in the formation of many public and private agencies organized to promote occupational programs. Fostered by the hope that it holds the key to the solution of our urban problems, especially the employment of disadvantaged youth, vocational education receives added attention and support.

T. J. Watson, chairman of the board of directors of IBM, favors organizing more junior colleges and the development of career programs "to help correct the nation's serious manpower problems" (Erickson, 1970)'. In its second report, the National Advisory Council on Vocational Education states as a fundamental policy: "The federal government should invest at least as much money in reducing the flow of untrained youth as it invests in reducing the pool of unemployed, and most of the federal investment should be concentrated in paying the additional cost of vocational and technical programs of career preparation (as compared with programs which prepare for further education)' in high school and post-secondary institutions" (1970)'. The council also points out that proposals for general federal aid "would do little to overcome our national preoccupation with general liberal arts education" and that the practice of earmarking funds for the disadvantaged classifies them "as second-class citizens who cannot make it in the mainstream."

President Nixon and his advisers place high priority on legislation assisting junior colleges and their vocational education programs, emphasizing the beneficial effects of vocational education in aiding the disadvantaged, the unemployed, and the minorities, and the low costs for both the students and the public. Early in 1969, the President's Task Force on Education stated that "for reasons of cost, educational policy, and social policy, a substantial proportion of higher education's future expansion . . . should take place at the junior college," since the "junior college[s] can help increase equality of access to higher education, provide occupational training directly related to productive employment opportunities, and become . . . genuine community institutions for the entire adult population." The Task Force advised Nixon that "the adequacy of federal aid to junior colleges should be examined carefully in the new fiscal 1970 budget review" (AAJC, *Developing Junior Colleges*, March 19, 1969, p. 1).

Subsequently, former Secretary Finch announced that the Department of Health, Education, and Welfare was drafting a comprehensive community college career education act, among other provisions, to "provide the chance for upward mobility for the disadvantaged." He noted that in all large cities more black students are enrolled in community colleges than in all other colleges combined and that over half of all entering freshmen are enrolled in junior colleges (AAJC, *Developing Junior Colleges*, October 10, 1969, p. 1).

Occupational education, the disadvantaged, ethnic minorities—all again received special attention in a speech by former Commissioner of Education Allen. He announced that the two-year colleges, which "have special links with the economic life of the community," were to be helped by proposed federal legislation in two ways: by direct aid to the colleges to improve their career programs, especially as they help expand opportunities for the disadvantaged; and by aid to the states to improve their management of career education (AAJC, *Developing Junior Colleges*, November 29, 1969, p. 2).

Less than a year later, President Nixon incorporated the ideas of Finch and Allen in a recommendation to Congress for the establishment of a Career Education Program to be funded with $100 million in fiscal 1972. In his message, the President pointed to critical manpower shortages in police and fire science, environmental technology, and medical paraprofessions—shortages that community colleges and technical institutes are peculiarly suited to remedy through their vocational programs (Nixon, 1970). In November 1970, Health, Education, and Welfare Secretary Richardson announced a work-study program for students whose families earn $3,000 a year or less. He estimated that 340 million dollars would be available for this purpose in 1971–1972. Thus, vocational education enjoys support at the highest reaches of government and the business community. The officials are behind it because they feel it will solve certain urban and economic problems. Although they may become disillusioned if their fond hopes for a docile, urban labor force do not materialize, at least they are providing much fiscal support. Vocational education floats on a sea of money.

Status

Paradoxically, vocational education does not have the status that its fortunate fiscal condition should give it; in fact, just the opposite is true. In one publication, the comments of five educators ranged from oblique references about its low status to the dogmatic assertion that "vocational, technical, or occupational education is on the bottom rung of the status ladder as judged by every significant population on our campuses: students, faculty, administration, and parents" (Sheldon, 1970b, p. 18). In another context, President Cosand of the St. Louis Junior College District also referred to the low status of vocational education, a condition he attributed to the misunderstanding that "technical programs mean vocational programs in terms of the connotation used in the past with respect to high school programs which emphasize only skills training" (Cosand, 1969, p. 5).

Student Attitudes. Lack of status is reflected in a relative lack of student interest in vocational programs. The students do not enroll because of the unfortunate social hierarchy of occupations "based on an intangible scale," rating one occupation as better than another (Barlow, 1962, pp. 9–11). Many administrators have known the disappointments experienced by those at the College of the Virgin Islands, where expectations of large enrollments in technical courses failed to materialize (Jerome, 1970).

In preferring the liberal arts, students reflect the views of the community and the feelings of the academic faculty that vocational programs are useless and suitable only for the training of low-aptitude students (Ibid., p. 18). Studies showing that the average academic ability of occupational students is much lower than that of transfer students do not help the prestige of the former; neither do studies pointing out that a larger proportion of vocational students than of academic students are first-generation college students and children of skilled, semiskilled, or unskilled workers.

Sensitivity to status is particularly acute among members of minority groups. Because of the implication that vocational courses are less rigorous and therefore more suited to students of lesser scholastic ability, any statement that minority students should attend community colleges to enroll in vocational rather than academic programs arouses resentment. Blacks and Mexican-Americans maintain a continuous attack on the "tracking" system, which they claim relegates them to vocational programs. During the student activist period of 1968–1969, black students demanded that entrance evaluation should be such that a student can be free from a career-tracking system. The Seattle Black Student Union vigorously opposed a management firm's recommendation that trade and technical programs be concentrated in the central (black) campus while the "higher" semiprofessional programs be allocated to the northern and southern (white) campuses.

Most black educators are unopposed to vocational education. They recognize that jobs in business, industry, and service occupations offer opportunities to black students trained to perform essential semiprofessional and other tasks competently. Colleges like Malcolm X in Chicago, with an almost all-black administration and student body, have developed programs in major categories such as engineering and technology; business, office services, and data processing; health and paramedical occupations; and public and social service, as well as in other areas (Malcolm X College, 1969).

However, black educators object to the assumption held by the white community that black students do not have the ability to succeed in transfer programs. On May 16, 1970, a group of black junior college leaders set forth their objection to the "natural aristocracy pronouncements of Vice President Agnew" and to "President Nixon's emphasis in his message on higher education of March 19, 1970, on vocational training at the expense of greater black participation in higher education." The black educators made it clear that "providing terminal skills, where appropriate," is a proper function of the junior college, but they strongly disagreed with the view that the community college is a ceiling for black educational achievement (Goodrich, 1970).

The prevalence of the stereotype that blacks are capable of succeeding only in vocational programs has produced a deep antipathy among black students and educators in urban colleges. The difficulties experienced at Seattle Community College have been duplicated at urban colleges in Chicago, Detroit, and Los Angeles.

At Los Angeles Trade-Technical College, Burns (1970) reports an internal struggle between black educators, students, and community leaders—who want to reorient the college's philosophy toward the comprehensive concept—and their white counterparts—who are determined to maintain its occupational emphasis.

    Educator Attitudes. A major share of the responsibility for the low prestige of vocational education is placed on community college educators; they are criticized for being "committed to the more respectable high-level occupational programs . . . giving lip-service only to the others" (Carey, 1968). Some critics watch "with a somewhat ambivalent feeling . . . the proliferation of junior colleges," which they welcome because they bring college closer to the young people, but which make them apprehensive because of the contrast between the neglect of vocational-industrial education and the excessive concern with college-transfer and technical education. They accuse "junior college status-seekers of building a moat around their academic tower" (Ibid.). In a speech, former Secretary of Health, Education, and Welfare Finch alluded to the "prestige syndrome of those two-year colleges trying to transform themselves into little universities" (Finch, 1969).

    Unfortunately, educators often inadvertently downgrade vocational education when they attempt to defend it. For example: "Two-year occupational education is not an inferior type of college education—it is just a different kind of education, which is designed for the competencies of the majority of high school graduates" (Peterson, 1962). The qualification in that sentence approaches an aristocratic viewpoint, and it is essentially this implication that made vocational education less desirable than academic education in high schools and continues to make it so in community colleges. Both students and parents substitute the word "inferior" for "different" (Jerome, 1970).

    For a variety of reasons, vocational educators do not feel secure in their relations with academic instructors and administrators, particularly because of differences in educational background. It is to be expected that vocational instructors, especially former artisans with at most a junior college education, would feel uneasy in the midst of the more numerous, degree-bearing academic personnel. Moreover, since administrators are usually academicians, vocational personnel believe that their problems are not understood, their interests neglected, and their welfare subordinated to the problems, interests, and welfare of the academic faculty. This is true even for high school instructors who transfer along with their programs. Although the move from high school or trade school to junior college usually confers a higher status for the trade program and its personnel, nevertheless the instructors believe that both are considered a little lower than the technical and much lower than the academic, in hierarchical status.

Insecurity also results from the relative instability of vocational programs. When a program is dropped, either because it has been upgraded to baccalaureate status or has become obsolete, personnel often are separated. It does not matter that forces outside the college are responsible for these circumstances; every time a program is dropped, it is interpreted by those involved (and by other vocational instructors) as another proof of academicians' indifference or lack of concern for the welfare of vocational programs. Because of their feelings of low status and insecurity, vocational educators are alert to actions or proposals that in any way may affect them or their programs. For example, they favor teaching credentials based on work experience, but they resist "with unusual ferocity" proposals requiring baccalaureate degrees or academic credits (*Los Angeles Times*, November 14, 1970).

Reconciling Differences. Many options are available to community college educators who want to move occupational education to a position of parity on the academic status ladder. First, they must examine their practices, policies, and published statements and eliminate those that have the effect of downgrading vocational education. For example, in some catalogs, educators unwittingly give second-class status to their vocational curriculums and courses by placing them after the academic and, more pointedly, by declaring them "nontransferable"—indicating that the Associate in Applied Science degree is not the equal of the Associate in Arts. Some do not offer academic rank to vocational instructors; they seldom promote them to general administrative assignments. The widespread practice of housing vocational education in separate facilities "erects unnecessary barriers to student interaction and may contribute to the permanent separation of the programs" (Schill and others, 1968, p. 7).

꜀ The widely used practice of separate numbering systems for vocational courses to distinguish them from transfer courses is another status symbol. It presumably helps four-year colleges in evaluating a student's record on transfer, but it does little for the prestige of the vocational student. Moreover, this practice implies a static rather than a dynamic concept of education. There are many illustrations of respectable courses that once were considered nontransferable. Why label any courses? May not a course be transferable in one college and nontransferable in another? Labeling it nontransferable makes it difficult for a four-year college to accept such a course even though it may be pertinent to the student's program.

꜀ Community college educators must also resist the attempts of accrediting agencies to downgrade their vocational programs. These agencies are part of the problem, going to great lengths to distinguish between technical and vocational education, giving their approval to the first as "college-type" education and relegating the latter to "less-than-college" grade. They argue that skilled or trade programs are not post-high school in either assumed prior educational competencies or inclusion of general education courses, although they may consist of structured learning experiences. In addition, community college educators are expected to differentiate between the degrees they offer by restricting the Associate in Arts to graduates of transfer programs and by awarding the Associate in Applied Science to graduates of semiprofessional programs. Furthermore, accrediting agencies often recommend that vocational/trade students be given only "certificates of completion" in order to maintain the "integrity" of the degree. If such plans are widely accepted, community college educators will have to do much more rationalizing to convince students that these programs and the A.A.S. degree are equal to the transfer and the A.A. degree.

The community college educator is not absolved from his responsibility even though resistance to suggestions made by accrediting commissions is not easy (since they are powerful and dominated by representatives from four-year colleges and universities). If the community college educator believes in the equality of ꜀

vocational education he must defend his belief against attempts to create hierarchical distinctions, whether among the various vocational programs or between them and the transfer program.

Community college educators should also emphasize the fact that occupationally oriented programs "have within their context skills and concepts that are of value to the population in general and thereby are a part of general education" (Schill and others, 1968, p. 7). What could be more valuable for providing students with "the broad outlines of human knowledge" than a course on the role of computers in modern life? Many other vocational courses could qualify for inclusion under this criterion; some may be even more relevant than many traditional courses included in academic and general education sequences. Typing is one of the most popular vocational courses, and for college students, it is a skill of inestimable value. Courses in ceramics, painting, music, theatre, and allied arts often serve the purposes of general education. Similar courses that can enrich a student's life are auto mechanics, drafting, horseshoeing for equestrians, cabinetmaking, other handicrafts, and machine tooling. A reexamination and reevaluation of vocational courses from this perspective will give them a broader base, enhancing their economic utility while recognizing their social and cultural significance.

In the areas of accreditation, transferability of courses, and general education, community college educators should concern themselves with the whole problem of certification for schools, programs, and individuals. In sum, educators can influence accrediting agencies since they are members but only if they do not assume a posture of subservience to the leaders, most of whom are university administrators. They will not overcome the "tyranny" of the universities over liberal arts by imitating their courses or by overlooking the general education values inherent in their own vocational courses.

Alternative Futures

The search for alternatives to the educational system has a bearing on vocational education. Proponents of alternatives attack the monopoly of the public school and its control over credentials and degrees, rarely attainable outside the traditional educational establishment—in this case, the community college. By law and custom, the ladder of educational progression rests on the traditional concept of education as a preparation for life prior to entering the "real" world. Some label this concept "credentialism"—a system basing qualification for a position on certain minimum educational requirements at an accredited institution in terms of attendance, credits, certificates, and degrees. Some of those interested in reform offer an alternative method of getting a credential, based on learning in vocationally-oriented programs and gained through such agencies as: first, Job Corps, Manpower Development Training Programs, Vista, Neighborhood Youth Corps; second, schools or educational programs maintained by business, industry, and the military services; third, cultural institutions such as libraries, museums, and botanical gardens; fourth, community educational programs conducted by the YMCA, Jewish Centers, and unions; and fifth, self-directed activities.

In these and many other agencies, much teaching and learning occur—often informal, sometimes highly organized. The problem is to translate this education into the units necessary for credentials. Much as we decry formal education's monopoly in granting credentials, its existence and entrenched position in society cannot be ignored—nor will it be easily displaced. All we can expect is a loosening of the grip. The ideal would be a condition similar to that of creative artists whose products serve as their credentials.

A few concessions have been made toward recognizing the learning that takes place outside the schools. For years, students in vocational courses have been placed in advanced classes on the basis of examinations before enrollment or of performance after enrollment. Then, in a limited way, credit or advanced placement has been offered through examination. Most noteworthy are the programs granting associate degree credits for nurse's aide and practical nurse experience, because they are occurring in a vocational area formerly marked by rigid state regulations. The discussions for granting transfer credit from associate degree to baccalaureate nursing programs are also significant (Kintgen, 1970).

The logical outcome of this development is the nonresidential degree plan instituted by some colleges. Most widely publicized is the New York plan of a flexible and open system to help those who are frozen in their positions because they do not have a credential based on formal education and a degree. Under this plan, the New York Board of Regents grants an associate or bachelor's degree by examination, regardless of where or how the knowledge was obtained. It is called appropriately an "external degree," fitting in with the career education emphasis so prominent in national efforts. If successful, the New York plan will help remove the stigma attached to vocational education; under this plan, no program becomes a dead end. Knowledge acquired on the job may enable one to obtain a degree in a related field. As was pointed out in a news report of the plan, it brings together "training, education, and [career] ladders." If it is impossible for a person to move toward a career by this method, he may still enroll in a college program (New Human Services, Fall 1970).

This and other similar plans are in line with recommendations made by the most severe critics of formal education. For example, one critic advocates eliminating obligatory schooling and qualification tests based on education, substituting specific tests of competence in the selection of employees (Illich, 1970, p. 68). Illich favors a constitutional provision, similar to the First Amendment, that "there shall be no law with respect to an establishment of education" and "forbidding discrimination in hiring, voting, or admission to centers of learning based on previous attendance in some curriculum." He asserts that "the belief in the ability of schools to label people correctly is already so strong that people accept their vocational and marital fates with a gambler's resignation." He adds that this faith in school slotting is leading to "meritocracy—a state of mind in which each citizen believes that he deserves the place assigned to him by school," a fate to be avoided since it is worse than hell (Ibid., p. 57). The external degree not only would aid vocational educators, but also it would mitigate some such valid criticism of schools in general.

In an effort to make education competitive, "vouchering"— giving to the parent a subsidy to cover the educational expenses of his child at any approved school—has been proposed. This proposal is similar to the various federal and state plans subsidizing the education of veterans and, under certain circumstances, their children. Some people who do not believe all high school graduates should go to college propose that the subsidy be given to everyone to use in or out of college. If adopted, vouchering would enable students to choose private vocational schools or even, perhaps, schools conducted by business firms. However, vouchering may increase junior college enrollment just as the GI Bills did after World War II and Korea, and it also may encourage an increase of tuition (Campbell and Boyd, 1970, p. 241). Regardless of the consequences, some form of vouchering is on the horizon; it will assuredly affect the future of vocational education.

Another suggestion is to create in high-density population centers an entirely new system flexible enough to cooperate with an educational or noneducational organization in providing a particular part of an individual's education; thus, education would be conceived of macroscopically rather than microscopically (Houska, 1970, p. 15). This is an extension of the arrangements in which public schools provide the education of parochial school students in science, vocational, and other nonreligious subjects. For a long period, many public school students have been receiving religious education in parochial schools or churches (Campbell and Boyd, 1970, p. 244).

New Course Patterns. For those not yet prepared for drastic alternatives to the existing educational system, more modest changes have been proposed for making vocational education more attractive to students. One worthwhile suggestion is to reduce the number of courses by developing basic skill courses for a variety of programs. The mutual relationships among trades and vocations make possible the development of common elementary courses for a wide group of programs and courses with varying levels of proficiency. If a common core of courses were developed for vocational nursing, registered nursing, inhalation therapy, radiological technology, and other health programs, students could benefit by more flexibility and colleges could conserve their resources (Schultz, 1970, p. 4; Schill and others, 1968, p. 9). The prevalent ladder concept would be much more successful if this suggestion were followed.

Common courses also may help overcome the narrow training for jobs that may become obsolete in a few years. Some educators recommend that half such courses be general education in nature—but not necessarily of the traditional variety. For example, the human services career programs, the general education courses in juvenile delinquency, theories of social change, criminology, racism, and family relations would be related to the students' careers (Ullrich, 1970–1971, p. 27).

Open-end vocational curriculums offer a transition from the "tracking" system to a "fusing" route. These open-end programs— as differentiated from closed-end or terminal vocational programs— include transferable general education courses for students who desire them and, whenever possible, transfer credit for vocational courses. In this there should be "no incongruity in a [student] studying drafting, the heat treatment of metals [or typing or medical library techniques], Renaissance history, and Elizabethan art, all at the same time. . . . Such combinations could supply the ingredients for very satisfying careers" (Houska, 1970, p. 14). Open-end programs make lateral transfer between academic and vocational programs easier for students. However, this transfer is difficult because students are penalized not only by loss of credit but also by payment of special fees and, in New York City, by imposition of tuition after two changes of program (Houska, 1970, p. 13).

Academic-Vocational Merger. One of the most far-reaching and ultimately necessary proposals for bringing about greater acceptability of vocational education is to merge it with the academic. Until its accomplishment, hierarchical distinctions will place the latter over the former. Unfortunately, even though fencing off "the vocational aspect of life in a compartment called vocational education, separate from the mainstream . . . and serving only one student in ten is an anomaly" (Feldman, 1967), it is unrealistic to expect the merging of general and vocational education in this century.

There are too many obstacles. Federal and state support plans, buildings and other facilities, instructor qualifications, course segregation in the catalog and on the campus, different types of degrees, and other practices encourage rather than discourage the desired duality. Also, do either academic *or* vocational educators want a merger? The former may be antagonistic because they look on vocational education as different from, if not inferior to, academic education; the latter because they distrust the commitment of academic educators to vocational education.

ꓥ   Before a merger can take place, vocational education must attain parity with academic education. Parity will not come until the label "vocational" disappears from the community college vocabulary. No amount of breast-beating will convince students or the public that vocational is equal to academic education. However, what will be effective is equating vocational courses with academic courses in units of credit, in transferability to senior colleges, in nonterminal career programs, and in acceptability for general education. This has been done from time to time with courses and curriculums in nonvocational and vocational areas. What is proposed is to do it for all. The present system represents tracking in practice, if not in theory.

ꓥ   Despite all that is said about merging vocational education with general education or academic programs, community college educators do not envision its early demise. Their commitment to vocational education as an integral part of a college's mission is reflected in their eagerness to develop new programs to replace or supplement current offerings. In fact, vocational courses and curricula multiply faster than academic courses. A college often boasts of thirty or forty programs—which means that it lists in its catalog from sixty to over one hundred courses. The Illinois Junior College Board (1969) lists 100 areas of specialization and 752 programs offered by the state's colleges. This record is matched by other states and systems of colleges (Los Angeles Community College District, 1970; Pratt and Frederick, 1970).

ꓥ   Regardless of the status of vocational courses and programs, a large proportion and number of students enroll in them. Over the years, the proportion of vocational to academic students has remained constant, varying slightly from a twenty-five to seventy-five ratio (recognizing, however, that on a single campus, the percentage of vocational students may range from sixty to ten). In this respect, vocational education is stable; figures over a period of more than twenty years show little deviation (Ward, 1948, p. 14; Martorana, 1966).

The question then arises: "Why be concerned with prestige and status?" The answer is that vocational programs would not survive without this concern. Community college educators constantly are making these programs attractive to students and counteracting the social forces that relegate vocational education to an inferior position in our education system. They critically scrutinize practices that hinder the development of vocational education and examine the proposals that encourage changes in the educational system. Though they may not enjoy the criticism leveled at them, they give it serious attention. And they are less than eager to risk having their positions compromised by effecting an alliance with the academicians.

Centrifugal Forces

Federal legislation probably will continue to favor vocational education; however, these laws are a mixed blessing. With safeguards against diversion of funds to nonvocational purposes, the laws tend to deepen the division within community colleges and may in time destroy what they are attempting to do—make vocational programs acceptable. By fostering separate administrative organizations, separate brochures, and separate facilities, federal laws reduce rather than enhance the desirability of vocational programs. They magnify the differences of the programs rather than emphasize their interrelatedness and thereby contribute to the development of a rigid track system. This criticism is not directed against federal aid, for we recognize that without federal subsidies to the colleges and to the students, vocational education would have fewer programs and fewer students. The point here is that educators must call attention to the dangers of federal policies and at the same time assure Congress that they are concerned with the promotion and development of vocational education.

A serious danger mentioned previously is the growing tendency to make vocational education a vehicle for relieving unemployment by keeping young people off the labor market. Educators look forward to legislation similar to that passed by the Senate on September 16, 1970, authorizing two, two-and-one-half, and three billion dollars for the three years beginning July 1971. This manpower bill has overtones of unemployment relief and welfare, however. Its purpose is to subsidize programs that will permit young (and older) people to qualify for employment in areas of unfilled public needs, such as health, recreation, housing, public safety, maintenance of streets and parks, rural development, transportation, beautification, and conservation. At least one-third of the appropriations must be used for public service employment.

Juxtaposing jobs and public works points to the strong assumption that more than education is involved in this and other federal legislation. Keeping people in school reduces unemployment; training them to meet unfilled public needs removes the possibility of further glutting an employment market already supplied with a surplus of workers (American Vocational Association, October 27, 1970). This policy may make vocational education the WPA of the 70s. One cannot quarrel with efforts to relieve unemployment or to aid the disadvantaged or the minorities, but if vocational education becomes associated exclusively with these objectives, it will never obtain parity with academic education. And, if this form of social welfare is to be the ultimate purpose of the community college, the educators should be aware of its implications. Many people (including Vice President Agnew, other Nixon administration officials, and community leaders) openly suggest that four-year colleges and universities be reserved for the elite; the rest have or should have community colleges. Their attitude affects the prestige of the whole community college, not only that of vocational education. Community college educators should read carefully the 1970 statements of Agnew (1970, pp. 12–15), Nixon (1970), and Kerr (1970, pp. 34–35), in which the concept of universal higher education is reexamined. They should then read "Crisis in the Country" (Goodrich, 1970), a statement issued by black community college educators.

Nevertheless, vocational education enjoys tremendous support among Washington's influential leaders, and among many educators—a statement that cannot be made for the students and many faculty members. Large federal appropriations for its support are almost certain and they will receive widespread approval from many segments of the public.

Therefore, it is unlikely that many radical changes will occur. Suggestions for revolutionizing the relationship of vocational to academic education meet with little favor. Weak centripetal forces are opposed by too many powerful centrifugal forces. The separatism is fostered or encouraged by federal legislation, vocational educators, and academic instructors.

The concept of area vocational education schools and the establishment of regional accrediting commissions on vocational education in the Southern and New England Association(s) of Schools and Colleges are potent centrifugal forces that encourage continued separation. For the seventies and eighties—probably even into the next century—the prospects are dim for fusing vocational and academic education. The most that can be expected is to make vocational education more acceptable to students, academic educators, and the parents of students by reforming certain practices that have made vocational education ostensibly inferior to academic.

Bearing on this problem is a shift in emphasis from universal higher education to open access to higher education, as a national goal. If adopted, this shift will break a long series of official pronouncements that began in 1948 with President Truman's Commission on Higher Education. The Truman Commission's advocacy of universal higher education as a national policy was followed by a similar statement by an Eisenhower Commission, by President Johnson, by the national political parties in their platforms, and by the Educational Policies Commission of the NEA. Nevertheless, a commutation seems imminent.

Also associated with vocational education are problems and issues involving minorities and the disadvantaged. How to bring these groups into the mainstream of American economic activity without relegating them exclusively to vocational programs is complex and difficult. Helping them learn employable skills through vocational programs and, at the same time, offering them opportunities to upgrade themselves in the traditional academically accepted manner are tasks confronting the community college educators.

Further complicating the whole complex of relationships so far mentioned are the technological, economic, and cultural forces that make occupations obsolete, make jobs unavailable, or create unfavorable attitudes toward certain vocations. Automation affects occupations and vocational programs; unemployment has a discouraging effect on programs associated with the industries most affected; and intense feelings against war often have an adverse effect on programs that cater to the war effort. Cultural attitudes, as many educators observe, have great influence on student acceptance of vocational programs.

In this connection, the concept of the "open door" is involved, since open admission provides a rationalization for those favoring restrictive admission policies for the senior institutions. As long as access to higher education is open to young people, the reasoning goes, no injustice is committed by denying any group admission to the senior institutions. But this distinction introduces the problem of the status and acceptability of vocational programs; for, underlying this shift, is the assumption that those not eligible to enter a senior institution are not qualified for academic work and therefore should be encouraged to enroll in community college vocational programs. This attitude also prevailed (and probably still prevails) in high schools with vocational programs. As a result, vocational programs, rated inferior to academic programs, have been shunned by all who could do so.

Along with professional education, vocational education must contend with problems relating to supply and demand. How to obtain a reasonable balance between vocational-technical manpower needs is a perennial topic at educational conferences. Moreover, the unchallenged claims of unmet needs for skilled employees became hollow during unemployment periods such as that of 1969 to 1971. Associated with supply and demand is the problem of selection of vocational education programs. Medsker (1963) observed that "not even the experts can predict the upsets and the other changes which will result from the accelerating pace of technology and automation. . . . How to plan a curriculum that is not out of date before it is implemented is provocative." If community college educators introduce programs indiscriminately, disregarding demand for skilled workers, they will be subject to the kind of accusation leveled by unemployed aerospace engineers at colleges, universities, and the National Science Foundation for creating a surplus of trained personnel by encouraging students to go into science and engineering.

Problems of status or prestige stand out as the most difficult to resolve. They are so deeply seated that years of effort to mitigate their effects have been unsuccessful. The American Dream, the prestige syndrome, the national preoccupation that everyone must go to college for an academic education all complicate the problems of the community college. Our economic system places such a premium on the bachelor's degree that, as Jencks and Riesman point out, even business cannot compete with four-year colleges for high school graduates (Jerome, 1970, p. 20). In a special article on junior colleges, the *U.S. News and World Report* (May 17, 1965)' listed lack of prestige as the most serious problem. High school counselors, it stated, "think of the junior colleges as places for 'rejects' unable to gain admission to four-year colleges." And, remembering the role vocational education played in the high school as a dumping ground for "rejects," high school graduates exhibit wariness toward community college programs. Ironically, the open-door policy "designed to help young people to enter college is interpreted to mean that junior colleges are second-rate institutions" (Cosand, 1965).

\   Subsidies for vocational education may make it more palatable to students and attractive to educators, but they do not necessarily enhance its prestige. The opposite may result, especially if vocational education is associated with relief and the disadvantaged. These subsidies, together with the reemergence of the elitist theory that not all should attend a four-year college or university, may exact a usurious repayment in the form of revision of the concept of the comprehensive community college. During periods of stringent finances, community college educators understandably may be tempted to accept almost any conditions in return for federal aid. They may live to regret their eagerness.

Black Studies as a

Curriculum Catalyst

10

The advent of black studies in the curriculum may become the most far-reaching reform in the history of the community college, for it has forced a reexamination of the colleges' educational philosophy. The college—though it claims to be community-oriented—was caught by surprise. It was no more attuned to the aspirations and needs of the large groups of black students than were the four-year colleges and universities. The initial impetus for reexamination came from the students and their allies in the community; much momentum continues to come from them.

Ever since its inception around 1967, the movement has attracted wide attention. Few educational changes have had as much publicity in popular and scholarly journals. Black and nonblack scholars, columnists, and community leaders carry on a war of words over the relevancy of black studies, especially to black students. The criticism and defense of black studies in schools cut across racial and generation gaps. Some of its major critics are black educators and leaders of black organizations; some of its stoutest defenders are influential nonblack schoolmen and scholars. The unending interest and controversy force continual evaluation of the rationale for black studies programs, a controversial dialogue that may be the key to their survival.

The survey of black studies reported here was conducted as

part of a study, funded by the U.S. Office of Education, to furnish certain audiences in the junior college field with information about the development and implementation of black studies in two-year colleges. It was a formative effort, conducted in 1970, to find out about practices within the field, since the development of black studies programs in two-year colleges (and in other schools) has clearly outdistanced efforts to understand the phenomena that gave rise to them. The complete report was published as *Black Studies in the Community Colleges: A Survey* (Lombardi and Quimby, 1971).

Data collected included responses from a mail-out questionnaire, interviews with California-based program directors and teachers of black studies, correspondence with a number of junior college educators who have been active in the implementation of black studies, and countless institutional documents: catalogs, brochures, class schedules, and so on. This data collection was supplemented by a bibliographic search for all available literature on the topic of black studies. However, the general direction of inquiry was shaped by an advisory board recruited from all sections of the United States. The questionnaire, by the way, was addressed to the 807 institutional members of the American Association of Junior Colleges (1970) in the fifty states and the District of Columbia. Response to it was excellent—nearly 80 per cent of the colleges replied—and 67 per cent (543) of the replies were returned in some usable form.

Since the black studies idea was, in Bornholdt's words, "accepted before it was defined" (1970), the questionnaire allowed community colleges to respond in terms of a very loose definition. On the one hand, "black studies" was defined as "courses of instruction [that] deal directly with the culture, history, sociology, psychology, language, and so on of the black man." Respondents were asked to take into consideration traditional African area studies and languages, besides more recent courses in the many facets of what is described as the "black experience." On the other hand, if the respondents replied they offered no black studies courses, they were asked: "Insofar as you know, have any of your college's courses of instruction been placing greater emphasis—since the mid-1960s— on the blacks' contribution to and accomplishments in American society?" A positive reply to this question was interpreted as involvement in black studies—even though we recognize that this interpretation may be questionable.

Who Offers Black Studies?

The results of the survey suggest the impact of the black studies movement on community colleges. By the end of the school year 1969–1970, nearly 45 per cent (242 institutions) of the colleges participating in the survey claimed to offer at least one course of instruction under the rubric of black studies. An additional 31 per cent (168 colleges) of the respondents—at institutions that did not offer black studies courses—reported that since the mid-1960s their traditional course offerings place greater emphasis on the black man's contributions to and accomplishments in American society.

The widespread adoption of black studies courses in community colleges started in the late 1960s. Before 1965, only ten of the respondent colleges (five in California, two in Illinois, and one each in Alabama, Michigan, and Washington) claimed to offer courses that dealt with American Negro or African history and culture. Even by spring 1967, only twenty-three of the respondent colleges were offering courses in black studies. The pace quickened somewhat during 1967–1968 for, by spring 1968, forty-seven of the respondent institutions had adopted black studies courses. In 1968–1969, the school year immediately following Martin Luther King's assassination, 100 of the respondent colleges inaugurated their first course in black studies. By spring 1970, another ninety-five began courses of instruction in black studies.

The heaviest concentration of colleges with black studies courses is in California, where sixty-one colleges—75 per cent of the respondents in that state—reported offering black studies learning opportunities in 1969–1970. Though other parts of the country are not as deeply involved as California in this development, its overall growth is remarkable. In the Middle States, for example, 64 per cent of the respondent colleges offered black studies courses in 1969–1970. Almost half of those in New England offered them, while 60 per cent of the colleges in the Northwest had them under way.

The adoption of black studies courses in the North Central

region and in the southern colleges has not kept pace with developments elsewhere. A third of the North Central colleges and 25 per cent of the southern colleges reported offering at least one course in black studies during 1969–1970. Significantly, in both regions, a large number of colleges—twenty-one in the South and twenty-two in the North Central states—were planning to offer courses in black studies within the following two or three school years. In addition, many colleges in the South and North Central regions reported that their conventional curriculums have been emphasizing the role and contribution of the black man in America.

At the time we designed the study, we did not expect community colleges to be so heavily involved in the development of black studies courses, though we assumed many would report that their curriculums placed more emphasis on the history and culture of black America. (After all, such a response would be both socially desirable and impractical to challenge.) Yet the adoption of distinct courses in black studies is the chief means by which community colleges approach this ethno-curricular innovation. The pell-mell rush to adopt black studies courses does not necessarily reflect a deep commitment to the aims of the black studies movement, but it highlights the programmatic approach most community junior colleges take to keep abreast of contemporary social reality. This report, then, can be viewed both as a chronicle of the development of black studies in two-year colleges through 1970 and as a statement that reveals much about their institutional functioning in general.

Black studies courses are offered at virtually every type of two-year college, but they prevail in the large community junior colleges (5,000 or more students in California institutions, 3,000 or more students elsewhere). About 20 per cent of all two-year colleges in the United States are large institutions; collectively they enroll over half of all community college students. We received responses from 138 (or three-fourths) of these large colleges; black studies courses were offered at 119 or 86 per cent of them. Ten of the large colleges that did not offer black studies courses in 1969–1970 reported they would be developing them in the next year or two. Thus, the study of black America is becoming commonplace in large community junior colleges—an unsurprising development as the largest are in or near urban population centers. They are heterogeneous and comprehensive social institutions in almost every respect, and they enroll most of the black students in the two-year colleges outside the South.

However, attempts to infer relationships between the number of black students on a campus and the development of black studies courses must be viewed with caution, even though the black studies movement in community colleges was addressed primarily to the needs of black students. We found virtually no reliable longitudinal data on black student enrollments for the three years during which these courses emerged in so many community colleges. Only a handful of respondent institutions reported that they had undertaken ethnic surveys during 1969–1970. And distinguishing colleges with significant numbers of black students from those with only a few begs the question: what constitutes a significant black enrollment on a community college campus?

One hypothesis did emerge from our attempts to secure reliable data on black student enrollments in large community colleges. It appears that some, possibly many, of these colleges are enrolling an increasing percentage of black students. If this indicates a trend, the changing racial composition of large two-year colleges is attributed best to factors unrelated to the development of black studies (for example, minority student recruitment campaigns, unemployment, and changes in the boundaries of attendance districts), though the implementation of black studies courses between 1967 and 1970 may have been stimulated at some colleges by an upsurge in black student enrollments perceived by college officials.

Although inadequate, this test of significant black enrollments nonetheless yielded one tentative conclusion: irrespective of size, colleges with "significant" black student enrollments (greater than 10 per cent) do not adopt black studies courses any more readily than colleges with less. In short, the black studies movement has "captured" the junior college movement.

Politics

Obviously, the black studies movement has political overtones; the battle over black studies represents one element in the black students' attempts to establish themselves on campus (Jerome, 1969, p. 38). Or, as Hamilton puts it in other words, "it is a political struggle for academic innovation." The advanced group in the black studies movement wants nothing less than "the total reorganization of . . . knowledge and curriculum from a black perspective." Since "the educational systems of the white West have had their chance" and failed, the blacks "demand the right to experiment with new directions, if initially only in black studies programs" (1970, p. 84). Black colleges such as Malcolm X in Chicago are expected to serve the political, social, and economic as well as the educational needs of black people. To the advanced group, black studies implies a total transformation of the educational system, not a patchwork of isolated modifications. Harding, an educational leader with wide influence among black educators, believes that education for blacks "must be developed always within the context of the needs of black community here and abroad, and not the needs of American space, business or weapons technology" (1970b, p. 158).

Much of the politics of black studies in community colleges has been equally concerned with the knotty problem of institutional racism. In nearly all instances, black student demands for black studies also have been demands for bringing an end to various discriminatory practices. Black students frequently attack community colleges for their white, middle-class, antiblack bias, repeating the premise of black activist leaders that schools and colleges perpetuate injustices because they make the black man invisible by denying his contribution to the social and cultural tradition of America and the world. In brief, they echo the charge of a black psychologist that education has crippled more people than all of the diseases of mankind.

At the outset, possibly the overriding aim of the black studies movement in community colleges was to galvanize black students on college campuses into constituencies that could press for both the implementation of black studies courses and the reform of any number of institutional policies and practices that governed the education of young black men and women. Black student organizations sought a separate educational setting under black control within the colleges to mount a permanent attack on racism and to promote the special interests of black student constituencies. To a great extent, the formation of viable black student constituencies in community colleges resulted in hurried efforts to implement black studies courses and to undertake a host of institutional reforms in the face of real or possible confrontations. Confrontations initiated by black student organizations took place mainly on large two-year college campuses with many black students. That these confrontations produced results satisfactory to the black students strongly suggests the effiacy of what a historian calls collective bargaining through protest.

From its inception, the black studies movement has been closely identified with the notion of separate educational settings for black students—a notion that has been dealt with from three vantage points. First is the continuing call by some black leaders for virtually separate educational facilities (see Harding, 1970b). This concept of institutional separateness is promoted in earnest, for example, by Hurst at Malcolm X College. Second have been the demands of black student organizations on biracial and multiethnic campuses for separate black studies departments, centers, or institutes under black control, that is, control by black faculty members, administrators, and others who value the premise of black liberation from white domination. This demand was met at Merritt College (California) after a long confrontation episode. A third vantage point has been the relatively tame demand for greater representation of black people on community college faculties and in administrative positions, and on boards of control, a demand that has occupied the attention of many community colleges since 1967.

Black autonomy in bisocial and multiethnic community college settings is the immediate goal of most black advocates, but separatism in the form of black colleges is the ultimate goal of a smaller avant-garde group. In a few preponderantly black colleges controlled by black educators, the programs approximate the ideal of the advanced group. In these colleges, every facet of the educational enterprise is directed toward fulfillment of the aims of black studies. The reorganization of knowledge from a black perspective is a total activity. This group of about ten colleges is growing; possibly every large urban center outside the South will have at least one college controlled by blacks. Moreover, in some communities black colleges are being formed as offshoots of mother colleges located in suburban areas distant from the ghettos.

Undeniably, the black quest for autonomy has challenged a host of institutional conventions in junior colleges. The more militant blacks—students, faculty, and community leaders—demand not only a black studies curriculum, but participation in institutional decision making. In some instances, control over the educational system that shapes the minds of black youth has been the central policy conviction. Such autonomy was achieved easily at the institutional level, where now black educators chair and teach in black studies departments. Since such control usually is in the context of the overall organizational pattern of the colleges, this pattern of black autonomy raises the larger issue of black independence from supervision by white administrators at the institutional level.

In urban communities with densely populated black areas, where colleges have largely black enrollments, control over the institution is passing to black administrators. By 1970, at least fifteen nonsouthern public community colleges had black presidents, and in some of them black instructors formed the majority of the staff. In these colleges the presidents, their staffs, and faculty have the opportunity to shape the institution in terms of the aims of the black studies movement.

Malcolm X College comes closest to the black militants' ideal of control by the black community—students, faculty, staff, administrators, and community people. It is considered "a prototype of the kind of educational system needed to solve the problems of black people" (Poinsett, 1970). On a smaller scale is Oak Park School of Afro-American Thought, established in a Sacramento (California) black community by the Los Rios Community College District. The school offers courses in the late afternoon and evening hours and maintains a counseling service from ten o'clock in the morning until nine in the evening. Community participation is a feature of its operating procedure. The supervision of the school by a student is also unique.

During the spring of 1969, students led a campaign for community control of Seattle Community College. The effort failed, but it resulted in the selection of a black president and the resignation of a white board member to make way for the appointment of a black trustee. Community involvement, which was an issue at Merritt College for more than five years, came to a head with the decision to move the college to another location. After considering a request for community control of its Merritt College flatlands campus, the Board of Trustees adopted a resolution expanding the concept of community participation to all of the district's colleges.

As the number of black presidents, faculty members, and trustees increases, the movement for black control of segregated colleges will accelerate. In addition to the fifteen presidents, many black trustees and considerably more black instructors are now in community colleges. The developments at Malcolm X College, the Oak Park School of Afro-American Thought, Seattle Community College, and Merritt College may forerun varied strategies for black autonomy in community college schooling. In predominantly white colleges, black studies involves the introduction of a few courses and the modification of the standard courses to include a balanced treatment of the black experience in the United States, as well as its relationships to its African roots and to comparable developments in other countries.

Division or disagreement over the extent of black studies is most severe in colleges with mixed or integrated student bodies. There, pressure is more insistent and criticisms are more outspoken regarding the programs (especially where black students are not permitted to participate in their development), and charges of tokenism are made against administrators for not introducing more black studies courses. From this large group of colleges, many patterns of black studies programs are evolving to meet the needs of the various ethnic mixes.

In ethnically mixed colleges, greater insistence centers on the employment of black instructors, as well as of counselors and other administrators. Full-time black instructors are the barometer of these colleges' commitment to black studies. If a college cannot provide a full program of black studies classes to an instructor, black students insist that the college should permit him to teach courses in other departments. The reverse process of taking an instructor hired for the regular program to teach a black studies class or two is frowned upon. Part-time black instructors are considered a stopgap, a form of tokenism.

Aims

A few community colleges have formulated institutional aims for their black studies programs. These aims alert the public that the college seeks to attain certain educational ends through black studies. Significantly, in many instances where institutional aims for black studies have been set forth by community colleges, the aims recapitulate much of what black student leaders advocate in their position papers (Lombardi, 1970). This is a remarkable phenomenon, for it represents the first time in the history of the junior college movement that students have been directly involved in defining the goals of a collegiate educational program. Also, black studies have generated differentiated institutional aims in the colleges which have adopted them. Note, too, that where community colleges have adopted institutional aims dealing with the curricular ends of black studies, black students form a significant minority.

Merritt College in Oakland, where approximately 40 per cent of the students are black, has formulated an institutional aim for black studies that emphasizes the sociopsychological rehabilitation of Afro-Americans. Merritt argues for "the redefinition of Afro-Americans by themselves in order to develop a healthy psychological identity to which other ethnic groups may relate in a positive, dignified and humanistic manner." On the other hand, at Malcolm X College in Chicago, which has virtually an all-black student body, the aims of black studies are addressed to serving the goals of black people: "we must design our educational programs to promote the black agenda . . . [and] to prepare our young people to play a dynamic and constructive part in the development of a society in which all members share fairly in the good or bad fortune of the group." Wayne County Community College in Detroit, where less than half the student body is black, has addressed its institutional aims for black studies to both black and white students: they implicitly seek to deal with the knotty problem of racism. "The prime intent of the program must be to equip [all of] its students with the knowledge essential for the betterment of the black community."

In some instances, differentiation of institutional aims for black studies attempts to fashion curricular ends that reflect the particular expectations of the community served by each of the colleges. The special emphasis in urban community colleges on the sociopsychological needs of black students and on the social goals of black people is buttressed by the fact that the Kerner Commission found that these emphases were highly appealing to the urban black population.

However, most community colleges that offer black studies do not have stated institutional aims rooted in the raison d'être of black studies. These colleges offer one or more courses of instruction in black studies to keep pace with the revolution in ethnic relations or possibly to ward off student-generated protest. Their justification for black studies courses stems from such conventional notions as "extending the concept of liberal or general education" and "meeting the needs of minority students." These approaches often represent a genuine desire on the part of white administrators and teachers, in particular, to grapple with their own ignorance about black people in American history and contemporary society. Sauk Valley College (Illinois), for example, is now "committed to the progressive upgrading, expanding, and coordinating of teaching and research in black studies," though Sauk Valley does not offer any black studies courses. It has chosen to weave black studies learning opportunities throughout the fabric of conventional social science course work. In a similar vein, Diablo Valley College (California)—with an enrollment of only a few black students—requires that its students "examine their American institutions, including the contributions by and accommodations made to the many ethnic groups which comprise our complex American society." To achieve this end, Diablo Valley offers several black studies courses and other learning opportunities, including an annual film festival that deserves special recognition.

California community colleges are being required to formulate institutional aims and to adopt courses dealing with ethnic studies generally. The Board of Governors of the California Community Colleges has approved a resolution pointed to that end, an action urged on the Board by the California Junior College Association (in which nearly all community colleges hold institutional membership). No other state has moved this far in attempting to redirect the curriculums of community colleges; to be sure, very few states except California still employ state-mandated curriculums. The action of the Board of Governors of California Community Colleges is a pertinent commentary on the revolution in educational ideology taking place at all levels of American schooling. Com-

munity college students, according to the board, need exposure to
other cultural patterns and life styles to prevent friction and misun-
derstandings among diverse groups in American life. If the Board
has a pragmatic concern with civic peace in the United States, it is
equally concerned with recognizing—even legitimatizing—cultural
and social pluralism.

The framing of institutional aims by community colleges for
black and other ethnic studies places value on the reality of cultural
and social pluralism in American life. On campuses with a large
black student enrollment, institutional aims probably will continue
to center on the needs and goals of black people. These colleges have
a special obligation, in Hurst's words, "to promote the black
agenda."

Curriculum

The introduction of black studies into the curriculum is in
the tradition of higher education. Ethnic courses have been part of
the curriculum for many years. Negro history, Negro literature, and
African history did not evoke hysteria when first introduced in the
1950s, nor will the newer and more numerous black studies courses,
curriculums, and degree programs as time goes on. It is apparent
that white educators are not as disturbed as formerly by the black
students' challenge to the relevancy of the educational program and
by their insistence that a person's race is a valid qualification for
assignment as an instructor. In some colleges, white educators are
working with black students and staff members in the development
of courses and programs. In many urban colleges, black administrators and faculty are assuming a dominant role over, or achieving
independence of, white supervision.

In this, as in other reform and revolutionary movements,
different interpretations of the meaning of black studies are developing—even among the black educators who guide the development.
That the incorporation of their philosophies into educational programs takes different forms is shown in their writings, institutional
publications, and analysis of their practices. Those differences are not
surprising, nor do they diminish the stature of the individuals or the
significance of the movement. However, this lack of consensus may
diffuse the impact of black studies on the curriculum.

Practices in the colleges do not always conform to the theories of the black studies advocates, because translating theories into the curriculum patterns and life style of community colleges is done by a variety of practitioners, some of whom are more zealous than knowledgeable about higher education.

The black studies movement has made educators recognize the differences in the position of the many minority groups. These differences explain the relative inactivity of the European minorities who were neither assimilated nor forcibly kept apart from the mainstream of American life and culture. An ethnic group that has a cultural identity and has gained social and economic acceptance does not seem to mind if its particular ethnicity is neglected in education. Most of the European minority groups want it that way. If they maintain a separate existence culturally, it is because of a self-sufficiency and a knowledge that the barriers could be and are being scaled by those who so desire. This is hardly the case for other minority groups, and the blacks fare the worst despite the long history of their presence in America. Nevertheless, some educators, through ignorance of this distinction or through refusal to accept this interpretation, are including European ethnic groups in their ethnic studies programs.

Black studies courses have been variously categorized. At the University of California, Berkeley, they are classified as history, contemporary socioeconomic, cultural, community-related, and language and literature (Billingsley, 1970). Hamilton's (1969) six classifications (the Gaps Function, the Functional Theory, the Humanizing Function, the Reconciliation Theory, the Psychological Function, and the Ideological Function) stress the reasons or purposes of black studies programs rather than courses. A third classification of courses in the community colleges groups them into six categories: historical, literary, cultural, socioeconomic, integrated, and minority- and urban-oriented. As will be apparent in the description of these six categories, they resemble the other classifications:

Historical. By far the most popular are the history courses. History is included in nearly every college with one or more black studies programs. The classes revolve around some aspect of the black or Afro-American in American history and the history of Africa. Some are one-semester courses either of the survey kind, of the period variety, or of the contemporary urban setting. Others are two-semester (or three-quarter) courses covering, for example, history of America from its discovery and the span of civilization from the beginning of recorded history.

Literary. A larger variety of titles appears in the Afro-American literature sector of black studies. Although the course titles are more numerous than those in the history category, enrollment is smaller. Two reasons may account for this: English courses other than composition usually are not required in the general education pattern or for graduation as are courses in American history; and literature courses usually are restricted to second-, third-, and fourth-semester students who have completed the composition course.

Cultural. A third category of courses deals with Afro-American and African culture other than literature. These may be found under Afro-American studies, anthropology, art, sociology, and humanities. The number of courses in the group is large (although the number of enrollees is much smaller than in either the history or literature courses) but they are not usually found in catalogs listing fewer than three courses in the total black studies program.

Socioeconomic. The fourth category of courses relates to the socioeconomic aspects of the black people in the United States, with only an occasional course on Africa. These courses have an economic, sociological, or urban orientation. Some of them are being incorporated in two-year technical-vocational programs in education aide, community planning, urban government, environmental technology, and child care. In this category, the courses deal with the oppression and exploitation of blacks.

Integrated. Instead of developing separate black studies courses, some colleges are revising their standard courses to include material about Afro-Americans, Africa, and Africans. At Sauk Valley College (Illinois), "in most disciplines black studies are woven throughout the fabric of the courses, and are applied intensively where pertinent. Also, in some areas such as economics and major field requirements for child care aide, teacher aide, and law enforcement, black studies are more tangential than in other areas, but even in these, numerous areas exist where attention is focused on discrimination and minority group problems" (Nesbit, 1969).

Many colleges have separate black studies courses and, at the same time, are broadening their standard courses. At Forest Park Community College (Missouri), this is a long-range goal which proceeds side by side with the establishment of the new courses. The category may include all the courses offered at colleges like Malcolm X with an objective to become a black institution— one in which the educational services will be designed uniquely to serve the goals of black people. Among the standard courses included in the Afro-American Studies Program at Forest Park are: English Composition (Black Emphasis), Introduction to Sociology (Racial and Cultural Minorities Emphasis), and Introduction to Psychology (Afro-American Experience Emphasis). Similar practices are followed in the Los Rios District colleges (California) and in San Jose (California) City College. In the former, two sets of United States history courses are offered, one of which is labeled "Afro-American emphasis." In the latter, the black studies department issues a flyer to students with information on courses where the "emphasis is on the black perspective" and that focus "on the black point of view." Some courses are standard, others are black studies courses.

Minority- and Urban-Oriented. A group of related courses dealing with minorities is mentioned here, although they are not black studies courses in the strict sense of the definition. These courses do for the general area of minorities what black studies do for blacks. For example, the North Campus of the Community College of Denver offers a course in minority literature including Chicano, Jewish, black, and other groups. In addition, the courses cover subjects such as the composition and characteristics of ethnic groups and the relationships of minorities among themselves and with the dominant group, emphasizing the governmental structure and processes. Since so large a proportion of minorities lives in urban areas, courses dealing with problems connected with urban life are common. At Malcolm X College, a learning unit has been established under the heading of "urban survival." Many of these courses are found in the sociology departments of the colleges. A course on police-community relations appears frequently in the law enforcement curriculums. Often the courses in this category have the same content and purposes as some developed at Sauk Valley College (Illinois).

Among the experiments are those in which standard courses are being adapted, broadened in scope, or taught with a black emphasis. If these experiments satisfy enough black students, they may supplant the black studies courses. This is the hope of the black and white integrationists; it is the fear of the founders of the black studies movement. It is too early to determine the direction black studies will take—separate courses or infusion of the black experience into every course. Development is taking place in both directions.

Much work must be done before an effective integration of knowledge takes place. Even after the black studies ferment, American literature course syllabi rarely mention a black writer among those to be studied. The situation in American history is slightly better. Much depends on the instructors, many of whom introduce material on the black experience.

The absence of suitable textbooks retards the process of revision and integration of the regular courses, and many of them incorporate only minor comments or discussions. Often, the authors tack on a sentence or two about minorities at the end of each chapter or devote a single chapter to the subject. The interrelatedness of the black and white experience has not been achieved in textbooks.

Evaluation

From the beginning of the black studies movement, concern has been expressed about the quality of the courses, the qualifications of the instructors, and the performance of the students. Critics charge: first, the courses are substandard, designed for students who cannot succeed in the more rigorous intellectually-oriented courses; and, second, the courses are poorly conceived, irrelevant, and racist.

Proponents of black studies meet the charges head-on. President Hurst announced that at Malcolm X College the theme will be "better education than can be obtained anywhere else." "Some people," he said in his inaugural address, "would like to think that Malcolm X College will be synonymous with low standards and free rides to degrees." Far from it—but it will be different from the traditional "black education structured by white educators that was mediocre, encouraged failure and myths about black inferiority" (Hurst, 1969). To the charge that a proposal for a new teaching credential in black studies involved a lowering of standards, the reply was: "Black people aren't about to lower *any* standards; what we're doing is *raising* standards by considering new perspectives to define *'qualified.'* [The existent form of credentialing] preserved 'the white man's welfare system' " (Walton, 1969, pp. 51–52).

It is not surprising that some militants during the early days of the activist period expected to take advantage of the turmoil. The educational leaders of the black studies movement were alert to this possibility and took measures to counteract the tendency to lower standards. They deplored the anti-intellectualism prevalent among those student militants who wanted "to feel good," but opposed homework, research papers, and so on, on the specious ground that these were a "honky bag." They reminded these students that "a true revolutionary . . . is one who will fight to get a course implemented . . . but who will also attend that course *and study"* (Walton, 1969, p. 264).

The black instructors at Los Angeles City College indicated their concern for excellence by asking themselves: "how can we best protect the integrity and the quality of instruction" during the emergency when the demand for instructors exceeds the supply? They also asked: what can "be done for students who come . . . severely limited academically?" One of the most candid statements of a black instructor was: "we have assumed that . . . programs can be initiated for those limited academically; but we have not sufficiently questioned that assumption" (Ware, 1969).

Few people now challenge the academic quality of black studies courses or the qualifications of the instructors. The early insularity of excluding white students from the courses is disappearing. In time, the color of the instructor may also be a minor professional qualification. Emphasis is on academic excellence. No one can expect, however, that all black instructors will be superior or that all black studies courses will be taught excellently, any more than one expects the same for white instructors or for the standard subjects. "If black history is taught in the same pedantic manner as

our book-oriented courses in white history are, then black history
will be just as irrelevant" (Rainsford, 1970).

Proliferation of courses, because it implies dilution in content
and quality, may be as much a concern in black studies as it is in
most disciplines. The urge to create new courses is difficult to resist.
The evidence revealed in college catalogs does not indicate unusual
activity in this regard, however. Therefore, one may conclude that
restraint rather than proliferation prevails in the development of
black studies courses. Such restraint may be related to a concern for
quality and excellence.

In only a few cases do catalogs include courses on "soul
food" and other topics that are attacked as irrelevant and questionable. Language courses in Swahili or Ibo, another group under
attack, are offered in very few colleges. When enrollments are examined, it becomes evident that black students are as indifferent to
language courses as are white students.

If one were to judge by the number of courses in community
college catalogs and schedules of classes, the verdict would be that
black and white administrators have been exceedingly restrained, if
not actually reluctant, to introduce black studies courses. For example, a college with a 60 per cent black enrollment offered only three
such courses for its 3,100 black students. Another, with 2,500 black
students, offered eight, including three standard courses with a black
emphasis. A third college, with an 80 per cent black enrollment,
offered five for 2,500 students. A fourth college, with a 95 per cent
black enrollment of 1,660 students, offered four courses. These
hardly can be cited as examples of proliferation, but as of fall 1970,
they represented the situation in community colleges.

From the categories of the black studies courses, a definition
of black studies in the community colleges would parallel the one
used to define the standard curriculum. It is apparent that black
studies embody the totality of knowledge of the black community in
the United States, Africa, and elsewhere in that order of importance.
In the majority of courses, positive aspects of black civilization are
featured. Only a few courses deal with the oppression and exploitation of blacks by whites, though these negative aspects are incorporated in many of them (they could no more be ignored than
Hitler's treatment of the Jews in a Jewish studies curriculum). In

their comprehensiveness and scope, these courses attempt to destroy the negative image of blacks created by the traditional curriculum but, more importantly, they aim to create self-respect for blacks by building an identity rooted in American and African history and culture.

A category or description of courses cannot capture or reveal the spirit, the inner essence, the idealism, and the righteous indignation experienced by leaders of the black renaissance of the 1960s. For this, the reader must dip into their speeches and writings, readily available in numerous periodicals and anthologies. Unless he does, the dramatic success of this black renaissance and curriculum revolution is incomprehensible to him.

Just Another School?

11

Thus far we have traced certain aspects of the community junior college. The institution itself has been examined, its people described, and its processes analyzed as they relate to and reflect institutional values. There are various ways to conclude such a book. One could plot trends in institutional functioning, speculate on future enrollments and staffing patterns, and/or make recommendations for functional changes in institutional operations. Or we could end by offering platitudes ("many challenges remain; much needs to be done if institutional promise is to be fulfilled"). Another way, of course, is merely to recapitulate the preceding chapters, repeating what has already been said.

However, we chose to do none of these. Instead, we will restate some major premises covered in the book and then we will introduce a new thesis developing the premise that the institution's unstated social functions maintain tensions and not only subvert its educative functions but are in conflict with them. Finally, we will recommend alternative institutional forms that would acknowledge the disparate functions.

Something for Everyone

The community junior college is built on principles set down in the nineteenth century by educators who foresaw the societal changes that would put increasing numbers of young people into post-secondary school. Unable to reconcile their visions of the research-oriented university with the hordes of students who soon

176

would be seeking some form of higher education, they postulated a system of two-year colleges to relieve the senior institutions from dealing with freshmen and sophomores. As buffer schools, these colleges would act as feeders to the universities, screening and sorting the matriculants, allowing the fit to continue on to higher education, shunting the unfit to the nether reaches of society. As they developed, the colleges took on other activities—remedial and vocational education, guidance, and community services.

The comprehensive community college of the 1970s has grown large by promising something for everyone. It allows the universities to maintain restrictive admissions by offering an alternative to those who cannot gain admittance. (In most states, the two-year college bars no one who has graduated from high school and/or who has attained the age of 18.) It promises the young an opportunity to go to college in their home town at minimum expense and with little advance commitment. Admission is easy, fees are small. The student may work and go to school at the same time. He need not lay long-range plans for college attendance and neither he nor his family must commit large sums for tuition. The two-year college promises the industrial community a ready source of workers trained at public expense. And it offers the allure of a respectable community agency that attempts to mitigate all urban ills. As a result, the more than 1,000 two-year colleges grow in number and size at a rate considerably greater than that of any other segment of higher education.

Higher education is in a bear market. The universities, accused of being elitist, archaic, restrictive, unresponsive to their students, and indifferent if not downright antagonistic to the people of the cities where they are located, are under attack from within and without. However, the community college has escaped nearly all such criticism. Its remedial programs are viewed as correcting the defects in education with which lower schools are unable to cope. Its open admissions stand as evidence that no one—regardless of ability or aptitude—is barred. Its variety of programs offer something for everyone. The promise of the college maintains currency.

Because the promise is there, the two-year college rides high in popularity. The student activism that has plagued the universities has skirted the junior colleges. Most college officials believe the relatively few incidents that have occurred were fomented by "outside agitators" (Lombardi, 1969). The popular press, frequently critical of senior institutions, has pointed with pride to two-year colleges as sensible structures, responsive to community needs. And elected officials who for years have made political capital by attacking the university support the colleges that promise to keep the young off the streets, sort them ostensibly according to their abilities, and offer everyone a chance to succeed. In the 1960s, while everyone was attacking or defending the university, criticizing and questioning its motives, the two-year college grew significantly, mushroomed in the backyard of higher education, as it were, and took its place as a major force. (The state colleges and regional universities have been in much the same position. See Dunham's *Colleges of the Forgotten Americans,* 1969.)

Thus, on the crest of a wave of support, the two-year colleges remain symbols of achievement. They have high enrollments and concomitantly high claims on public funds. Their total financial support is minute in comparison with that of the universities, but it grows at a faster rate. Because community college libraries are smaller, salaries lower, and physical plants less elaborate, a student costs the taxpayer less than half the amount his university counterpart costs—a fact of considerable political importance. And in a skittish social climate, an institution filled with docile, pragmatic students who usually live with their parents and work part time seems idyllic.

Community college advocates are quick to capitalize on the expanding enrollments by remarking in the following vein: "Here are students who would never have gone to college had it not been for our institution." (This point has considerable validity because each time a community college opens, the number of high school graduates in that area who go to college jumps dramatically.) The colleges recognize and readily acknowledge the challenge of handling many tasks that other higher educational enterprises have not been able to manage adequately—keeping the young out of the labor force, training them for jobs, inculcating them with basic skills, helping them gain a feeling for their place in society—in short, providing an overflow receptacle for those whom the universities are unwilling or unable to serve. As long as the majority of their constituents accept these premises, the colleges avoid severe criticism.

Occasional demurrers by critics of the system are heard. Jencks and Riesman, for example, aver that because the proportion of bachelor's degrees awarded since the community colleges began enrolling sizable percentages of students has not increased, the community colleges are not "an alternative path to the top for individuals, but rather a safety valve . . . that . . . allows the universities to go their own way without facing the full consequences of excluding the dull-witted or uninterested majority" (1968, p. 492). And a high level task force of the U.S. Department of Health, Education, and Welfare sees the promise of the community college "rapidly being undermined [because] the public, and especially the four-year colleges and universities are shifting more and more responsibility onto the community colleges for undertaking the toughest tasks of higher education" (Newman, 1971, p. 57). However, such criticism is rare. Most commentators on higher education either offhandedly applaud the community college or, more frequently, totally ignore it.

Unstated Functions

The community college presents a remarkable success story, one that attests to our faith in institutions as solutions to social ills. How then view this school? Is it all it purports to be? What does it really offer?

The questions may be answered from any of several points of view. To an individual student graduating from high school and unsure of his next move, the college provides a socially acceptable place to spend time. A young man may take a few courses, drop out when he finds a job, drop back in if he loses the job, study a while longer, and then drift on. He may go into the armed services and find the college waiting for him when he returns. Prior academic failure is not a deterrent; universal absolution is granted—there is always a new program in which to enroll.

To the staff, the colleges provide prestigious positions. Nationwide, less than 7 per cent of the faculty holds doctoral degrees; hence most are disqualified from obtaining positions in major universities. Over one-third of the instructors are former secondary school teachers who may view junior college teaching as a step upward on the occupational ladder. The college also offers the allure of work in a growing enterprise with relatively fluid forms.

The college means many things to the community at large. Corporate managers view it as a source of trained personnel— an announcement of a need for skilled workers causes college administrators to trip over each other in their haste to organize a new technical curriculum. The parent of children who must be "educated" if they are to maintain a satisfactory social position sees his tax money well spent in an institution that guarantees their admission regardless of academic competition; in the large cities he may balk at supporting the elementary and secondary schools because of their top-heavy administrations and archaic practices, but the junior college promises new vision and offers different dreams.

Sorting and Certifying.   Above all, the community college must be viewed in the context of the public schools. Contrary to the claims of some of its well meaning advocates, it is not a magical entity that has arisen in a class by itself to solve the social ills of its time. Instead, it can be seen as one element in an educational establishment that is a straight-line system leading from kindergarten to the Ph.D. Since Ph.D.'s are being awarded at a rate of approximately one for every 112 children who entered elementary school twenty-five years ago, obviously, 111 people must be dropped along the way. Two generations ago, most of the dropout occurred between elementary school and high school. In this generation, more people leave between high school and the completion of the first two years of college than at any other point. Assuming that these trends continue, in a generation or two the problem of sorting and screening out will be one for the graduate schools to handle, but now it resides with the community colleges.

Illich (1970, 1971) and Reimer (1970) describe this sorting function, adding that the schools also act as indoctrinational agencies—convincing the young that people who have been to school are in some way better than people who have not and that, if a young person does not graduate, it is his own fault—not that of the school. For it is not enough for the college to screen its matriculants; it must make them believe they have an equal chance to succeed.

Defended and maintained assiduously, this (allocative) function is one of the strongest in the community college. Its manifestations are so entrenched that it is difficult for staff members to perceive how many of their practices are based on it. Beginning with the use of placement examinations—devices created for the purpose of finding dissimilarities among people—and grade marks earned at the lower schools, the institution places students into particular curriculums. Clark spells it out in *The Open Door College:* "The assistance is initially gentle. A common case is the student who wants to be an engineer but whose test scores and school grades indicate that he is a nearly hopeless candidate." The counselors do not insist that he stay away from the transfer program but push him gently toward a trades program, one more "consistent with his abilities." If the student insists on entering the college level courses, the "counselors can become more severe later in the sequence when they have grades as a talking point and the student is in trouble" (1960, pp. 71–72). Gradually the student is boxed in, forced to the decision that he cannot obtain an academic degree, that he must redirect his life goals.

The counselors are not alone the sorting agents; most other institutional procedures are based on "norms"; that is, whether a student is enrolled in a remedial course or a transfer course, he is sorted, judged, and screened in comparison with his fellows. The instructor whose mission is to sort people shuffles student responses to vague questions, placing ever finer discrimination upon them until the scores conform to a curve of normal distribution probabilities. He adjusts his "objective" test items so that his examinations are better able to discern shades of difference among the students. When his students cluster near the top of the scale on one examination, he makes the items more "difficult" on the next; if the scores are too low he prepares "easier" items. Back and forth he adjusts the "difficulty index" so that by the end of the course, if he has done well, his students' scores on a 100-item quiz range from 45 to 95 with a mean, median, and mode of 70. Whereupon the instructor announces, mirabile dictu, students *are* innately different and he has distinguished the differences. The allocative function has been well served. (This phenomenon is not confined to the community colleges by any means; it is a reality of schools at all levels. In 1970, the

Regents of the University of California appointed a committee to
investigate why so many A's were being given in certain classes.)

In defense of instructors and counselors, it must be said that
often they are unaware of the way they impose a selection process.
However, the sorting function is not always inadvertent. Frequently
it is defended as a genuine service to protect the higher schools from
the less able students and to accommodate the employers. If community colleges did not fail half of their entrants, universities would
be overrun. If they do not "redirect" sizeable numbers of the remaining students into occupational programs, the trades programs
would find few takers. For most students *go* to college to *be* in college; only rarely have they made fixed and firm occupational choices.
And if it were not for diplomas, how would employers know which
job applicants would tend to show up regularly and do what they
are told? The community must be served; the community college
must sort and certify the young. So the reasoning goes. Institutional
success in maintaining the allocative function is evidenced by high
and rapid student drop-out figures. On the average, one-half the
first-year dropout occurs during the first six weeks of the fall semester. Thus at minimum public expense, the student has been led
to believe that he has had a chance at college.

Sorting and certifying, then, is a major function of the community college. Formerly, public universities used the freshman year
as a protracted admissions screen. Those who failed abandoned college; the remainder were accorded serious treatment in upper-
division courses. Since community college systems have been developed in most states, the university is free to select its students by
use of College Board scores and high school grade-point averages,
sending the remainder to the community college. The fact that
many students still pound at university doors demanding open admissions merely points out that some refuse to accept an implied
second-class status.

Custodial. The custodial function, another in the educational critic's list of unacknowledged services performed, is played
well by the community college. Schools traditionally serve as cus-
todians. Elementary schools baby-sit; high schools keep young people off the streets; the community colleges hold them well into what
would have been adulthood in an earlier era. And strong remnants

of the custodial function still are found in the universities, particularly in residential institutions. The importance of the custodial function is well documented. Kistler, in a *Los Angeles Times* article (1971), noted how much crime had dropped during the day as soon as police instituted a campaign to pick up school truants. This is precrime incarceration, similar in intent to the pretrial detention of persons accused of crimes. It points up one of the most serious obstacles to true school reform at any level—the question of where young people would be if they were not in school.

The custodial function insures the continuation of many practices in the two-year college. Young people come to school and socialize. It is important that they be entertained because they might leave if the college were to become less attractive than a park, a neighborhood youth center, or the street. Thus "student activities" —a generic term for sports, clubs, and other functions—is continued in junior colleges even though these organized activities are played down in universities. Funding patterns support the custodial function. Roll is taken, and if the student is not in school, the institution does not get paid. Some states have allowed district reimbursement on the basis of credits obtained (Michigan, for example); but in most, the public school pattern of average daily attendance is retained. And what is the practice of granting draft deferments to students "in good standing" if it is not custody in another guise? School, jail, or the army—the young man is offered his choice of an institution with which to affiliate.

Enhancing Inequality. The community college fits in well with other elements that characterize the public schools. For example, each institution includes buildings and classrooms on a campus. No catalog states that such an institution tends to teach that education is a thing apart, a matter divorced from life or reality; yet campus and classroom communicate that message ever so firmly to the students. And the more instructional hardware that is placed within those buildings, the stronger the message.

The colleges also imply that some people are innately better than others. The magnitude of this assumption is best illustrated by perusing the array of euphemisms designed to describe the young people who attend. The phrase, "new" students, is being used as a synonym for "untraditional" students and is replacing earlier terms

such as "high risk," "culturally disadvantaged," or "culturally deprived." Yet the latter terms, out of favor, were introduced as substitutes for "slow learner" and "developmental" student. "Bonehead"
was abandoned even earlier. Each term communicates the true feelings of staff members about inequalities among people. Each is more
revealing than all protestation to the effect that the schools truly
maintain "open doors to opportunity" and "pathways to higher
status."

And, in the community college, the master-servant relationship that characterizes teachers and students at other levels of education is continued. Students learn that to suceed, one must perform meaningless tasks under direction, accept authority, and maintain an air of obsequiousness while speaking to superiors. Most community colleges are commuter institutions; students and instructors
alike drive to campus, park, meet in the highly stylized environment
of the classroom, and then part. Except for the few students who
join faculty-sponsored clubs, there is little teacher-student interaction
outside the confines of the classroom. Any human interchange that
does occur is fortuitous, similar to that which occurs at a rock concert or other place where young people gather. High school students
rebel; university students form "free" universities and "experimental"
colleges. Community college students accept the pattern of teacher-
student relationships or drop out.

Resultant Tensions.   The community colleges thus have
taken a place in the mainstream of education. Their apologists insist
they are dynamic and responsive to their communities. No doubt
they are, in comparison with most high schools and universities.
However, the dynamism is not a deliberate posture; it results from
tensions among disparate functions.

Examples of tensions abound. The sorting and certifying
function that insists students enter a fixed program and be judged
according to performance in relation to their fellows conflicts with
the custodial function that demands the students be kept in school
at any cost. It also conflicts with the belief that the more students
who are given an opportunity to go to college, the better off we are.
Or as Featherstone stated, "The notion of enlarging the potential of
bottom dogs flies in the face of one of the important, unstated func-

tions of the schools, which is to act as social sieves separating out those who make it from those who don't" (1969, p. 18).

Occasionally the underlying disparities surface as, for example, when a proposal is made to lower the minimum score a student must make on an entrance test if he is to be admitted to the "university parallel" courses. Which students are eligible for the transfer courses? Which require further developmental studies? Here the philosophical cleavage lines become apparent. For in this comprehensive institution, for every staff member who thinks the college should make a concerted effort to educate all students to the limit of their abilities, another one feels it his mission to protect the university from the unworthy because he uses the graduate department from which he obtained his degree as a reference group.

So far the tensions have been subordinated by rapid expansion of the colleges. Staff members have been so busy trying to meet ever-increasing enrollments (they rose thirteen per cent in 1970) that they have not had to reconcile the basic conflict in educational purposes. The colleges pride themselves on innovations and their readiness to institute new procedures. Does it matter that they rarely determine which procedures lead to greater satisfactions and better learning? Something newer will be introduced soon, anyway. Does it matter if hundreds of students drop out of school in the first few weeks of a semester? As soon as the new term begins, thousands will be there to take their places. A day of reckoning, of young people turning their backs on the whole enterprise, appears far off.

Trends

Where are they going? Separating recommendations from expectations is difficult but certain trends are evident. The Carnegie Commission (1970) envisions 230 to 280 new community colleges enrolling 35 to 40 per cent of all undergraduate students by 1980—providing that federal and state financial aid is augmented markedly. Medsker and Tillery (1971) anticipate increased centralization with state plans establishing guidelines for curriculum development, finance, and interinstitutional coordination. But the Newman report warns that this trend will lead to "the transformation of community institutions into amorphous, bland, increasingly large, increasingly state-dominated, two-year institutions which serve a number of interests other than that of their own students" (1971, p. 59). The colleges do seem destined to become more like each other with the long-applauded distinctive mission being swallowed up by comprehensiveness and by the tendency to absorb problems that the older, more prestigious segments of higher education have not been able to solve.

The function of the community college as a custodial institution is growing. The various Stay in School campaigns—coupled with the scarcity of attractive options—are having the intended effect. Fifty new colleges open each fall, teasing the last recalcitrant youths away from alternative pursuits. A college soon will be within commuting reach of nearly everyone. And when such a school stands ready to enroll a young person, it is difficult for him to find excuses for not attending.

Support for the custodial function comes from all quarters. The colleges provide opportunity for people of low socioeconomic status to move up through employment certification; hence, they delight the "new careers" protagonists. They also provide a net to keep the children of higher status parents from dropping down in social class. Barred from enrollment in any other institution of higher learning because of poor academic qualifications and/or a lackadaisical attitude toward school, these young people are being served in increasing number. They must be in college lest they drop out of the stratum in which their parents—skilled workers and professional people—are based. Thus, the same institution that allows for upward mobility also helps to prevent downward movement and gains the support of people who want to maintain position.

The allocative or sorting and certifying function is weakening; the trend is to move it to a higher-level school. One indication of this is the de facto abandonment of grade marks. In an increasing number of community colleges, a student may withdraw from a course without penalty at any time until the last week of the term. Many colleges no longer put failing marks on transcripts; if the student cannot earn a "C" or better, nothing appears on his record and he is given additional chances to "pass" the course. These practices seem to presage a "pass only" student marking system, one that will see courses open to students indefinitely or until they obtain certain levels of content mastery.

This increase in custodial effort and decrease in allocation has been occasioned, not by a philosophical shift, but by the fact that as more and more young people go to college there is less margin for allocating them to higher or lower positions based on the level of schooling attained. This phenomenon has long been felt in secondary schools. Two generations ago, when high schools were still dropping out large percentages of their entrants, allocation was one of their main functions. Now it has nearly disappeared, to be replaced with custody as the central effort. Two-year colleges are beginning to experience the same phenomenon. Practically everyone can attain an associate degree or a trade certificate; the question of who shall attain further schooling will be pushed back to the doors of universities where it was before community colleges came on the scene—this time to the upper division and graduate levels.

The community service function slowly is gaining strength. The use of community college students as tutors in the lower schools, the employment of noncertificated personnel as teacher aides, the branch counseling centers and other forms of reaching out from behind the college walls into the community are expanding in importance. An entire new career line titled "community service aide" has been designated as a way of formalizing the relationship between the college and the many people who associate with it in one capacity or another while working with other social agencies.

The future of the teaching/learning function itself is less clear. Community colleges long have prided themselves on their instructional operations, claiming that students receive more personal attention than they would get if they went to the university where professors are busy with other activities. And instructional technology makes steady inroads. There is no question that the community colleges adopt new hardware and instructional techniques more quickly than the universities or the secondary schools. Although a variety of teaching forms do not in themselves evidence a commitment to instruction as a central thrust, educational hardware and technological concepts may eventually push *instruction*—here defined as *a deliberate sequence of events arranged so that learning occurs*—to the fore. However, instruction in the two-year colleges—as in other schools—is still subordinate to the custodial and allocative functions and shows little upward movement.

Comprehensiveness of Intent. Comprehensiveness of intent demands large size and, indeed, many community college spokesmen point with pride to the growth in student enrollments (most community college students are on campuses with greater than 5,000 enrollment). It is difficult to attain comprehensiveness in a small institution—a complete offering of vocational-technical and liberal arts courses, counseling services, student activities, community services, teaching and testing, demands a large school. Each service calls forth its complement of professional and supportive staff. State level finance, region-wide accreditation, and newly emergent opportunities for service also point to larger structures. And enrollments show no sign of abating. However, it is possible that responsiveness to control by the community—the ideological cornerstone of the community college—will be weakened as the institutions and the concomitant administrative bureaucracies grow even larger.

When the community college was new and struggling for fiscal support, its leaders quickly seized upon every apparent function and offered to fulfill it. Now we should face the question of whether or not one institution can perform with equal facility all the tasks that have been undertaken by this post-secondary parvenu. Tension within an educational structure can be healthy if it leads to constant reexamination of function. However, the obvious anomalies in the custodial, allocative, and educative functions are not examined often enough. Decisions are made ad hoc, in a political arena; the philosophical bases to which they relate are left unstated. Whether one agency can do it all under one roof is unclear.

The issue is not that people do or do not possess different capabilities; it is whether or not it is the function of a school to attempt to find out whether it *can* so determine without adversely affecting its other roles. The issue is not that we do or do not need to keep our young off the streets and out of the labor force; it is whether or not a school can do this without affecting their growth untowardly. The question of whether or not people need to learn is not at issue; it is the extent to which they can do so in an institution that has taken on so many other functions. Perhaps the community needs separate agencies to perform all the functions of the community college. Perhaps not. It depends on one's view of society and one's faith in social institutions.

Alternative Functions. Are there better ways of performing the same functions? Illich (1970, 1971) insists we are so captured by schools that other schools are the only alternatives we can postulate. His "society without schools" has the appeal that most utopias possess; it also has the same likelihood of attainment. Some viable alternatives to improve the system can be formulated, however, short of the "de-schooling" called for by Illich. These would be community colleges that have freely acknowledged their real purposes, taken on deliberate functions, and made their institutional forms fit their purposes and objectives. They would still be subject to the ills of "institutionalization," but at least they can be built feasibly within the existing social context.

One plan sees the community colleges as attending strictly to teaching and learning on a defined outcomes basis, with the custodial and allocative functions being abandoned along with the massive buildings and campuses. This hypothetical college, detailed in *Dateline '79: Heretical Concepts for the Community College* (Cohen, 1969), has a corps of professional instructors specifying and articulating particularized learning objectives and preparing varieties of media to insure that all matriculants attain them. Not only have grade marks and other forms of sorting people been abandoned, students are also involved in situations other than the classroom; that is, many of its objectives have the students working in the community and learning on their own. In addition, whenever a person demonstrates his ability to achieve the prestated criterion level on the objectives—regardless of where he learned the skill or concept—he is given his credit and sent on.

Another type of community college could be set up to serve the guidance function only. This would be an agency that abandons all pretense of formalized classroom instruction, that offers only counseling services, psychological testing, and information about the various opportunities available for work, education, and community involvement. The sole intent of the institution would be to aid people in goal formulation and redirection. Still another college could be a true community service agency that would act as a coordinating form for a domestic Peace Corps. "Students" would tutor in the lower schools, serve as recreation counselors and parks attendants, and have their work apprenticeship experiences coordinated.

The custodial function is the most difficult to satisfy, primarily because a truly humanistic custodial institution is a contradiction. Still, each community could support a "place" for young people to go and learn, mature, and be entertained at public expense. It would offer concerts and films, records and paperback books, food and drink. It would have student-run shops, an open forum, the right of free assembly, and would promise no wider goals. No one would be certified for attending.

We do not suppose that the community college is about to divorce its present functions. Specialization demands deliberate vision, overt recognition of specific purpose. However, a voucher plan is on the horizon, and it will bring forth alternative formulations—if not different structures. Not that increasing the demand for services increases the supply (doubling the number of students who want to get into Harvard does not create new Harvard Colleges), but vouchering does hold the possibility of opening professional as well as public debate on what is being offered and what is being achieved in the colleges.

Institutionalism is insidious. We have a penchant for believing that, once a problem has been defined and an institution created to deal with it, we no longer need to think about it—the veteran has not been a "problem" since the Veterans Administration was organized. Similarly, education is not seen as a problem as long as schools are accessible. The community colleges thrive on this illusion. Their success is marked by their "providing opportunity for education." They are not called to account—nor do they hold themselves accountable—for the learning achieved by their students. They allow all people to attend; perhaps that is all they really ever promised.

No screening device—whether birth, status, money, or score attained on any test—ever has adequately predicted who will eventually perform society's tasks and attain personal satisfaction. Perhaps it is best to assume that intelligence is normally distributed, like any other trait, and that by expanding the absolute numbers of people who feel they have had a chance to be "educated," the schools have done all that can be done. If so, the community colleges are a roaring success. Still, such a view makes formal education seem a random event. One would hope we could do more with what we know about the processes of human learning.

ERIC: Educational Resources Information Center

Appendix

The Educational Resources Information Center (ERIC) is a program funded by the U.S. Department of Health, Education, and Welfare, Office of Education. It is dedicated to serving the field of education through the acquisition, analysis, synthesis, and dissemination of information. ERIC includes a central office staff in Washington, D.C., the ERIC Document Reproduction Service, and a network of twenty decentralized Clearinghouses. Each Clearinghouse gathers the documents pertinent to the segment of education it represents, indexes and abstracts them, and puts them into the ERIC system, where they are made available as follows: The abstracts are printed in *Research in Education,* a monthly publication available from the Government Printing Office, Washington, D.C. Full documents may be ordered in microfiche or hard copy form from ERIC Document Reproduction Service. The Clearinghouses also index journal articles and submit them to *Current Index to Journals in Education,* a publication of CCM Information Corporation, New York. Thus, the ERIC network operates as a documentation service bringing bibliographic order to the literature of education.

In addition to putting documents into the ERIC system, each Clearinghouse is charged with information analysis and synthesis. The Clearinghouses publish a variety of periodicals and occasional reports including bibliographies, document analyses, and information syntheses. Several hundred periodicals, journals, state-of-the-art reports, newsletters, and monographs emanate from the Clearinghouses annually.

ERIC Clearinghouse for Junior Colleges

The ERIC Clearinghouse for Junior Colleges, a joint project of the UCLA Graduate School of Education and the University Library, has as its target audience the community colleges of America. It acquires documents from, by, and about these colleges and processes them for the ERIC system. Junior college institutional research studies; dissertations and theses; miscellaneous reports, including surveys and other forms of studies prepared by state agencies and independent researchers; journal articles—all are grist for the ERIC mill. The Clearinghouse sorts the documents, sending some into the system and disposing of others in various ways. The staff also aids researchers and practitioners directly by performing literature searches, compiling special bibliographies—the extensive bibliography for this volume, for example—and instructing people in the use of the ERIC system. The Clearinghouse staff includes educational researchers, editors, and bibliographers, along with support personnel.

The Advisory Board to the Clearinghouse is made up of educators with primary interest in the community college. The following groups are permanently represented: the UCLA Graduate School of Education, the University Library, the Council of State Directors of Community Colleges, the American Association of Junior Colleges, and the American Educational Research Association's Special Interest Group in Junior College Research. Other delegates to the twelve-man board are appointed for two-year terms.

Publications

The Clearinghouse has three major publication series of its own: *Junior College Research Review,* Monographs, and Topical Papers. The *Research Review* is a synthesis of documents pertaining to single topics. Published ten times a year, it is available from the American Association of Junior Colleges at $3 per subscription. Articles in 1970–1971 issues of the *Review* have summarized research in the following areas: long-term research trends; cooperative work-experience programs; occupationally oriented students; entrance and placement testing; teacher education programs; paraprofessional programs; studies of student populations; alternatives in junior college education; and the teaching of English. Sample copies and back issues of the *Review* may be obtained from the Clearinghouse on request.

The Monographs are lengthy research syntheses. Each includes a literature review, a core of original research, and conclusions and recommendations. The following titles are available from the American Association of Junior Colleges at $2 each.

Salvage, Redirection, or Custody? Remedial Education in the Community Junior College. By John E. Roueche. 1968.

Junior College Institutional Research: The State of the Art. By John E. Roueche and John R. Boggs. 1969.

Personality Characteristics of College and University Faculty: Implications for the Community College. By Florence B. Brawer. 1969.

Measuring Faculty Performance. By Arthur M. Cohen and Florence B. Brawer. 1969.

Institutional Administrator or Educational Leader? The Junior College President. By Arthur M. Cohen and John E. Roueche. 1969.

Student Activism in Junior Colleges: An Administrator's Views. By John Lombardi. 1969.

The Multi-Institution Junior College District. By Frederick C. Kintzer, Arthur M. Jensen, and John S. Hansen. 1969.

State Master Plans for Community Colleges. By Allan S. Hurlburt. 1969.

Student Characteristics: Personality and Dropout Propensity. By Arthur M. Cohen and Florence B. Brawer. 1970.

Orientation for Faculty in Junior Colleges. By M. Frances Kelly and John Connolly. 1970.

Values and the Generation Gap: Junior College Freshmen and Faculty. By Florence B. Brawer. 1971.

Junior College Faculty: Their Values and Perceptions. By Young Park. 1971.

The Chief Student Personnel Administrator in the Public Two Year College. By Alice S. Thurston, Fredric B. Zook, Timothy Neher, and Joseph Ingraham. 1971.

The Topical Papers, the third series of Clearinghouse publications, offer research designs, statements of exemplary practices, and medium-length research reports. The following titles are available.

1. A Developmental Research Plan for Junior College Remedial Education. July 1968.

2. A Developmental Research Plan for Junior College Remedial Education; Number 2: Attitude Assessment. November 1968.

3. Student Activism and the Junior College Administrator: Judicial Guidelines. December 1968.

4. Students as Teachers. January 1969.

5. Is Anyone Learning to Write? February 1969.

6. Is It Really a Better Technique? March 1969.

7. A Developmental Research Plan for Junior College Remedial Education; Number 3: Concept Formation. August 1969.

8. The Junior College in International Perspective. January 1970.

9. Identifying the Effective Instructor. January 1970.

10. Financing Higher Education: A Proposal. February 1970.

11. The Person: A Conceptual Synthesis. March 1970.

12. The Position Papers of Black Student Activists. September 1970.

13. Case Studies in Multi-Media Instruction. October 1970.

14. The Laws Relating to Higher Education in the Fifty States, January 1965–December 1967. October 1970.

15. Nationwide Pilot Study on Articulation. November 1970.

16. The President's Reaction to Black Student Activism. January 1971.

17. The Dynamic Interaction of Student and Teacher. February 1971.

18. Directions for Research and Innovation in Junior College Reading Programs. February 1971.

19. Some Philosophical and Practical Concepts for Broadening the Base of Higher Education in Virginia. May 1971.

20. Skill Development in Junior College Reading Programs. April 1971.

21. Community College Reading Center Facilities. May 1971.

22. Black Studies as a Curriculum Catalyst. May 1971.

23. Exemplary Practices in Junior College Reading Instruction. May 1971.

24. Training Faculty for Junior College Reading Programs. May, 1971.

Clearinghouse staff members also prepare other information analysis products such as books and journal articles, discussing trends in the study of people and institutions, and examining value positions underlying the current ideas in the field of the community college. For a current publications list and other information, write to the ERIC Clearinghouse for Junior Colleges, 96 Powell Library Building, University of California, Los Angeles 90024.

Bibliography

Entries available through the ERIC Document Reproduction Service (P.O. Drawer O, Bethesda, Maryland 20014) are indicated by ED (ERIC Document) number. Prices for hard copy (HC) are $3.29 per unit of 100 pages or fewer; microfiche (MF) is $.65 per title, regardless of size. Payment should accompany orders of $10 or less and include state sales tax where applicable. No handling charge is required. ERIC documents may also be found in more than 400 libraries throughout the country.

ABBAS, R. D. *Interpersonal Values of the Junior College and University Student.* Columbia, Mo.: NDEA Institute, University of Missouri, 1968. 11 pp. (ED 023 390)

AGNEW, S. T. "Spiro T. Agnew on College Admissions." *College Board Review,* Spring 1970, 12–15.

AIKEN, J. *A Comparison of Junior College Withdrawees.* Columbia, Mo.: University of Missouri, 1968. 15 pp. (ED 023 389)

ALDRIDGE, J. H. "A Comparative Study of Ideas and Theories Concerning Junior Colleges of Educational Leaders: 1900–1935 and 1945–1960." Unpublished doctoral dissertation, Stanford University, 1968. 302 pp.

ALLEN, J. A. "The Community College and the Office of Education's Goals." In *Developing Junior Colleges.* Washington, D.C.: American Association of Junior Colleges, Nov. 29, 1969, 2–3.

American Association of Junior Colleges. *Developing Junior Colleges,* Mar. 19 (31); Oct. 10 (49); Nov. 29 (53). Washington, D.C., 1969.

American Association of Junior Colleges. *In-Service Training for Two-Year College Faculty and Staff: A Survey of Junior and Com-*

munity College Administrators. Washington, D.C., 1969. 80 pp. (ED 034 519)

American College Testing Program. *College Student Profiles—Norms for the ACT Assessment.* Iowa City, Iowa, 1966. 310 pp. (ED 011 763)

American Vocational Association. *AVA Washington Letter,* Oct. 27, 1970.

ANDERSON, J. E. *The Auto-Critique Method of Instructional Evaluation.* Pensacola, Fla.: Junior College Administrative Teams Institute, 1964. 15 pp. (ED 013 634)

ANDERSON, R. C. "Control of Student Mediating Processes During Verbal Learning and Instruction." *Review of Educational Research,* June 1970, *40*(3), 349–369.

ANDES, J. *"Due Process" for Junior College Students in Academic and Discipline Cases.* Gainesville, Fla.: Florida Community Junior College Inter-Institutional Research Council, University of Florida, 1970. 13 pp. (ED 038 126)

ANTHONY, D. M. "The Relationship of Certain Socioeconomic and Academic Factors to Student Choice of Occupation and Program in the Public Junior College." Unpublished doctoral dissertation, University of Texas, 1964. 240 pp. (ED 019 088; not avail. EDRS)

Appalachian State University. *A Preliminary Survey of the Academic Performance of Transfer Students Who Graduated in June, 1967.* Boone, N.C.: Appalachian State University, 1968. 8 pp. (ED 022 446)

Appalachian State University. *Improving Instruction in Two-Year College: Proceedings of a Conference for Two-Year College Teams.* Boone, N.C.: Appalachian State University, 1969. 86 pp. (ED 038 979)

APUZZO, M. P. *Summary Report on the Sixth Annual Conference on the Nature and Demands of Two-Year College Teaching.* Millbrook, N.Y.: Bennett College, June 16–21, 1968. 7 pp. (ED 025 232)

Arizona University. *Proposal for a Program for the M.A. in English with Emphasis on Teaching in the Junior College.* Tucson, Ariz.: Department of English, University of Arizona, 1969, 11 pp. (ED 027 866)

ARNWINE, J. E., AND JUBY, B. *An Objective Evaluation of the Success of Audio-Tutorial Course in General Biology.* Independence,

Kan.: Independence Community Junior College, 1969. 5 pp.
(ED 037 207)

AXEN, R. "Faculty Response to Student Dissent." In G. K. Smith
(Ed.), *Stress and Campus Response: Current Issues in Higher
Education 1968*. San Francisco: Jossey-Bass, 1968. pp. 106–114.

BAEHR, R. F. *Project Success*. Chicago: City Colleges of Chicago and
Kennedy-King College, 1969. 64 pp. (ED 039 870)

BAILEY, S. K. "Education and the Pursuit of Happiness." Sir John
Adams lecture given at the Graduate School of Education, University of California, Los Angeles, Apr. 28, 1971.

BAIRD, L. L. *The Undecided Student—How Different Is He?* Iowa City,
Iowa: American College Testing Program, 1967. 24 pp. (ED
017 230)

BAIRD, L. L., RICHARDS, J. M., JR., SHEVEL, L. R. "A Description of
Graduates of Two-Year Colleges." In *The Two-Year College
and Its Students: An Empirical Report*. Iowa City, Iowa:
American College Testing Program, 1969. 152 pp. (ED 035
404)

BANATHY, B. H. *Instructional Systems*. Belmont, Calif.: Fearon, 1968.
106 pp.

BANISTER, R. E. *Setting the Stage for Change in the Junior College—
A Case Study*. Los Angeles: Graduate School of Education,
University of California, 1968. 32 pp. (ED 019 056)

BANISTER, R. E. *Case Studies in Multi-Media Instruction*. ERIC Clearinghouse for Junior Colleges, Topical Paper 13. Los Angeles:
University of California, 1970. 61 pp. (ED 044 098)

BANNISTER, J., AND OTHERS. "Evaluating College Teaching." In
Curriculum Reporter, Supplement #1. San Jose, Calif.: San
Jose State College, 1961. 8 pp. (ED 022 450)

BARLOW, M. L. "Vocational Education in the Fabulous Future." *American Vocational Journal*, Oct. 1962, *37*, 9–11.

BARNES, D. *Teaching Strategies for the Clarification of Values*. Grand
Rapids, Mich.: Northview Public Schools, 1968. 23 pp. (ED
025 784)

BEAN, A., AND HENDRIX, V. L. *The Mini-College, Spring 1968*. Dallas:
Dallas County Junior College District, 1968. 24 pp. (ED 029
640)

BERG, E. H., AND AXTELL, D. *Programs for Disadvantaged Students in
the California Community Colleges*. Oakland, Calif.: Peralta
Junior College District, 1968. 97 pp. (ED 026 032)

BERTRAMI, A. *A Description of the Psychological Environment of Students at the Agricultural and Technical College at Delhi*. Delhi, N.Y.: Agricultural and Technical College at Delhi, 1969. 23 pp. (ED 034 512; avail. EDRS on MF only)

BESSIRE, J. D. *Student Rights Statement*. Monterey, Calif.: Monterey Peninsula College, 1969. 8 pp. (ED 030 426)

BETZ, R. *The Project Consultant: His Unique Role*. Washington, D.C.: American Personnel and Guidance Association, 1969.

BILLINGSLEY, A., AND OTHERS. "Ethnic Studies at Berkeley." *California Monthly*, June–July 1970, *80*, 12–20.

BIRKHOLZ, J. R. *A Faculty Internship Program for William Rainey Harper College*. Palatine, Ill.: William Rainey Harper College, 1969. 108 pp. (ED 035 407)

BLAI, B., JR. *Job Satisfactions and Work Values for Women*. Bryn Mawr, Pa.: Office of Institutional Research, Harcum Junior College, 1970a. 15 pp. (ED 040 705)

BLAI, B., JR. "Values and Attitudes of Harcum Students and Faculty-Staff." Bryn Mawr, Pa.: Office of Institutional Research, Harcum Junior College, 1970b. 13 pp.

BLOCKER, C. E. *Dissent and the College Student in Revolt*. Paper presented to the Annual Convention of the American Association of Junior Colleges, Atlanta, 1969. 21 pp. (ED 027 900)

BLOCKER, C. E., PLUMMER, R. H., RICHARDSON, R. C. *The Two-Year College. A Social Synthesis*. Englewood Cliffs, N.J.: Prentice-Hall, 1965. 298 pp.

BLOESSER, R., AND OTHERS. *Study Skills Project, Spring, 1968, Foothill College*. Cupertino, Calif.: Foothill Junior College District, 1968. 17 pp. (ED 022 437)

BLOOM, B. S. (Ed.) *Taxonomy of Educational Objectives, I*. New York: McKay, 1956. 207 pp.

BOGUE, J. P. *The Community College*. New York: McGraw-Hill, 1950. 390 pp.

BORNHOLDT, L. "Black Studies: Perspective, 1970." *Danforth News and Notes*, March 1970, *5*, 1.

BOSSEN, D. A., AND BURNETT, C. W. "What Happens to the Withdrawal Student?" *Junior College Journal*, June–July 1970, *40*, 30–36.

BOSSONE, R. M. *The Reading-Study-Skills Problems of Students in Community Colleges of the City University of New York*. New York: City University of New York, 1970. 110 pp. (ED 039 866)

BRADLEY, R. L. "Lecture Demonstration Versus Individual Laboratory

Work in a General Education Science Course." *Journal of Experimental Education,* 1965, *34,* 33–42.

BRANN, J. "Guest Opinion . . . ." In *Edcentric.* Washington, D.C.: Center for Educational Reform, Sept.–Oct. 1970.

BRAWER, F. B. "The Concept of Ego Strength and Its Measurement Through a Word Association Technique." Unpublished doctoral dissertation, University of California, Los Angeles, 1967.

BRAWER, F. B. *Personality Characteristics of College and University Faculty: Implications for the Community College.* ERIC Clearinghouse for Junior Colleges, Monograph 3. Washington, D.C.: American Association of Junior Colleges, 1968. 104 pp. (ED 026 048)

BRAWER, F. B. *The Person: A Conceptual Synthesis.* ERIC Clearinghouse for Junior Colleges, Topical Paper 11. Los Angeles: University of California, 1970. 63 pp. (ED 037 219)

BRAWER, F. B. "Student Studies: Comparative and Remedial Populations." *Junior College Research Review,* Mar. 1971a, *5*(7). 4 pp. (ED 047 665)

BRAWER, F. B. *Values and the Generation Gap: Junior College Freshmen and Faculty.* ERIC Clearinghouse for Junior Colleges, Monograph 11. Washington, D.C.: American Association of Junior Colleges, 1971b. 66 pp. (ED 050 724)

BRAWER, F. B., AND COHEN, A. M. "Global and Sign Approaches to Rorschach Assessment of Beginning Teachers." *Journal of Projective Techniques and Personality Assessment,* Dec. 1966, *30,* 536–542.

BRIGGS, L. G., AND OTHERS. *Instructional Media: A Procedure for the Design of Multi-Media Instruction.* Pittsburgh: American Institute for Research, 1967.

BRIGHT, R. L. "Research in Educational Technology." *Educom,* Dec. 1967, *2,* 6–9.

BRIGHTMAN, R. W. *Strategies for Change: A Case Study of Innovative Practices at the Coast Community College District.* Costa Mesa, Calif.: Orange Coast College, May 1971. 152 pp.

BROWN, J. W., AND THORNTON, J. W., JR. *College Teaching.* New York: McGraw-Hill, 1963a. 260 pp.

BROWN, J. W., AND THORNTON, J. W., JR. *New Media in Higher Education.* Washington, D.C.: Association for Higher Education, 1963b.

BURNS, H. "To: Friends of the Inner-City Minority Community and

Friends of the Los Angeles Trade-Technical College." Los Angeles, Nov. 12, 1970.

BURNS, M. A. *New Careers in Human Service: A Challenge to the Two-Year College.* Report 8. University Park, Pa.: Center for the Study of Higher Education, Pennsylvania State University, 1971. 87 pp. (ED 049 732)

BUTLER, R. R. *Differences in Need-Press Variables as Perceived by University and Junior College Students.* Columbia, Mo.: NDEA Institute, University of Missouri, 1968. 11 pp. (ED 023 386)

CALHOUN, C. E. "Some Thoughts I Leave Behind: The Exposure of a Soul." Address presented at Miles College, Miles City, Mont., Sept. 13, 1970.

California Junior College Association. *Automation and Agitation: Today's Junior College Student (Do Not Fold, Spindle, Mutilate, or Bend).* Pacific Grove, Calif.: Conference for Chief Administrators of Student Personnel, Jan. 10–12, 1968. 44 pp. (ED 024 398)

California State Department of Education. "Summary of Source and Education Background of New Teachers in California Junior Colleges, 1963–1964." n.p.: n.d.

CAMPBELL, C. E. *Innovation in Health Education at the Junior College.* Los Angeles: University of California, 1968. 25 pp. (ED 019 054)

CAMPBELL, R., AND BOYD, W. L. "Organizational Alternatives for Secondary Schools." *The North Central Association Quarterly,* Fall 1970, *45,* 239–247.

CAPLOW, T., AND MC GEE, R. J. *The Academic Marketplace.* New York: Basic Books, 1958. 226 pp.

CAPPER, M. R. (Comp.) *Instructional Objectives for Junior College Courses.* Los Angeles: ERIC Clearinghouse for Junior Colleges, University of California, 1969. (ED 033 679 to ED 033 717)

CAREY, R. V. "The Need for Vocational-Industrial Education in the Junior College." *California Industrial Education Association News,* Apr.–May 1968 (22).

Carnegie Commission on Higher Education. *The Open-Door Colleges: Policies for Community Colleges. A Special Report and Recommendations by the Commission.* New York: McGraw-Hill, 1970. 74 pp.

Carnegie Corporation of New York. "The Doctor of Arts: A High Degree of Teaching Competence." *Carnegie Quarterly,* Winter–Spring 1970, *18,* 1–3.

CARPENTER, M. "The Role of Experimental Colleges in American Higher Education." In W. H. Stickler (Ed.), *Experimental Colleges.* Tallahassee, Fla.: Florida State University, 1964. 185 pp.

CARZO, R., JR., AND YANOUZAS, J. N. *Formal Organization: A Systems Approach.* Homewood, Ill.: Irwin, 1967. 501 pp.

CELLURA, A. R. "The Application of Psychological Theory in Educational Settings: An Overview." *American Educational Research Journal,* May 1969, *6,* 349–382.

CHADBOURNE, J. P. *The Future Is Now! Report of a Workshop for New Junior College Deans of Instruction.* Los Angeles: Junior College Leadership Program, University of California, 1969. 22 pp. (ED 032 885)

CHALGHIAN, S. "Success for Marginal Students." *Junior College Journal,* Sept. 1969, *40,* 28–30.

CHRISTOPHER, J. L. *Certain Aspects of the Teachers' Role in Wyoming Junior Colleges with Implications for Program Planning and Improvement.* Laramie, Wyo.: University of Wyoming, 1966. 230 pp. (ED 014 312)

CLARK, B. R. *The Open Door College: A Case Study.* New York: McGraw-Hill, 1960. 207 pp.

CLARKE, J. R. "A Curriculum Design for Disadvantaged Community Junior College Students." Unpublished doctoral dissertation, University of Florida, 1966. 151 pp. (ED 015 754; not avail. EDRS)

COHEN, A. M. "Teacher Preparation—Rationale and Practice." *Junior College Journal,* May 1967, *37,* 21–25. (ED 013 088)

COHEN, A. M. *Dateline '79: Heretical Concepts for the Community College.* Beverly Hills, Calif.: Glencoe, 1969. 234 pp.

COHEN, A. M. "A Hierarchy of Disciplinarianism." Los Angeles: Graduate School of Education, University of California, 1970a.

COHEN, A. M. "Education in the Two-Year College." In D. G. HAYES (Ed.), *Britannica Review of American Education.* Vol. 1. Chicago: Encyclopaedia Britannica, 1970b. pp. 123–136.

COHEN, A. M. *Objectives for College Courses.* Beverly Hills, Calif.: Glencoe, 1970c. 140 pp.

COHEN, A. M. "Technology: Thee or Me? Behavioral Objectives and the College Teacher." *Educational Technology,* Nov. 1970d, *10,* 57–60.

COHEN, A. M., AND BRAWER, F. B. "Adaptive Potential and First-Year

Teaching Success." *Journal of Teacher Education,* Summer 1967, *18,* 179–184.

COHEN, A. M., AND BRAWER, F. B. *Focus on Learning—Preparing Teachers for the Two-year College.* Los Angeles: University of California Junior College Leadership Program, 1968. 66 pp. (ED 019 939)

COHEN, A. M., AND BRAWER, F. B. *Measuring Faculty Performance.* ERIC Clearinghouse for Junior Colleges, Monograph 4. Washington, D.C.: American Association of Junior Colleges, 1969. 90 pp. (ED 031 222)

COHEN, A. M., AND BRAWER, F. B. *Student Characteristics: Personality and Dropout Propensity.* ERIC Clearinghouse for Junior Colleges, Monograph 9. Washington, D.C.: American Association of Junior Colleges, 1970. 69 pp. (ED 038 130)

COHEN, A. M., AND BRAWER, F. B. *Confronting Identity: The Community College Instructor.* Englewood Cliffs, N.J.: Prentice-Hall, 1972.

COHEN, A. M., AND SHAWL, W. F. "Coordinating Instruction Through Objectives." *Junior College Journal,* Oct. 1970, *41,* 17–19.

COHEN, E. *Faculty for Teaching-Learning: Proposed New Graduate Centers for the Systematic Preparation of Community College Teachers.* Pennington, N.J., 1970. 281 pp. (ED 038 133)

College Entrance Examination Board. *Comparative Guidance and Placement Program for Junior Colleges.* Princeton, N.J.: Educational Testing Service, 1968. 85 pp. (ED 026 053)

COLLINS, C. C. *Junior College Student Personnel Programs—What They Are and What They Should Be.* Washington, D.C.: American Association of Junior Colleges, 1967. 57 pp. (ED 011 459)

COLVERT, C. C., AND BAKER, M. L. *The Status of College and University Offerings and Services in the Area of Junior College Education and Professional Upgrading of Junior College Faculty Members.* Austin, Tex.: Research Office, American Association of Junior Colleges, 1955.

COOLEY, W. W., AND BECKER, S. J. "The Junior College Student." *Personnel and Guidance Journal,* Jan. 1966, *44,* 464–469. (ED 012 609)

COREY, G. F. *An Investigation of the Outcomes of Introductory Psychology.* Whittier, Calif.: Rio Hondo Junior College, 1967. 12 pp. (ED 014 966)

GOSAND, J. P. "Community/Junior Colleges: An Analysis of Their Sociological Impact." Address delivered at the annual meeting of the College Entrance Examination Board, New York, Oct. 28, 1965. 5 pp.

COSAND, J. P. "The Community College in 1980." In A. C. Eurich (Ed.), *Campus 1980*. New York: Delacorte, 1968.

COSAND, J. P. Address delivered at the annual meeting of the College Entrance Examination Board, New York, Oct. 28, 1969. 14 pp.

COUCH, J. R. *An Experiment to Determine the Effectiveness of a Summer Preparatory Program at Spartanburg Junior College.* Spartanburg, S.C.: Spartanburg Junior College, 1969. 41 pp. (ED 031 242)

CROSS, K. P. *The Junior College Student: A Research Description.* Princeton, N.J.: Educational Testing Service, 1968. 56 pp. (ED 024 354)

CROSS, K. P. "The Quiet Revolution." *The Research Reporter,* 1969, *4,* 3.

CROSS, K. P. "Occupationally Oriented Students." *Junior College Research Review,* Nov. 1970. 4 pp. (ED 043 328)

DALTON, M. *Men Who Manage.* New York: Wiley, 1961. 318 pp.

DAVE, J. P. *Evaluation of the Developmental Program: Fall 1967–1968.* Chicago: Central YMCA Community College, 1968. 116 pp. (ED 024 357)

DE LOACHE, D. F. "Attitudes and Opinions of Faculty Members and Junior College Presidents Toward Selected Descriptions of the Office of College President." Unpublished doctoral dissertation, University of Oklahoma, 1966. 134 pp. (ED 022 433; not avail. EDRS)

DENNISON, J. D., AND JONES, G. *A Study of the Characteristics and Subsequent Performance of Vancouver City College Students Who Transferred to the University of British Columbia in September 1967.* Vancouver, B.C.: Vancouver City College, 1968. 84 pp. (ED 026 061)

Diablo Valley College. "Ethnic Studies." In *Schedule of Classes, 1970.* Pleasant Hill, Calif., 1970. pp. 57–62.

DISTASIO, P. J., AND GREENBERG, B. *Community Services: A Center for Community Development.* Washington, D.C.: American Association of Junior Colleges, 1969. 8 pp. (ED 032 053)

DODDS, H. W. *The Academic President—Educator or Caretaker?* New York: McGraw-Hill, 1962. 294 pp.

DRESSEL, P. L. *College and University Curriculum.* Berkeley, Calif.: McCutchan, 1968. 232 pp.

DRESSEL, P. L., AND DE LISLE, F. H. *Undergraduate Curriculum Trends.*

Washington, D.C.: American Council on Education, 1969. 83 pp.

DRUCKER, P. F. *The Age of Discontinuity: Guidelines to Our Changing Society.* New York: Harper and Row, 1969. 402 pp.

DUBIN, R., AND TAVEGGIA, T. C. *The Teaching-Learning Paradox: A Comparative Analysis of College Teaching Methods.* Eugene, Ore.: Center for the Advanced Study of Educational Administration, University of Oregon, 1968. 78 pp.

DUNHAM, E. A. *Colleges of the Forgotten Americans: A Profile of State Colleges and Regional Universities.* New York: McGraw-Hill, 1969. 206 pp.

EATON, J. M. "A Study of Orientation of New Faculty Members in Michigan Community Colleges." Unpublished doctoral dissertation, Michigan State University, 1964. 115 pp. (ED 023 373; not avail. EDRS)

EBLE, K. E. *The Recognition and Evaluation of Teaching.* Washington, D.C.: American Association of University Professors, 1970.

EELLS, W. C. *The Junior College.* Boston: Houghton Mifflin, 1931. 833 pp.

ELLERBROOK, W. L. "Pre-Service and In-Service Training of Junior College Teachers." Unpublished term paper, University of Texas, 1968. 23 pp. (ED 026 983)

ELSNER, P. A. *The Presidential Prism: Four Views: A State Officer's View of the Community College President.* Address given at the Junior College Leadership Program's Presidents' Institute, Scottsdale, Ariz., May 6, 1969. 14 pp. (ED 032 059)

ERICKSON, C. G. "The Two-Year College." *Journal of Higher Education,* May 1970, *41,* 409–412.

Erie County Technical Institute. *Recruitment Survey, 1968: An Institute Research Report.* Buffalo, N.Y., 1968. 19 pp. (ED 027 864)

EVANS, R. I., AND LEPPMANN, P. K. *Resistance to Innovation in Higher Education: A Social Psychological Exploration Focused on Television and the Establishment.* San Francisco: Jossey-Bass, 1967. 198 pp.

FEATHERSTONE, J. "The Talent Corps: Career Ladders for Bottom Dogs." *The New Republic,* Sept. 6/13, 1969, *161*(10/11), 17–23.

FEIRER, J. L., AND LINDBECK, J. R. *Development of Junior-Community College Curricula for Future Teachers of Industrial Education.*

Interim report. Washington, D.C.: Bureau of Research, U.S. Office of Education, 1970. 580 pp. (ED 039 884)

FELDMAN, K. A., AND NEWCOMB, T. M. *The Impact of College on Students.* San Francisco: Jossey-Bass, 1969. 474 pp.

FELDMAN, M. J. *Public Education and Manpower Development.* New York: Office of Reports, Ford Foundation, 1967.

FELTY, J. *A Feasibility and Planning Study for an Experimental, Two-Year Community College for Rural and Urban Youth.* Final report. Washington, D.C.: Bureau of Research, U.S. Office of Education, 1969. 512 pp. (ED 040 704)

FENSKE, R. H. "Who Selects Vocational-Technical, Post-High School Education?" In *The Two-Year College and Its Students: An Empirical Report.* Iowa City, Iowa: American College Testing Program, 1969. 152 pp. (ED 035 404)

FERRARI, M. R., AND BERTE, N. R. *American Junior Colleges: Leadership and Crucial Issues for the 1970's.* Kent, Ohio: Department of Management, Kent State University, 1969. 20 pp. (ED 035 398)

FIELDS, R. R. *The Community College Movement.* New York: McGraw-Hill, 1962. 360 pp.

FIGHTMASTER, W. J. *Establishing and Expanding a Community Services Program.* Community Services Working Paper 4. Washington, D.C.: American Association of Junior Colleges, 1969. 61 pp. (ED 037 193)

FINCH, R. "Secretary Finch Outlines Community College Plans." In *Developing Junior Colleges.* Washington, D.C.: American Association of Junior Colleges, Oct. 10, 1969. p. 1.

FISHER, J. R., AND LIEBERMAN, L. R. *Student and Faculty Views Concerning the Summer Trial Program at GSC.* Americus, Ga.: Georgia Southwestern College, 1965. 23 pp. (ED 015 737)

FITCH, R. J. *An Investigation of the "Cooling-Out" Process in the Junior College as Indicated by Changes of Major.* Los Angeles: University of California, 1969. 59 pp. (ED 039 868; avail. EDRS on MF only)

FLIZAK, C. W. *Organizational Structure and Teacher Role Orientation.* Chicago: University of Chicago, 1968. 4 pp. (ED 027 628)

Florida Community Junior College Inter-Institutional Research Council. *Where Are They Now? A Follow-up of First Time in College Freshmen in Florida's Community Junior Colleges in Fall 1966.* Gainesville, Fla., 1969. 56 pp. (ED 035 396)

FOX, L. J. "A Study of Relationships Between Grades and Measures of

Scholastic Aptitude, Creativity, and Attitudes in Junior College Students." Unpublished doctoral dissertation, University of Southern California, 1967. 312 pp.

FRASE, L. T. "Boundary Conditions for Mathemagenic Behaviors." *Review of Educational Research,* June 1970, *40,* 337–347.

FRENCH, S. J., AND COOPER, R. M. *Pilot Project for Improving College Teaching—The Florida College Teaching Project.* Tampa, Fla.: University of Southern Florida, 1967. 142 pp. (ED 013 083)

FRIEDMAN, N. L. "The Public Junior College Teacher in Unified Public School System Junior Colleges: A Study in the Sociology of Educational Work." Unpublished doctoral dissertation, University of Missouri, 1965. 145 pp. (ED 034 550; not avail. EDRS)

FRIEDMAN, N. L. "Career Stages and Organizational Role Decisions of Teachers in Two Public Junior Colleges." *Sociology of Education,* Summer 1967, *40,* 231–245. (ED 018 178; not avail. EDRS)

GADDY, D. *Student Activism and the Junior College Administrator: Judicial Guidelines.* ERIC Clearinghouse for Junior Colleges, Topical Paper 3. Los Angeles: University of California, 1968. 47 pp. (ED 026 039)

GADDY, D. *The Scope of Organized Student Protest in Junior Colleges.* Washington, D.C.: American Association of Junior Colleges, 1970. 30 pp. (ED 045 076)

GALLAGHER, E. A. "From Tappan to Lange: Evolution of the Public Junior College Idea." Unpublished doctoral dissertation, University of Michigan, 1968. 259 pp. (ED 041 584; not avail. EDRS)

GARRISON, R. H. *Junior College Faculty: Issues and Problems.* Washington, D.C.: American Association of Junior Colleges, 1967. 99 pp. (ED 012 177)

GETZELS, J. W. "Administration as a Social Process." In A. W. Halpin (Ed.), *Administrative Theory in Education.* New York: Macmillan, 1958. 185 pp.

GILES, F. T. "Selecting and Securing a Junior College President." In *The Junior College President.* Occasional Report 13. Los Angeles: Junior College Leadership Program, University of California, 1969. pp. 33–41. (ED 031 227)

GILLILAND, J. R., AND NUNNERY, M. Y. "Florida Trustees: Characteristics and Opinions." *Junior College Journal,* Feb. 1970, *40,* 25–29.

GLADSTONE, D. (Ed.) *1969 Guide to In-Service Training for Two-Year College Faculty and Staff Members*. Washington, D.C.: American Association of Junior Colleges, 1969. 35 pp. (ED 027 019)

GLEAZER, E. J., JR. "Preparation of Junior College Teachers." *Educational Record*, Spring 1967, *48*, 147–152. (ED 016 489; not avail. EDRS)

GLEAZER, E. J., JR. *This Is the Community College*. Boston: Houghton Mifflin, 1968. 151 pp. (ED 026 063; not avail. EDRS)

GOLD, B. K. *Religious Attitudes of College Students at Harvard University, Radcliffe College, and Los Angeles City College—Highlights of Comparative Studies Made in 1946–48 and in 1966–67*. Los Angeles: Los Angeles City College, 1967a. 18 pp. (ED 013 073)

GOLD, B. K. *Some Characteristics of Los Angeles City College Transfers Who Earned Academic Honors at UCLA*. Los Angeles: Los Angeles City College, 1967b. 8 pp. (ED 016 478)

GOLD, B. K. *The Developmental Studies Program: Some Scholarship and Persistence Statistics*. Los Angeles: Los Angeles City College, 1968a. 20 pp. (ED 026 043)

GOLD, B. K. *Project Summer '67, An Experimental Program for Educationally Disadvantaged Youth—An Evaluation*. Los Angeles: Los Angeles City College, 1968b. 35 pp. (ED 018 180)

GOLD, B. K. *Survey of Faculty Regarding Campus Incidents of March 10–14*. Los Angeles: Los Angeles City College, 1969. 15 pp. (ED 030 423)

GOLDBERG, I., AND DAILEY, J. T. "Research on Academic Degree Projections: The Identification and Development of Talents of 1960 High School Graduates." Unpublished manuscript, Project Talent (Palo Alto, Calif.), 1963.

GOOD, W. E., AND OTHERS. *Faculty Profile: Kansas Community Junior Colleges*. Hutchinson, Kan.: Hutchinson Community College, 1968. 17 pp. (ED 023 392)

GOODLAD, J. I., AND RICHTER, M. N., JR. *The Development of a Conceptual System for Dealing with Problems of Curriculum and Instruction*. Los Angeles: Institute for Development of Educational Activities, University of California, 1966. 59 pp.

GOODRICH, A. "Crisis in the Country: Statement by Black Junior College Leaders." Washington, D.C.: American Association of Junior Colleges, 1970.

GORDON, S. B., AND WHITFIELD, R. P. "A Formula for Teacher Preparation." *Junior College Journal,* May 1967, *37,* 26–28. (ED 016 488)

GREENBERG, B. *Inner College: A Report of the Spring, 1970 Experiment.* Miami: Miami-Dade Junior College, 1970. 16 pp. (ED 040 712; avail. EDRS on MF only)

GROSS, R., AND MURPHY, J. *Learning by Television.* New York: Fund for the Advancement of Education, 1966. 95 pp.

GROUT, D. R. "Psychological Security-Insecurity of Illinois Central College Students." Unpublished master's thesis, Illinois State University, 1969. 130 pp. (ED 037 196)

GUSFIELD, J., AND RIESMAN, D. "Faculty Culture and Academic Careers." In K. Yamamoto (Ed.), *The College Student and His Culture: An Analysis.* Boston: Houghton Mifflin, 1968. 493 pp.

HADDEN, J. K. "The Private Generation." *Psychology Today,* Oct. 1969, *3,* 32–36.

HALL, C., AND LINDZEY, G. "The Relevance of Freudian Psychology and Related Viewpoints for the Social Sciences." In G. Lindzey and E. Aronson (Eds.), *The Handbook of Social Psychology.* Vol. 1. Reading, Mass.: Addison-Wesley, 1957.

HALL, L. H. "Personality and Attitude Variables Among Achieving and Nonachieving College of the Sequoias Freshmen from Different Socioeconomic Backgrounds." n.p.: 1968. 6 pp. (ED 027 016)

HAMILL, R. E. "The Effects of Teachers in Four-year Colleges and Universities as Reference Groups for Teachers in Community Colleges." Unpublished doctoral dissertation. Eugene, Ore.: University of Oregon, 1967. 98 pp. (ED 017 260; not avail. EDRS)

HAMILTON, C. V. "Relevance of Black Studies." In G. K. Smith (Ed.), *Agony and Promise: Current Issues in Higher Education 1969.* San Francisco: Jossey-Bass, 1969.

HAMILTON, C. V. *Journal of Black Studies,* Sept. 1970, 8.

HARDING, V. "Black Students and the Impossible Revolution." *Journal of Black Studies,* Sept. 1970a, *1,* 75–100.

HARDING, V. "Toward the Black University." *Ebony,* Aug. 1970b, *25,* 158.

HARLACHER, E. L. *The Community Dimension of the Community College.* Englewood Cliffs, N.J.: Prentice-Hall, 1969. 140 pp.

HARMON, S. J. "Effects of a Multi-Media Environment in College-Level Electronics." Unpublished doctoral dissertation, Colorado State College, 1969. 167 pp.

HARPER, W. A. (Ed.) *1970 Junior College Directory.* Washington, D.C.: American Association of Junior Colleges, 1970. 112 pp.

Harrisburg Area Community College. *Meeting the Changing Needs of Students: Curriculum Development.* Monograph 2. Harrisburg, Pa., 1970. 16 pp. (ED 038 136)

Harrisburg Area Community College. *Meeting the Changing Needs of Students: Variations in Methods of Instruction.* Monograph 3. Harrisburg, Pa., 1970. 22 pp. (ED 038 137)

HAYES, G. E. *Junior College Work Experience Education.* Los Angeles: University of California, 1969. 24 pp. (ED 035 397)

HEATH, R. *The Reasonable Adventurer.* Pittsburgh: University of Pittsburgh Press, 1964. 165 pp.

HECHINGER, F. M. "A Call for More and Better Community Colleges." *New York Times,* June 28, 1970, Sec. 4, p. 9.

HEINKEL, O. A. *Evaluation of a General Studies Program for the Potentially Low Academic Achiever in California Junior Colleges: Final Report.* Washington, D.C.: Bureau of Research, U.S. Office of Education, 1970. 75 pp. (ED 039 881)

HEINZ, E. *Student Opinion Survey.* El Cajon, Calif.: Grossmont College, 1967. 45 pp. (ED 017 233)

HEIST, P., AND OTHERS. *Omnibus Personality Inventory.* New York: Psychological Corporation, 1968.

HENDRIX, V. L. "Relationships Between Personnel Policies and Faculty Life-Record Data in Public Junior Colleges." *California Journal of Educational Research,* 1964, *15*(3), 150–157. (ED 015 747)

HENDRIX, V. L. *Functional Relationships of Junior College Environments and Selected Characteristics of Faculties, Students, the Administration, and the Community.* Minneapolis: University of Minnesota, 1967. 421 pp. (ED 026 986)

HENRY, N. B. (Ed.) "The Public Junior College." In *The Fifty-Fifth Yearbook of the National Society for the Study of Education.* Part 1. Chicago: University of Chicago Press, 1966.

HIGHET, G. *The Art of Teaching.* New York: Vintage, 1950. 291 pp.

HILLS, J. R. "Transfer Shock—The Academic Performance of the Junior College Transfer." *Journal of Experimental Education,* Spring 1965, *33,* 201–215. (ED 010 740)

HILLWAY, T. *The American Two-Year College.* New York: Harper and Row, 1958. 276 pp.

HORVATH, R. J. *Community Relations: A Practical Approach.* n.p.: 1969. 8 pp.

HOUSKA, R. B. "Postsecondary Education: A Model for Getting It All Together." *College Board Review,* Fall 1970, *77,* 13–15.

HOYT, D. P., AND MUNDAY, L. "Academic Description and Prediction in

Junior Colleges." In *The Two-Year College and Its Students: An Empirical Report.* Iowa City, Iowa: American College Testing Program, 1969. pp. 108–120. (ED 035 404)

HUGHES, H. G., AND OTHERS. *A Follow-up Study of Discontinuing Students at Grossmont College.* El Cajon, Calif.: Grossmont College, 1968. 36 pp. (ED 019 985)

HUNT, B. J. "Characteristics, Perceptions and Experiences of Married Women Students at Lansing Community College, 1965." Unpublished doctoral dissertation, Michigan State University, 1966. 227 pp.

HUNT, F. J. "The Role of the Faculty in Organization Change in Junior Colleges." Unpublished doctoral dissertation, Stanford University, 1964. 258 pp. (ED 024 396; not avail. EDRS)

HUNTER, W. E. "A Systems Approach to Teaching and Learning." In B. L. Johnson (Ed.), *The Improvement of Junior College Instruction.* Junior College Leadership Program, Occasional Report 15. Los Angeles: University of California, 1970. pp. 55–61 (ED 040 707)

HUNTER, W. E. *A Systems Approach to the Instructional Process.* St. Louis: Meramec Community College, 1970. 93 pp. (ED 040 696)

HURST, C. G. *President's Newsletter.* Vol. 2. Chicago: Malcolm X College, Oct. 20, 1969.

HUTCHINS, R. M. *The Learning Society.* New York: Praeger, 1968. 142 pp.

ILLICH, I. "The False Ideology of Schooling." *Saturday Review*, Oct. 17, 1970, *53*, 53–68.

ILLICH, I. "The Alternative to Schooling." *Saturday Review*, June 19, 1971, *54*, 44–48, 56–60.

Illinois Junior College Board. *Career Programs: Technical Vocational Education.* n.p.: 1969.

JACOB, P. E. *Changing Values in College.* New York: Harper and Row, 1957. 174 pp.

JENCKS, C., AND RIESMAN, D. "Patterns of Residential Education: A Case Study of Harvard." In N. Sanford (Ed.), *The American College.* New York: Wiley, 1962. pp. 731–773.

JENCKS, C., AND RIESMAN, D. *The Academic Revolution.* Garden City, N.Y.: Doubleday, 1968. 580 pp.

JENSEN, A. R. "How Much Can We Boost I.Q. and Scholastic Achievement?" *Harvard Educational Review*, Winter 1969, *39*, 1–123.

JENSEN, M. E. "The Preparation of Faculty for the Implementation of

Innovations in Curriculum and Instruction. University of California, Los Angeles, 1969. 37 pp. (ED 031 221)

JEROME, J. "The American Academy 1970." *Change*, Sept.–Oct. 1969, *1*, 10–47.

JEROME, J. *Culture out of Anarchy: The Reconstruction of American Higher Learning.* New York: Herder and Herder, 1970. 330 pp.

JOHNSON, B. L. *General Education in Action.* Washington, D.C.: American Council on Education, 1952. 409 pp.

JOHNSON, B. L. *Islands of Innovation.* Los Angeles: Junior College Leadership Program, University of California, 1964. 77 pp. (ED 012 605)

JOHNSON, B. L. *Islands of Innovation Expanding.* Beverly Hills, Calif.: Glencoe, 1969. 352 pp.

JOHNSON, C. E. "A Study of the Scholastic Achievement of Junior College Transfer Students at the University of Missouri." Unpublished doctoral dissertation, University of Missouri, 1965. 125 pp. (ED 022 464; not avail. EDRS)

JOHNSON, S. R. *Students as Teachers.* ERIC Clearinghouse for Junior Colleges, Topical Paper 4. Los Angeles: University of California, 1969. 15 pp. (ED 026 999)

JOHNSON, S. R., AND JOHNSON, R. B. *Developing Individualized Instructional Material.* Palo Alto, Calif.: Westinghouse Learning Press, 1970. 108 pp.

JONES, G. *Community College Accessibility to the Economically Disadvantaged.* Vancouver, B.C.: Vancouver City College, 1969. 82 pp. (ED 032 055)

JONES, T. *Some Comments on the Role of Junior College Counselors.* Normal, Ill.: Illinois State University, 1969. 7 pp. (ED 034 541)

JUNG, C. G. *Psychological Types; or, The Psychology of Individuation.* H. G. Baynes (trans.). London: Routledge and Kegan Paul, 1949. 654 pp.

JUSTIZ, T. B. "A Method for Identifying the Effective Teacher." Unpublished doctoral dissertation, University of California, Los Angeles, 1968. 100 pp.

KELLEY, W., AND WILBUR, L. *Teaching in the Community-Junior College.* New York: Appleton-Century-Crofts, 1970. 295 pp.

KELLY, M. F., AND CONNOLLY, J. *Orientation for Faculty in Junior Colleges.* ERIC Clearinghouse for Junior Colleges, Monograph 10. Washington, D.C.: American Association of Junior Colleges, 1970. 85 pp. (ED 043 323)

KERNER, O. (Chm.) *Report of the National Advisory Commission on Civil Disorders.* New York: Bantam, 1968. 654 pp.

KERR, C. "Access." *College Board Review,* Summer 1970, 34.

KIBLER, R. J., BARKER, L. L., AND MILES, D. T. *Behavioral Objectives and Instruction.* Boston: Allyn and Bacon, 1970. 196 pp.

KILPATRICK, G. *In-Service Education with Recommendations Concerning Its Implementation in American Junior Colleges.* El Camino, Calif.: El Camino College, 1967. 21 pp. (ED 020 721)

KINTGEN, J. *Interpretation of Literature on Career Ladders and Lattices in Health Occupations Education.* Columbus, Ohio: Center for Vocational and Technical Education, Ohio State University, 1970. 29 pp. (ED 042 919)

KINTZER, F. C. *Nationwide Pilot Study on Articulation.* ERIC Clearinghouse for Junior Colleges, Topical Paper 15. Los Angeles: University of California, 1970. 135 pp. (ED 045 065)

KISTLER, R. "Drive on Truants Cuts Crime Rate." *Los Angeles Times,* Jan. 20, 1971, Part 1, pp. 1, 28.

KLUCKHOHN, C. K. M. "Values and Value Orientations in the Theory of Action." In T. Parsons and E. A. Shils (Eds.), *Toward a General Theory of Action.* Cambridge, Mass.: Harvard University Press, 1954. 506 pp.

KNOELL, D. M. "Potential Student Clienteles." *Junior College Research Review,* Oct. 1969, *4,* 2–5. (ED 032 872)

KNOELL, D. M. *People Who Need College: A Report on Students We Have Yet to Serve.* Washington, D.C.: American Association of Junior Colleges, 1970. 204 pp. (ED 041 573)

KNOELL, D. M., AND MEDSKER, L. L. *From Junior to Senior College: A National Study of the Transfer Student.* Washington, D.C.: Joint Committee on Junior and Senior Colleges, 1965. 65 pp. (ED 013 632)

KOOS, L. V. *The Junior-College Movement.* Boston: Ginn, 1925. 436 pp.

KRATHWOHL, D. R., AND OTHERS. *Taxonomy of Educational Objectives II: The Affective Domain.* New York: McKay, 1964. 196 pp.

KUNHART, W. E., AND ROLEDER, G. "Counseling Techniques with Potential Drop-Out Students in Junior Colleges." *Journal of Counseling Psychology,* Summer 1964, *11,* 190–191.

KUUSISTO, A. A. *Report of the Conference on Two-year Colleges and the Disadvantaged.* Albany, N.Y.: State University of New York and State Education Department, 1966.

LACKEY, R. D., AND ROSS, G. N. *Project SPEED: Final Report of a Summer Program to Prepare Educationally Deficient Students for*

College. Douglas, Ga.: South Georgia College, 1968. 65 pp. (ED 024 389)

LAMKE, T. A. "Personality and Teaching Success." *Journal of Experimental Education*, Dec. 1951, *20*, 2, 217–259.

LANGE, A. F. *The Lange Book: The Collected Writings of a Great Educational Philosopher*. A. H. Chamberlain (Ed.). San Francisco: Trade Publishing, 1927. 302 pp.

LIDZ, T. *The Person: His Development Throughout the Life Cycle*. New York: Basic Books, 1968. 574 pp.

LOMBARDI, J. *Student Activism in Junior Colleges: An Administrator's Views*. ERIC Clearinghouse for Junior Colleges, Monograph 6. Washington, D.C.: American Association of Junior Colleges, 1969. 83 pp. (ED 028 767)

LOMBARDI, J. *The Position Papers of Black Student Activists*. ERIC Clearinghouse for Junior Colleges, Topical Paper 12. Los Angeles: University of California, 1970. 19 pp. (ED 042 453)

LOMBARDI, J. *The President's Reaction to Black Student Activism*. ERIC Clearinghouse for Junior Colleges, Topical Paper 16. Los Angeles: University of California, 1971. 33 pp. (ED 046 390)

LOMBARDI, J., AND QUIMBY, E. A. *Black Studies in the Community Colleges: A Survey*. Washington, D.C.: Bureau of Research, U.S. Office of Education, 1971. 89 pp. (ED 048 851)

LOOMIS, W. G. "A Study of the Formal Preparation of Academic Teachers in Community Colleges with Proposals for Oregon." Unpublished doctoral dissertation, Oregon State University, 1964. 269 pp. (ED 019 931; not avail. EDRS)

Los Angeles Community College District. *College Courses and Curriculums 1970–71*. Los Angeles, 1970.

MC CALLUM, H. N. "A Comparative Study of Male Junior College Graduates Who Made Initial or Deferred Decisions to Major in Vocational/Technical Programs." Unpublished doctoral dissertation, University of California, Berkeley, 1968. 227 pp. (ED 022 453)

MC CLELLAN, J. E. *Toward an Effective Critique of American Education*. Philadelphia: Lippincott, 1968. 324 pp.

MC CONNELL, T. R., AND OTHERS. *Junior College Student Personnel Programs—Appraisal and Development*. Washington, D.C.: American Association of Junior Colleges, 1965. 352 pp. (ED 013 065)

MAC MILLAN, T. F. *NORCAL Project: Phase II; Final Report*. Northern California Cooperative Research Project on Student Attrition. Napa, Calif.: Napa College, 1970. 51 pp. (ED 039 879)

MAGER, R. F. *Preparing Instructional Objectives.* Belmont, Calif.: Fearon, 1962. 62 pp.

MAGER, R. F. *Developing Attitudes Toward Learning.* Belmont, Calif.: Fearon, 1968. 104 pp.

MAGER, R. F., AND BEACH, K. M. *Developing Vocational Instruction.* Belmont, Calif.: Fearon, 1967. 83 pp.

Malcolm X College, City Colleges of Chicago. *Malcolm X El Shabazz Community College: Raison d'Etre.* Chicago, 1969. 25 pp.

MALONEY, C. M. *Attitudes of Missouri Public Junior College Faculty Toward Objectives of the Comprehensive Junior College.* Columbia, Mo.: NDEA Institute, University of Missouri, 1969. 8 pp. (ED 031 247)

MARTIN, W. "A Conservative Approach to Radical Reform." In J. W. Minter (Ed.), *The Individual and the System.* Boulder, Colo.: Western Interstate Commission for Higher Education, 1967. 187 pp.

MARTORANA, S. V. "Progress and Plans in the Empire State." In R. Yarrington (Ed.), *Junior Colleges: 20 States.* Washington, D.C.: American Association of Junior Colleges, 1966.

MASLOW, A. *Motivation and Personality.* New York: Harper and Row, 1954. 411 pp.

MAXWELL, J., AND TOVATT, A. *On Writing Behavioral Objectives for English.* Champaign, Ill.: National Council of Teachers of English, 1970.

MAYHEW, L. B. (Ed.) *General Education: An Account and Appraisal.* New York: Harper and Row, 1960. 212 pp.

MAYHEW, L. B. *Colleges Today and Tomorrow.* San Francisco: Jossey-Bass, 1969. 200 pp.

MEDSKER, L. L. *The Junior College: Progress and Prospect.* New York: McGraw-Hill, 1960. 367 pp.

MEDSKER, L. L. "The Choice Is Not Ours." Speech delivered at Student Personnel Leadership Conference, California Junior College Association, Jan. 10–12, 1963.

MEDSKER, L. L., AND TILLERY, H. D. *Breaking the Access Barriers: A Profile of the American Junior College.* New York: McGraw-Hill, 1971. 183 pp.

MEDSKER, L. L., AND TRENT, J. W. *The Influence of Different Types of Public Higher Institutions on College Attendance from Varying Socioeconomic and Ability Levels.* Cooperative Research Report 438. Berkeley, Calif.: Center for Research and Development in Higher Education, University of California, 1965. 110 pp.

Merritt College. "Afro-American Studies Program." Oakland, Calif., 1968.

Midwest Technical Education Center. *Teaching Internships—CORE Program.* Joint Project of the St. Louis Junior College District, St. Louis County, Clayton, Mo., and Southern Illinois University, Carbondale, Ill. n.p.: 1967. 9 pp. (ED 015 758)

MILTON, O. *Survey of Faculty Views on Student Participation in Decision Making.* Final report. Knoxville, Tenn.: University of Tennessee, 1968. 35 pp. (ED 024 332)

MITCHELL, J. A., AND MOOREHEAD, R. *A Study of Full-time Students Who Discontinued Their Attendance at A.W.C. After Attending One or Both Semesters of the 1966–67 School Year.* Yuma, Ariz.: Arizona Western College, 1968. 73 pp. (ED 024 360)

MOEN, N. W., AND SHANER, J. P. (Eds.) *Minnesota Junior College Faculty 1969 Conferences. Reports and Papers from Three Conferences on Innovation.* Minneapolis: University of Minnesota, 1969. 62 pp. (ED 038 953)

MOORE, W., JR. *Against the Odds: The High-Risk Student in the Community College.* San Francisco: Jossey-Bass, 1970. 244 pp.

Moraine Valley Community College. *The Moraine Valley Resident: His Attitude Toward the Community College and His Socioeconomic Characteristics.* Oak Lawn, Ill., 1969. 39 pp. (ED 032 064)

MORGAN, D. A. *Perspectives of the Community College Presidency.* Occasional Report 14. Los Angeles: Junior College Leadership Program, University of California, 1970. 115 pp. (ED 038 955)

MORIN, L. H. "A Feasible Scheme for the Evaluation of Instructors." Unpublished seminar paper, University of California, Los Angeles, 1968. (ED 024 361)

MORRIS, W. H. (Ed.) *Effective College Teaching.* Washington, D.C.: American Council on Education, 1970. 82 pp.

MORRISON, J. L. "The Relationship of Socialization Experience, Role Orientation, and the Acceptance of the Comprehensive Junior College Concept by Public Junior College Faculty." Unpublished doctoral dissertation, Florida State University, 1969. 225 pp. (ED 031 229; not avail. EDRS)

MUNDAY, L. A. "A Comparison of Junior College Students in Transfer and Terminal Curriculum." In *The Two-Year College and Its*

Students: An Empirical Report. Iowa City, Iowa: American College Testing Program, 1969. 152 pp. (ED 035 404)

MURRAY, H. A., AND OTHERS. *Explorations in Personality.* New York: Wiley, 1938. 761 pp.

MYERS, I. B., AND BRIGGS, K. C. *Myers-Briggs Type Indicator.* Princeton, N.J.: Educational Testing Service, 1962.

MYRAN, G. A. *Community Services: An Emerging Challenge for the Community College.* Washington, D.C.: American Assocation of Junior Colleges, 1969. 12 pp. (ED 032 051)

National Advisory Council on Vocational Education. "Second Report, 1970." *Occupational Education Bulletin,* Feb. 15, 1970, *5,* 2.

National Faculty Association of Community and Junior Colleges. *Guidelines for the Preparation of Community/Junior College Teachers.* Washington, D.C., 1968. 12 pp. (ED 031 205)

National Science Foundation. *The Junior College and Education in the Sciences. Report to the Subcommittee on Science Research and Development of the Committee on Science and Astronautics.* Washington, D.C.: Government Printing Office, 1967.

NESBIT, F. L. "A Survey of Black Studies Taught in the Social Science Division." Dixon, Ill.: Sauk Valley College, 1969.

New Human Services Newsletter. New York: New Careers Development Center, New York University, Fall 1970, *1,* 84.

NEWCOMB, T. M. "Student Peer Group Influence." In N. Sanford (Ed.), *The American College: A Psychological and Social Interpretation of Higher Learning.* New York: Wiley, 1962. pp. 469–88.

NEWCOMB, T. M. "The General Nature for Peer Group Influence." In T. M. Newcomb and E. K. Wilson (Eds.), *College Peer Groups.* Chicago: Aldine, 1966. 303 pp.

NEWMAN, F. *Report on Higher Education.* Washington, D.C.: Government Printing Office, 1971. 130 pp.

NEWSHAM, L. R. "Iowa Sets Its Course." In R. Yarrington (Ed.), *Junior Colleges: 50 States/50 Years.* Washington, D.C.: American Association of Junior Colleges, 1969.

NIXON, R. M. "Message on Higher Education." *American Education,* May 1970, *6,* 4, 28–31.

O'CONNELL, T. E. *Community Colleges: A President's View.* Urbana, Ill.: University of Illinois Press, 1968. 172 pp.

O'CONNOR, E. F., JR., AND JUSTIZ, T. B. *Identifying the Effective Instructor.* ERIC Clearinghouse for Junior Colleges, Topical Paper 9.

Los Angeles: University of California, 1970. 34 pp. (ED 035
416)

OPPELT, M. L. "Attitude of Community College Instructors Toward
Student Groups as a Function of Certain Teacher Characteristics." Unpublished doctoral dissertation, University of Washington, 1967. 166 pp. (ED 026 072; not avail. EDRS)

Orange Coast Junior College District. *A Comparison of California
Junior College Active Enrollments with the Orange Coast Col-
lege and Golden West College Enrollments, Spring, 1968.* Costa
Mesa, Calif., 1969a. 7 pp. (ED 028 776)

Orange Coast Junior College District. *Project Follow-Through:
Progress Report II.* Costa Mesa, Calif., 1969b. 157 pp. (ED 035
410)

Orange Coast Junior College District. *Ins and Outs, How They
Answer: Fall 1968–Spring 1969.* Costa Mesa, Calif., 1970. 20
pp. (ED 038 970)

ORT, V. K. "A Study of Some Techniques Used for Predicting the
Success of Teachers." *Journal of Teacher Education,* Mar.
1964, *15,* 67–71.

OVERTURF, C. L., JR., AND PRICE, E. C. *Student Rating of Faculty at St.
Johns River Junior College.* Palatka, Fla.: St. Johns River
Junior College, 1966. 34 pp. (ED 013 066)

PACE, C. R. *College and University Environment Scales.* Princeton, N.J.:
Educational Testing Service, 1969. 7 pp.

PAETZ, C. G. "A Comparison of Perceived Educational Values of Community College Students, Their Parents, and Faculties in Five
Oregon Community Colleges." Unpublished doctoral dissertation, University of Oregon, 1966. 170 pp. (ED 016 477; not
avail. EDRS)

Palomar College. *Insight: A View of the Faculty Through the Eyes of
Their Students.* San Marcos, Calif.: 1968. 128 pp.

PARK, Y. "The Junior College Staff: Values and Institutional Perceptions." Unpublished doctoral dissertation, University of California, Los Angeles, 1970.

PARK, Y. *Junior College Faculty: Their Values and Perceptions.* ERIC
Clearinghouse for Junior Colleges, Monograph 12. Washington,
D.C.: American Association of Junior Colleges, 1971. 68 pp.
(ED 050 725)

PARKER, P. *Escrow College: The Superior High School Student and the
Community College.* Pittsburg, Kan.: Department of Admin-

istration and School Services, Kansas State College of Pittsburg, 1970. 17 pp. (ED 042 454)

PARSONS, T., AND SHILS, E. A. (Eds.) *Toward a General Theory of Action.* Cambridge, Mass.: Harvard University Press, 1954. 506 pp.

Pasadena City College. *General Bulletin, 1967–1968.* Pasadena, Calif., 1967.

PEARCE, F. C. *Basic Education of Teachers: Seven Needed Qualities.* Modesto, Calif.: Modesto Junior College, 1966. 20 pp. (ED 010 677)

PEARCE, F. C. *A Study of Pre-Registration Counseling.* San Mateo, Calif.: San Mateo Junior College, 1967. 28 pp. (ED 017 231)

Pennsylvania Association of Junior Colleges. *Minutes of the 25th Annual Convention.* Pittsburgh, Oct. 1967. 49 pp. (ED 019 086)

PEPPER, S. C. *World Hypotheses.* Los Angeles: University of California Press, 1966. 348 pp.

PETERSON, B. "The Multipurpose Junior College in California." n.p.: 1962.

PHAIR, T. S. "Third Year Survey Results: An Analysis of the Characteristics of New Full-Time Faculty in California Community Colleges." Berkeley, Calif.: Office of Educational Career Services, University of California, 1969.

PHAY, J. E., AND MC CARY, A. D. *Undergraduate Transfer Students at the University of Mississippi, 1963–1966.* Oxford, Miss.: University of Mississippi, 1967. 57 pp. (ED 012 098)

PIFER, A. "Is It Time for an External Degree?" *College Board Review,* Winter 1970–1971, 8–10.

POINSETT, A. "Dr. Charles G. Hurst: The Mastermind of Malcolm X College." *Ebony,* Mar. 1970, *25,* 29–38.

POPHAM, W. J. *The Teacher Empiricist.* (2nd ed.) Los Angeles: Aegeus, 1970. 76 pp.

POPHAM, W. J., AND BAKER, E. L. *Establishing Instructional Goals.* Englewood Cliffs, N.J.: Prentice-Hall, 1970. 130 pp.

POSTLETHWAIT, S. N., MURRAY, H. T., JR., AND NOVAK, J. *An Integrated Experience Approach to Learning with Emphasis on Independent study.* Minneapolis: Burgess, 1964. 114 pp.

POSTLETHWAIT, S. N., MURRAY, H. T., JR., AND NOVAK, J. *The Audio-Tutorial Approach to Learning, Through Independent Study and Integrated Experiences.* (2nd ed.) Minneapolis: Burgess, 1969. 149 pp.

POWELL, H. M. *Administrative Procedures Involved in Stimulating, Developing, and Implementing a Curriculum for Low-Ability Students at Los Angeles City College.* Los Angeles: Los Angeles City College, 1966. 31 pp. (ED 012 167)

PRATT, A. L., AND FREDERICK, M. *Your Career and Two-Year Colleges.* Washington, D.C.: American Association of Junior Colleges, 1970.

PRATT, G. L. B. *Flexibility of Personality as It Relates to the Hiring and Retention of Public Community College Faculty in New York State.* New York: School of Education, New York University, 1966. 110 pp. (ED 023 382)

The President's Task Force on Education. Washington, D.C.: American Association of Junior Colleges, Mar. 19, 1969.

QUIMBY, E. A. "Needed: Rational Curriculum Planning." *Junior College Research Review,* Feb. 1970, *4,* 2–4. (ED 035 415)

RAINES, M. R., AND MYRAN, G. A. "Community Services: A University-Community College Approach." *Junior College Journal,* Oct. 1970, *41,* 2, 41–49.

RAINSFORD, G. N. "What Honor Students Don't Like About Honors Programs." *College Board Review,* Summer 1970, 18–21.

Regional Education Laboratory for the Carolinas and Virginia. *Long Term Goals of the Educational Improvement System.* Durham, N.C., 1970.

REIMER, E. *An Essay on Alternatives in Education.* (2nd ed.) CIDOC Cuaderno 1005. Cuernavaca, Mexico: Centro Intercultural de Documentacion, 1970. 181 pp.

REITAN, H. M., AND LANDER, R. E. *Educational Innovation in Community Colleges of the Northwest and Alaska.* Seattle: Center for the Development of Community College Education, 1968. 82 pp. (ED 028 765)

REYNOLDS, J. W. *The Comprehensive Junior College Curriculum.* Berkeley, Calif.: McCutchan, 1969. 224 pp.

RICHARDS, J. M., JR., AND BRASKAMP, L. A. "Who Goes Where to Junior College?" In *The Two-year College and Its Students: An Empirical Report.* Iowa City, Iowa: American College Testing Program, 1969. 152 pp. (ED 035 404)

RIESS, L. C. *Faculty Governance in Turmoil—Who Speaks for the Junior College Professor?* Long Beach, Calif.: Junior College Faculty Association, 1967. 12 pp. (ED 017 250)

ROBINSON, R. B. *Survey of Personal Attitudes About Cerritos College from Full-Time Day Students of Mexican Heritage.* Norwalk, Calif.: Cerritos College, 1968. 13 pp. (ED 024 355)

ROGERS, C. R. *Freedom to Learn.* Columbus, Ohio: Merrill, 1969. 358 pp.

ROGERS, J. T. "Retired Military Personnel as Junior College Instructors: An Analysis Conducted in Florida Public Junior Colleges." Unpublished doctoral dissertation, Florida State University, 1965. 146 pp. (ED 012 578; not avail. EDRS)

ROKEACH, M. *Beliefs, Attitudes, and Values: A Theory of Organization and Change.* San Francisco: Jossey-Bass, 1968a. 214 pp.

ROKEACH, M. "The Role of Values in Public Opinion Research." *Public Opinion Quarterly,* 1968b, *32,* 547–559.

ROMAN, P. A. "Effects of a Career Planning Course on the Career Choice Strategies of Students in Junior College." Unpublished doctoral dissertation, University of California, Los Angeles, 1969. 200 pp.

RORSCHACH, H. *Psychodiagnostics.* (7th ed.) P. Lemkan and B. Kronenberg (Trans.). Berne, Switzerland: Hans Huber, 1969. 217 pp.

ROSENTHAL, A. (Comp.) *Governing Education: A Reader on Politics, Power, and Public School Policy.* Garden City, N.Y.: Doubleday, 1969. 500 pp.

ROUECHE, J. E. *Salvage, Redirection, or Custody?* ERIC Clearinghouse for Junior Colleges, Monograph 1. Washington, D.C.: American Association of Junior Colleges, 1968. 77 pp. (ED 019 077)

ROUECHE, J. E., AND BOGGS, J. R. *Junior College Institutional Research: The State of the Art.* ERIC Clearinghouse for Junior Colleges, Monograph 2. Washington, D.C.: American Association of Junior Colleges, 1968. 76 pp. (ED 021 557)

ROWBOTHAM, N. D. "The Comparison of an Auto-Tutorial Laboratory and a Traditional Laboratory in Physical Science." Unpublished doctoral dissertation, University of Arkansas, 1969. 85 pp.

SALATINO, A. (Ed.) *Teaching in the Junior College.* Providence, R.I.: Roger Williams Junior College, 1967. 50 pp. (ED 013 100)

SANFORD, F. H., AND WRIGHTSMAN, L. S., JR. *Psychology: A Scientific Study of Man.* Monterey, Calif.: Brooks/Cole, 1970. 736 pp.

SANFORD, N. (Ed.) *The American College: A Psychological and Social Interpretation of the Higher Learning.* New York: Wiley, 1962. 1084 pp.

Sauk Valley College. "Black Studies at Sauk Valley College." Dixon, Ill.: Sauk Valley College, June 6, 1969.

SCHILL, W. J., OLSON, O. L., AND REITAN, H. M. *An Analysis of the Role of Lewis-Clark Normal School in Idaho Higher Education with Recommendations.* Seattle: Center for the Development of Community College Education, University of Washington, 1968. 32 pp.

SCHMIDT, R. (Ed.) *Insight: A View of the Faculty Through the Eyes of Their Students.* San Marcos, Calif.: Palomar College, 1968. 128 pp. (ED 023 405)

SCHRAG, P. "Miami-Dade's Encounter with Technology." *Change in Higher Education,* Mar.–Apr. 1969, 24–27.

SCHULTZ, R. E. "The Junior College President: Who and Where From?" In *The Junior College President.* Occasional Report 13. Los Angeles: Junior College Leadership Program, University of California, 1969. pp. 7–19.

SCHULTZ, R. E. "Will Tradition Keep Occupational Education from Meeting Its Potential?" In *Occupations and Education in the 70's: Promises and Challenges.* Washington, D.C.: American Association of Junior Colleges, 1970. 18 pp.

SCHULTZ, R. E., AND GARRETT, L. W. *Junior College Honor Students Who Were Initiated into Phi Theta Kappa for Selected Years During the Period 1947–1965.* Tallahassee: Florida State University, 1967. 149 pp. (ED 014 308)

SCHWAB, J. J. *College Curriculum and Student Protest.* Chicago: University of Chicago Press, 1969. 303 pp.

SEASHORE, C. E. *The Junior College Movement.* New York: Holt, Rinehart, and Winston, 1940. 160 pp.

SENSOR, P. *Analysis of Student Reactions to Counseling.* Riverside, Calif.: Riverside City College, 1962. 15 pp. (ED 014 287)

SHELDON, M. S. "Entrance and Placement Testing for the Junior College." *Junior College Research Review,* Dec. 1970a, 5, 1–4.

SHELDON, M. S. "Occupational Education—A Touch of Reality." In *Occupations and Education in the 70's: Promises and Challenges.* Washington, D.C.: American Association of Junior Colleges, 1970b. 18 pp.

SIBLEY, A. M. *A Study of Selected Characteristics of Transfer Students at Appalachian State University.* Boone, N.C.: Appalachian State University, 1968. 11 pp. (ED 022 445)

SIEHR, H. E. *Problems of New Faculty Members in Community Colleges.* East Lansing, Mich.: Michigan State University, 1963. 78 pp. (ED 013 093)

SILVER, A. B. *English Department Large-Small Class Study: English 50–60.* (Rev. ed.) Bakersfield, Calif.: Bakersfield College, 1970. 9 pp. (ED 041 586)

SIMPSON, R. H., AND SEIDMAN, J. M. *Student Evaluation of Teaching and Learning.* Washington, D.C.: American Association of Colleges for Teacher Education, 1962. 38 pp.

SINGER, D. S. "Do We Need a Community College Institute?" *Junior College Journal,* Oct. 1968, *39,* 36–41. (ED 024 388)

SKILLING, H. H. *Do You Teach?* New York: Holt, Rinehart, and Winston, 1969. 150 pp.

SMITH, R. B. "Do Curriculums Reflect Purposes?" Provo, Utah: Brigham Young University, 1969. 15 pp. (ED 038 972)

SNYDER, F. A., AND BLOCKER, C. E. *A Profile of Non-Persisting Students: A Description of Educational Goals and Achievements, Activities, and Perceptions of Non-Graduates, Spring 1969.* Research Report 3. Harrisburg, Pa.: Harrisburg Area Community College, 1969. 67 pp. (ED 037 218)

SNYDER, F. A., AND BLOCKER, C. E. *A Profile of Students: A Description of the Characteristics, Attitudes, and Concerns of Students, Spring 1969.* Research Report 10. Harrisburg, Pa.: Harrisburg Area Community College, 1969a. 63 pp. (ED 037 203)

SNYDER, F. A., AND BLOCKER, C. E. *A Profile of Students: A Description of the Characteristics, Perceptions, and Activities of Graduates, Spring 1969.* Research Report 2. Harrisburg, Pa.: Harrisburg Area Community College, 1969b. 67 pp. (ED 037 204)

SOGOMONION, A. *Report of a Survey of Attitudes on Current Political Issues.* San Bernardino, Calif.: San Bernardino Valley College, 1965. (ED 012 618)

SPECTOR, I. L., AND GARNESKI, T. M. *Summer Group Counseling of Phoenix College Freshmen.* Phoenix: Maricopa County Junior College District, 1966. 9 pp. (ED 013 071)

SPINDLER, G. D. "Education in a Transforming American Culture." *Harvard Educational Review,* Summer 1955, *25,* 145–156.

STEIN, R. S. *Some Concepts Held by Los Angeles City College Entrants on Probation Because of Low SCAT Scores.* Los Angeles: Los Angeles City College, 1966. 27 pp. (ED 014 274)

STERN, G. C. *Stern Activities Index.* Minneapolis: National Computer Systems, 1950–1963. 7 pp.

STERN, G. C., AND PACE, C. R. *College Characteristics Index.* Syracuse, N.Y.: Psychological Research Center, Syracuse University, 1963. 6 pp.

SUMMERSKILL, J. "Dropouts from College." In N. Sanford (Ed.), *The American College.* New York: Wiley, 1962. pp. 627–657.

SWANSON, H. L. "An Investigation of Institutional Research in the Junior Colleges of the United States." Unpublished doctoral dissertation, University of California, Los Angeles, 1965. 37 pp. (ED 013 089; not avail. EDRS)

TETER, R. O., AND PATE, T., JR. *Creating a Climate for Innovation: Report of a Conference for Community College and Public School Administrators, Supervisors, Personnel, and Teachers.* Baytown, Tex.: Lee College, 1967. 51 pp. (ED 018 208)

THELEN, A. M. *The Effectiveness of Acquired Individual and Group Guidance Procedures in Promoting Changes in Selected Characteristics of Junior College Freshmen.* Madison, Wis.: University of Wisconsin, 1968. 211 pp.

THOMPSON, J. R. *Why Students Drop Courses.* Warren, Mich.: Macomb County Community College, 1969. 33 pp. (ED 026 994)

THOMSON, J. "Institutional Studies of Junior College Students." *Junior College Research Review,* May 1967, *1,* 1–2. (ED 013 070)

THORNTON, J. W., JR. *The Community Junior College.* (2nd ed.) New York: Wiley, 1966. 300 pp.

TILLERY, H. D. "Differential Characteristics of Entering Freshmen at the University of California and Their Peers at California Junior College." Unpublished doctoral dissertation, University of California, Berkeley, 1964. 254 pp. (ED 019 953; not avail. EDRS)

TODD, C. E. "The Perceived Functions of the Junior College Academic Dean in the Improvement of Instruction." Unpublished doctoral dissertation, University of Alabama, 1965. 286 pp. (ED 034 548; not avail. EDRS)

TOWNSEND, R. C. *Up the Organization.* New York: Knopf, 1970. 202 pp.

TRAICOFF, G. *Obtaining Financial Support for Community Services Programs.* Washington, D.C.: American Association of Junior Colleges, 1969. 14 pp. (ED 032 052)

TRENT, J. W., AND MEDSKER, L. L. *Beyond High School: A Psychosociological Study of 10,000 High School Graduates.* San Francisco: Jossey-Bass, 1968. 314 pp.

TRZEBIATOWSKI, G. (Ed.) *Guide to Audiovisual Terminology, Product Information Supplement No. 6.* New York: Educational Products Information Exchange Institute, 1968. (ED 021 440; not avail. EDRS)

TURNER, H. J., JR. *The Half That Leaves: A Limited Survey of Attrition in Community Colleges.* Gainesville, Fla.: Florida Community Junior College Inter-Institutional Research Council, University of Florida, 1970. 18 pp. (ED 038 127)

TYLER, R. W. *Basic Principles of Curriculum and Instruction.* Chicago: University of Chicago Press, 1950. 83 pp.

ULLRICH, M. "A Human Service Career Conference." *Junior College Journal,* Dec.–Jan. 1970–1971, *41,* 23–28.

U.S. News and World Report. "Junior Colleges—Students' Hope for the Future." May 17, 1965, *58,* 66–68.

VENN, G. *Man, Education, and Work: Post Secondary Vocational and Technical Education.* Washington, D.C.: American Council on Education, 1964. 184 pp.

VERBEKE, M. G. "The Junior College Academic Dean's Leadership Behavior as Viewed by Superiors and Faculty." Unpublished doctoral dissertation, State University of Pennsylvania, 1966. 146 pp. (ED 034 547; not avail. EDRS)

VOEGEL, G. H. *Update 1: A Report of the Beginning Efforts in Instructional Development at William Rainey Harper College.* Palatine, Ill.: William Rainey Harper College, 1970. 124 pp. (ED 038 112)

WALLER, W. W. *The Sociology of Teaching.* New York: Wiley, 1967. 467 pp.

WALTON, S. F., JR. (Ed.) *The Black Curriculum: Developing a Program in Afro-American Studies.* East Palo Alto, Calif.: Black Liberation, 1969. pp. 26, 29.

WARD, P. *Development of the Junior College Movement.* Washington, D.C.: American Council on Education, 1948, 21.

WARE, C. "The Dynamics of the Ethnic Studies Program." Los Angeles: Los Angeles City College, 1969.

WARREN, J. R. *Patterns of College Experiences.* Claremont, Calif.: College Student Personnel Institute and Claremont Graduate School and University Center, 1966. 149 pp. (ED 010 100)

WATTENBARGER, J. L., AND OTHERS. *State Level Staffs for Coordination and/or Control of Community Junior Colleges.* Gainesville, Fla.: Institute for Higher Education, University of Florida, 1970. 50 pp. (ED 038 114)

Wayne County Community College. *Catalog, 1970–71.* Detroit: Wayne County Community College, 1970.

WEBER, J. (Ed.) *Administration and Innovation*. Ann Arbor, Mich.: Midwest Community College Leadership Program, 1966. 118 pp. (ED 014 299)

WESSON, C. *Technological Changes in the Cement Manufacturing Industry*. Sacramento: California State Department of Employment, 1966. 31 pp. (ED 014 582)

WIEGMAN, R. R. *General Education in Occupational Education Programs Offered by Junior Colleges*. Washington, D.C.: American Association of Junior Colleges, 1969. 25 pp. (ED 031 233)

William Rainey Harper College. *Faculty Orientation for a New Community College*. Palatine, Ill., 1967. 105 pp. (ED 020 717)

WILLINGHAM, W. W., AND FINDIKYAN, N. *Patterns of Admission for Transfer Students*. New York: College Entrance Examination Board, 1969. 47 pp.

WILSON, R. S. *A Comparison of Student, Teacher, and Administrator Perceptions of the Junior College Environment*. Columbia, Mo.: NDEA Institute, University of Missouri, 1969. 10 pp. (ED 031 250)

WISGOSKI, A. E. "Attitudes of Community College Presidents, Chief Student Personnel Officers, and Faculty Toward the Student Personnel Point of View in Selected Illinois Community (Junior) Colleges, 1967–1968." Unpublished doctoral dissertation, Northern Illinois University, 1968. 211 pp. (ED 016 047; not avail. EDRS)

WITHERSPOON, F. D. *Group Guidance in Junior College—A Frame of Reference*. St. Louis: Forest Park Community College, 1967. 119 pp. (ED 016 487)

WRIGHT, S. J. *Faculty Participation in Academic Governance*. Washington, D.C.: American Association for Higher Education, 1967. 74 pp. (ED 018 218; avail. on MF only)

WYGAL, B. R. "Personal Characteristics and Situational Perceptions of Junior College Instructors as Related to Innovativeness." Unpublished doctoral dissertation, University of Texas, 1966. 100 pp. (ED 019 964; not avail. EDRS)

ZANDER, D. R. *Student Unrest: An Administrator's Point-of-View*. Minneapolis: University of Minnesota, 1969. 4 pp. (ED 039 875)

ZANE, L. F. H. *The Demand for Community College Teachers and the EPDA Program Under the College of Education*. Honolulu: University of Hawaii, 1969. 18 pp. (ED 036 291)

ZILLER, R. C. *The Alienation Syndrome: A Triadic Pattern of Self-*

Other Orientation. Eugene, Ore.: University of Oregon, 1969. 28 pp. (ED 032 606)

ZILLER, R. C. *A Theory of Self-Other Orientation and Interpersonal Conflict.* Eugene, Ore.: University of Oregon, 1969. 21 pp. (ED 032 608)

ZILLER, R. C., AND OTHERS. *Complexity of the Self-Concept and Social Acceptance.* Eugene, Ore.: University of Oregon, 1969. 38 pp. (ED 032 609)

ZILLER, R. C., AND OTHERS. *The Political Personality.* Eugene, Ore.: University of Oregon, 1969. 25 pp. (ED 032 603)

Name Index

Subject Index

Date Due

staff	AP 20 '81		
MY 10 '74	MY 1 '84		
AG 10 '74	MR 14 '84		
FE 3 '75	AUG 2 1985		
FE 14 '75	MAY 1 1987		
FE 28 '75	Res 1/88		
MR 21 '75	Res 8/S		
1/27/76	Res 3/90		
Res	Res 4/92		
MR 30 '77	MAR 24 '92		
	Res/93		
MR 30 '77	Res/93		
MR 17 '78	Res 10/9		
MY 3 '78	Res 5/94		
MR 30 '81			

Demco 38-297